BELIEF in the PAST
THEORETICAL APPROACHES to the ARCHAEOLOGY of RELIGION

BELIEF in the PAST
THEORETICAL APPROACHES to
the ARCHAEOLOGY of RELIGION

Edited by
Kelley Hays-Gilpin
David S. Whitley

Left Coast
Press Inc.

Walnut Creek, California

**Left Coast
Press** Inc.

LEFT COAST PRESS, INC.
1630 North Main Street, #400
Walnut Creek, CA 94596
http://www.LCoastPress.com

Library of Congress Cataloging-in-Publication Data

Belief in the past : theoretical approaches to the archaeology of
religion/[edited by] David S. Whitley and Kelley Hays-Gilpin.
    p. cm.
    Includes bibliographical references and index.
    ISBN 978-1-59874-341-8 (hardcover : alk. paper) – ISBN 978-1-59874-342-5
(pbk. : alk. paper)
    1. Archaeology and religion–Congresses. I. Whitley, David S. II. Hays-Gilpin,
Kelley, 1960–
    BL65.A72B46 2008
    200.9–dc22   2008024233

Printed in the United States of America

♾™ The paper used in this publication meets the minimum requirements of
American National Standard for Information Sciences—Permanence of Paper for
Printed Library Materials, ANSI/NISO Z39.48–1992.

08 09 10 11 12 5 4 3 2 1

CONTENTS

LIST OF ILLUSTRATIONS

Figures

Table

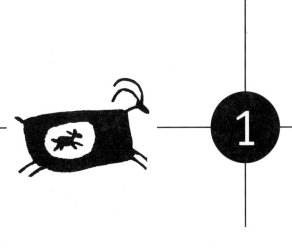

RELIGION BEYOND ICON, BURIAL AND MONUMENT: AN INTRODUCTION

David S. Whitley and Kelley Hays-Gilpin

A war is raging in the Middle East as you read this introduction or, at least, one is likely imminent and the world is on high alert. We can assert this with some certainty, regardless of the shelf-life of this volume, because this condition has characterized the region for most of the last 1000 years. During this same period various empires and nations have risen and fallen there. The regional economy region has shifted from mostly small-scale pastoralism, farming and trading to the epicenter of the global energy industry. Yet despite this history of change, there has been one constant in the Middle East. This is war, and its adjunct: whenever and wherever waged, Middle Eastern wars have divided along sectarian lines—Christian against Muslim, Muslim against Jew, Shia Muslim against Sunni Muslim, and factions within factions. Regardless of whether we view religion as consequence or cause, these conflicts have been, and promise to continue to be, *religious* wars.

The Middle East is hardly unique in this respect: many of the western European wars of the last half-millennium likewise involved battling Christian sects, pitting Roman Catholics against Protestants, and Christians against Jews. And lest you think that religious violence is an historical anachronism in the west, recall that sectarian strife only ended (we hope it has ended) recently in Northern Ireland and the Balkans.

Meanwhile the last half-century has also seen the development of a multi-billion dollar international tourist industry that is linked to the archaeological record. Tourists flock to Egypt, Latin America, Southeast

Asia and other regions in part to visit archaeological sites. When they arrive, they expect to see not house mounds and craft workshops so much as shrines, tombs, and temples. The Pyramids at Giza, the Great Kivas of Chaco Canyon, the Pyramids of the Sun and Moon at Teotihuacan, Stonehenge on the Salisbury Plain, the painted Paleolithic caves of France and Spain, and the temples at Angkor Wat are all remarkable archaeological tourist attractions. Each is also the product of intense if not preoccupying prehistoric concerns with religion.

What is missing from this picture?

The answer of course is archaeologists who, in the last half-century, have commonly given religion a wide berth[1]. This has occurred even though religion is implicated in and intimately connected with some of the most pressing issues that confront the world—not the least of which is the potential annihilation of the human race by nuclear warfare—and even though prehistoric religion is often the most compelling and visible aspect of the archaeological record, at least to non-archaeologists. Reasons for this archaeological neglect are several and varied, and some are discussed in subsequent chapters of this book. More pertinent to emphasize here is the current increase in professional archaeological interest in religion, as a series of recent volumes demonstrates (e.g., Hall 1997; Hayden 2003; Insoll 2001, 2003, 2004; Van Pool et al. 2006; Van Pool and Van Pool 2007). This collection of edited papers results from this same shift in interests[2]. It reflects both the changing nature of archaeological research, seen globally, and the specific concerns of a group of researchers interested in the developing sub-discipline we call the archaeology of religion.

Given this last fact, we begin this volume by assaying the texts and sub-texts of our contributors in order to identify the issues, themes and concerns highlighted in each contribution, and to explain what unifies the otherwise seemingly disparate discussions. The sub-text of our own statement is the notion that the archaeology of religion is still somewhere in its growth curve. What then does this group of archaeologists consider the main problems and prospects that confront research on belief in the past?

Studying Prehistoric Religion

Many of the founders of anthropology and sociology, including Durkheim, Weber, Marx and Tylor, accorded a great deal of importance to religion. Despite this long history of intellectual interest (e.g., see Morris 1987), our current understanding of religion as a social and cultural phenomenon still requires discussion. That religion is a system of beliefs and practices linked with supernatural agents is well understood, certainly (cf. Barrett 2004). Likewise the fact that some religions have explicitly defined theologies whereas others lack these entirely is also widely acknowledged (sometimes identified as "world religions" or "religions of the book" versus "folk religions," or "doctrinal" versus "imagistic" religions; cf. Whitehouse 2004). And that we can distinguish major religious systems from each other even in the absence of defined theology, such as shamanism and totemism, is also firmly established (Layton 2001; Winkelman 1992). What is at issue then is not the descriptive definition of religion or its various components—see Whitley (2008) for these—but instead an understanding of religion's origins, its social functions and its implications for daily life. How and why did religion(s) originate? How do religions operate at the individual and societal levels? How do religions change over time? Practically speaking, how can we interpret prehistoric religion, and how will our understanding of it improve our interpretations of ancient lifeways?

These types of process-[3] and method-oriented questions are raised explicitly and implicitly by all of the authors in this volume. They position religion not as an institution that must be understood in its own independent light so much as a fully integrated, and thus integral, part of human social life. The archaeology of religion, in this sense, is undertaken to enhance our understanding of prehistoric society and lifeways, not as an end in itself.

Despite slightly contrasting views of what religion is and does, and how archaeologists might best study it, all authors take as a starting point the need to redress traditional processual *and* post-processual archaeological approaches to social life. The place of religion in society is central to this reassessment, because it is exactly the religious component of ancient social life that archaeologists have traditionally overlooked.

Cognition and Religion

Much has been written about religion, as the histories of anthropology and sociology show (cf. Morris 1987) yet, despite this previous research, religion is still under-theorized. The first four chapters in this volume implicitly outline one reason why the intellectual contributions of researchers like Durkheim, Weber and other early theorists are alone inadequate for a plausible understanding of religion, contemporary or prehistoric. This involves cognition; specifically the rapid growth of cognitive neurosciences research over the last two decades. Cognitive science was not available to earlier researchers, and by now has fundamentally changed our understanding of the human mind-brain and the nature of human behavior, including especially our understanding of religion as a universal phenomenon (e.g., Atran 2002; Boyer 2001; McCauley and Lawson 2002; Pyysianen 2004; Whitehouse 2004).

The volume starts with a contribution by **David Lewis-Williams,** **"Religion and archaeology: an analytical, materialist account,"** that directly addresses the definition of religion, framed analytically, not descriptively. Lewis-Williams begins by distinguishing among "religious experience," grounded in universal characteristics of the human neuropsychological system; "belief," which is culturally and socio-economically contingent; and "practice," which mediates experience and belief. His ultimate concern is to unite the social and psychological elements of religion, in part based on a clearer understanding of human consciousness. Central to his argument is the point that social discrimination between those who obtain religious authority and those who do not is a *de facto* result of the appearance and practice of all religions, and this discrimination is likewise the basis for social change.

Lewis-Williams' emphasis on the control of the spectrum of human consciousness as a central component of religions is based on the perspective that the origin of religion may be partly understood in terms of natural neuropsychological processes. **Michael Winkelman,** in **"Cross-Cultural and Biogenetic Perspectives on the Origins of Shamanism,"** expands on this general idea in his discussion of shamanism both as the original religion, and as the product—not the by-product—of human biological evolution. Winkelman partly argues that shamanism represents a psychosocial adaptation reflecting mammalian social bonding and therapeutic needs. Importantly, he distinguishes between the cross-cultural universals of shamanism, *sensu stricto*, driven by underlying human biological structures, and the more generalized shamanistic elements that are common in many societies (especially shamanistic healing). Winkelman suggests that the cross-cultural universals of shamanism provide an etic model for the archaeologist that is analytically useful for studying archaic cultures.

That cognition can be explained in terms of biological and neuropsychological structures may be surprising to readers unfamiliar with the recent cognitive neurosciences literature. Yet the embodied basis of much of our thought is now well understood, as is the embodied origin for aspects of language, especially metaphoric language, and even emotion (e.g., Gibbs 2006). Although archaeologists have long emphasized behavior and, by that emphasis, assumed that it was distinct from cognition, neurosciences research has shown that the separation of mind and body is a false opposition that reflects our intellectual history rather than any useful empirical reality. The place of embodied conceptual metaphors in the archaeology of religion then is developed by **Elisabeth Culley,** in **"Supernatural Metaphors and Belief in the Past: Defining an Archaeology of Religion."** Conceptual metaphors are themselves universal, thereby providing an empirically verified cross-cultural model for understanding aspects of symbolism. They reflect the fact that our surrounding empirical world influences the way we think and, while we are not born with these conceptual structures already embedded in our thought processes, they develop (through repetition) to the point where they become neurologically hard-wired (Lakoff and Johnson 1999). Culley argues that conceptual metaphors serve as cognitive mechanisms for religiosity in general terms, as well as for specific beliefs and practices. Using an ethnographic and archaeological example from the Numic of the Great Basin of western North America, she shows both how conceptual metaphors are coherent and identifiable systems of perceptions, and how they provide the archaeologist access to beliefs.

In "Cognition, Emotion and Belief: First Steps in an Archaeology of Religion," David Whitley continues the discussion of embodiment, in this case with respect to emotions and their implications for understanding ritual. Though the importance of emotions is dismissed by many scientists, they are in fact closely associated with rational thought, and emotion and reason evolved together. Instincts, like the "fight or flight response" for example, are clear evolutionary products, representing our most basic set of emotions. Whitley considers the significance of emotions in ritual acts, especially in non-shamanistic/transcendental religions, providing a rationale for why ritual is so widespread.

Scientists have argued for decades (if not centuries) over the primacy of nature versus culture. Many cultural constructivists continue to dismiss the importance of biology in social life; meanwhile many neo-Darwinian evolutionists effectively ignore culture in their analyses of the archaeological record. Implicit to each of these first four papers is the idea that nature is expressed in our individual biological selves and that culture serves to mediate individual experiences resulting in the phenomenon we label society; both nature and culture then must be accommodated in any plausible account of social life. It follows that we cannot explain society or social life until we first understand the biological-self, countering the traditional "top-down" view that most social scientists favor, and which promotes the study of society but not so much its (individual) components. What these chapters offer instead is partly a "bottom-up" perspective that starts with biological and evolutionary processes and experiences, in order to develop a foundation on which a better understanding of social life can be built.

Archaeology and Text

A second concern in this volume is the relationship of the archaeological record to historical texts. **Andrzej Rozwadowski** addresses this issue first in "**Centering Historical-Archaeological Discourse: The Prehistory**

of Central Asian/South Siberian Shamanism." augmenting the earlier discussions of both Lewis-Williams and Winkelman on shamanism.
Ethnographic Asiatic shamanism has had a fundamental impact on western
views of the history (and thus the prehistory) of religions. Central/north-
east Asian shamanism in fact has been taken as a putative model of Paleolithic
religion in general and hunter-gatherer religions specifically, including the
belief that it served as the source for Native American religions. By combining linguistics, historical accounts and analyses of iconography (in the
form of rock art), Rozwadowski counters the prevailing views on a number
of central points. The most important of these are the possibility that the
term "shaman" may have originated in India, spreading to Central and
Eastern Asia with the diffusion of Buddhism; that archaeological evidence
for shamanism in this region extends back only to the second or third
millennium BCE; and that this was associated with metal-using pastoral-
ists, not with "stone-age" hunter-gatherers (cf. Whitley 2004). These are
fundamental revisions in our understanding of shamanism, with significant
implications for ongoing debates about this religious system.

The importance of the inter-play between archaeology and text is further emphasized in **"Text Versus Image: The Implications of Physical
Evidence for Buddhist History,"** by **Robert DeCaroli.** The concern in
this case is the use of religious documents as sources of historical data, a
task that (as DeCaroli acknowledges) is problematized by the fact that the
texts derive from an intellectual and spiritual elite. For this reason they tend
to emphasize the transcendental aspects of the religion although, as he also
notes, both texts *and* objects are laden with historical and religious implications. In the case of Buddhism, however, the focus on the metaphysical
aspects of the texts has resulted in a one-sided historical perspective. DeCaroli
looks to archaeological evidence juxtaposed against the textual evidence to
show that Buddhist religion was as much concerned with mortuary practices and local pre-existing spirit deities—as evidenced by the archaeological
record—as it was with metaphysics. The result is an improved understanding of the social dynamics of the spread of this major world religion.

Although the specifics of these two studies differ, the practical message
is the same: careful study of the archaeological *and* historical/ethnographic
records, if available, will greatly improve our understanding of ancient religions. Moreover, this is true regardless of whether the concern is with doctrinal faiths, like Buddhism, or imagistic ("theology-less") religious systems
like shamanism.

Practicing Faith

DeCaroli's interest in shifting our intellectual gaze beyond the metaphysical aspects of religion alone is further emphasized in the next series of

papers, where practice theory in different forms is raised as an appropriate means for analyzing faith in the past. **Lars Fogelin** perhaps of all the volume contributors most directly confronts the methodological issues in "**Delegitimizing Religion: The Archaeology of Religion as ... Archaeology.**" He confronts head-on Christopher Hawkes' (1954) famous—or perhaps better, *infamous*—essay on the archaeology of religion, which has been used by two subsequent generations of archaeologists to justify ignoring this topic. Fogelin's primary point is that religion is not entirely metaphysical; like all other aspects of social life, it also involves many kinds of routine behaviors. Practice theory, as one approach to the investigation of religion, then looks not to the metaphysical aspects of religion but instead to the way that it is manifest in people's daily lives. Religion in this sense is embedded in human action.

That religious practice is not just embedded in daily activities but also embodied in a fashion promoting the production and maintenance of sacred knowledge is emphasized by **Neil Price**. His chapter, "**Bodylore and the Archaeology of Embedded Religion: Dramatic License In The Funerals of the Vikings,**" contests what he refers to as the illusion of orthodoxy—the idea that all religions had a rigid set of precepts, beliefs and ritual routines that were always followed—as an imposition of modern western ideas and attitudes about religion on past societies. For Price, religion is a fluid and socially situated practice that we discover archaeologically by emphasizing individual acts of behavior rather than through the lens of our own preconceptions about the nature of ritual. What this will reveal are local patterns of personal belief and individual relationships with the supernatural rather than formal religious structures, thereby bringing us much closer to a reliable understanding of non-western/non-contemporary religions.

The importance of individual experience as opposed to formal creed is further emphasized in "**Historical-Processual Archaeology and Culture Making: Unpacking the Southern Cult and Mississippian Religion,**" by **Thomas E. Emerson and Timothy R. Pauketat**. Taking a "historical-processual" approach, these authors focus the analytical task on culture-making as a process rather than on the definition of culture as a structure or system. Religion then is an experience rather than a system, but recognizing this crucial fact archaeologically requires looking beyond the evidence of elite religion—often the most obvious aspect of the archaeological record—to the individuals acts of the "average" prehistoric person.

The great archaeological religious monuments, such as the temples at Teotihuacan or the pyramids at Giza, arguably were at least in part created to promote a particular view about religion, its place in society and the relationship of the elite to the supernatural. Our own archaeological emphasis on exactly these monuments has, in a sense, perpetuated the ideological message they were intended to encode, rendering into historical fact a message about the "natural" order of things that was instead negotiated and contested in the past, and may have had little everyday implication for the average person. Practice theory, involving analyses beyond the metaphysical aspects of religion and the elite experience in prehistory, is one way to correct this constructed view of the past.

Landscapes of Religion

The ideological implications of religion, particularly in terms of the interplay between religious and political power, are addressed directly by **Johannes H. N. Loubser** in his contribution, "**Discontinuity Between Political Power and Religious Status: Mountains, Pools, and Dry Ones Among Venda-Speaking Chiefdoms of Southern Africa.**" In the process Loubser raises two additional but important issues. The first concerns change over time in religious belief and practice. By carefully inter-weaving ethnographic and archaeological data, he demonstrates that religious change is in many respects an empirical process that is visible in the archaeological record. This substantiates careful use of the so-called Direct-Historical Approach (e.g., Wedel 1938), in part by negating the common archaeological attitude that a catastrophic break necessarily exists between the prehistoric and the recent (post-Western contact) past. Loubser also illustrates the importance of landscape, and especially landscape symbolism, in conceptualizations of settlement patterns and the internal arrangements of sites themselves. The message here is an important one: even in archaeological cases lacking obvious monumental constructions, religious (and political) symbolism permeated the surroundings of prehistoric peoples. Seen from the perspective of the previous group of papers, this fact emphasizes the embeddedness of religion in daily life.

The importance of landscape in the study of prehistoric religion is further emphasized by **Chris Scarre** in his paper "**Shrines of the Land and Places of Power: Religion and the Transition to Farming in Western Europe**." Scarre draws partly upon ethnographic analogy to consider the well-known megalithic monuments of the European Neolithic, suggesting that they may reflect animistic beliefs and concerns with ancestors. In both cases they are part of a numinous landscape and potentially may reflect, as he speculates, a transition from the use of natural places to the intentional creation of places for religious purposes. But whether natural or cultural, the message is that religious belief and practice were not necessarily isolated from the quotidian; instead mundane life transpired within the context of a world imbued with religious significance.

Lessons from Ethnography

The final group of papers considers the archaeology of religion in terms of some guidelines and cautionary suggestions derived from ethnographic and ethnological research. In his contribution, "**Northern Landscapes, Northern Mind: On the Trail of an** "*Archaeology of Hunter-Gatherer Belief*," **Peter Jordan** outlines some of the implications of his work with the Siberian Khanty for hunter-gatherer research specifically. Appropriately, given the theme of the previous papers, he emphasizes the importance of the articulation between worldview and landscape, including how religious sensibilities inform even movement across the landscape during the conduct of subsistence activities. The message again is that religious practice is part of all practices, full-stop, and cannot be treated as a phenomenon or entity in its own right.

Kelley Hays-Gilpin looks at an issue not otherwise considered in the volume in her chapter, "**Archaeology and Women's Ritual Business.**" Religion and gender are often inseparably related, and any attempt to consider one without attending to the other has the potential for leading to significant interpretive error. She identifies gender bias in some of the earliest ethnographic research on religion, shows how we inherited this historical bias, and warns that with the analogical use of this research in archaeology we perpetuate gender bias. Although most archaeologists have moved beyond the simplistic conceptualization of hunter-gatherers in terms of "Man the Hunter," too often these same archaeologists continue to consider religion as manifest in "Man the Ritual Official." More critical uses of ethnography—the importance of which Jordan also promotes—illustrate why gender matters, both in terms of female participation in ritual activities and the potential for other-gendered involvement in religion more widely.

The volume ends, appropriately enough, with a chapter that considers the archaeology of religion not from the perspective of traditional archaeological practice (regardless of how theorized), but from the view of our archaeological future. Here **María Nieves Zedeño** discusses collaborative research with indigenous consultants for the interpretation of the archaeological record, in her chapter "**Traditional Knowledge, Ritual Behavior, and Contemporary Interpretations of the Archaeological Record—An Ojibwa Perspective.**" Supporting the comments made by Jordan and Hays-Gilpin, Zedeño emphasizes first the need to approach contemporary sources critically but honestly. She also shows that traditional knowledge can be retained, even into contemporary times, and how this knowledge follows a cultural logic, albeit a cultural logic that may not be obvious to the western observer. One of her examples—a lithic scatter interpreted as a ritual offering by her consultants and, as she illustrates, so interpreted for good reason—should give pause to archaeologists otherwise blind to all but the most eco-functional of site interpretations. Inasmuch as archaeology in many parts of the world will require substantially more indigenous participation, Zedeño's contribution provides some guidelines for the future of archaeological research.

Belief in the Past

The chapters in this volume chart ongoing and potential future directions of and for an archaeology of religion. But like religion itself in the face of culture change (as many of the authors suggest), none of this necessarily requires a complete break with traditional approaches and practices. Burials, monuments and monumental architecture, and iconography continue to provide key data for many of our authors, and are likely to be evidential components of much future research on prehistoric ritual and belief. This is unlikely to change although, as many of these authors also contend, we need to look beyond these aspects of the archaeological record alone to explore religion in the past.

As the philosopher Mary Midgley (2003) has illustrated, the sciences largely have ignored religion as a topic of interest since the Enlightenment. This is not because the subject cannot be studied, however, but instead because, initially at least, science and religion were competing modes of thought. Science is now sufficiently mature as a mode of thought to turn its gaze towards its former rival, in order to understand religion as one of the universals of human social life. We believe the chapters in this volume contribute towards this understanding although, to be sure, there is still much to learn.

Notes

1. We recognize that archaeologists have never entirely ignored religion and that there is even a sub-discipline, biblical archaeology, which has always been explicitly tied to this topic. Instead our point, directed particularly at prehistoric archaeology—including both processual and post-processual prehistoric archaeologies—is that, when religious remains have been considered, interest in them has emphasized their socio-political implications with their religious nature barely if ever explicitly acknowledged. These socio-political implications are very important, to be sure, as emphasized in the discussion that follows. But to ignore the religious context and implications of these same remains is a bit like making a sandwich with only one piece of bread—the good stuff in the middle is likely to fall out. Not only is the result less than a full sandwich, but it leaves an untidy mess of lost ingredients behind.
2. With one exception, the papers in this volume originated in a session presented at the 2004 Society for American Archaeology meetings, in Montreal, "Faith in the Past: Theorizing an Archaeology of Religion." The exception is Michael Winkelman's paper, which was presented in 2005 at a meeting of the American Anthropological Association in Atlanta.

3. We refrain from use of the adjectival form of "process" here ("processual") because this word has been irremediably hijacked as the descriptor for a scientific approach to archaeology. Our point is that these kinds of explanatory and/or interpretive questions are likely of interest to both processual and post-processual archaeologists (as well as those in between and those who may consider themselves outside the debate—the elusive "extra-processualists").

References Cited

Atran, Scott
2002   *In Gods We Trust: The Evolutionary Landscapes of Religion.* Oxford University Press, Oxford.
Barrett, J.
2004   *Why Would Anyone Believe in God?* AltaMira Press, Walnut Creek.
Boyer, Pascal
2001   *Religion Explained: The Evolutionary Origins of Religious Thought.* Basic Books, New York.
Gibbs, Jr., Raymond W.
2006   *Embodiment and Cognitive Science.* Cambridge University Press, Cambridge.
Hall, Robert L.
1997   *An Archaeology of the Soul: North American Indian Belief and Ritual.* University of Illinois Press, Urbana.
Hawkes, Christopher
1954   Archaeological Theory and Method: Some Suggestions from the Old World. *American Anthropologist* 56:155–168.
Hayden, Brian
2003   *Shamans, Sorcerers, and Saints: A Prehistory of Religion.* Smithsonian Books, Washington, DC.
Insoll, Timothy (editor)
2001   *Archaeology and World Religion.* Routledge, London.
2003   *The Archaeology of Islam in Sub-Saharan Africa.* Cambridge University Press, Cambridge.
2004   *Archaeology, Ritual and Religion.* Routledge, London.
Lakoff, George, and Mark Johnson
1999   *Philosophy in the Flesh: The Embodied Mind and Its Challenge to Western Thought.* Basic Books, New York.
Layton, Robert (editor)
2001   Ethnographic Study and Symbolic Analysis, in D. S. Whitley, pp. 311–332. *Handbook of Rock Art Research.* AltaMira Press, Walnut Creek.
McCauley, R. N., and E. T. Lawson
2002   *Bringing Ritual to Mind: Psychological Foundations of Cultural Forms.* Cambridge University Press, Cambridge.
Midgley, Mary
2003   *The Myths We Live By.* Routledge, London.
Morris, Brian
1987   *Anthropological Studies of Religion: An Introductory Text.* Cambridge University Press, Cambridge.
Pyysianen, Ilkka
2004   *Magic, Miracles and Religion: A Scientist's Perspective.* AltaMira Press, Walnut Creek.
Van Pool, Christine S., and Todd L. Van Pool
2007   *Signs of the Casas Grandes Shamans.* University of Utah Press, Salt Lake City.

Van Pool, Christine S., and Todd L. Van Pool, and David A. Phillips, Jr., (editors)
2006   *Religion in the Prehispanic Southwest.* AltaMira Press, Lanham, MD.
Wedel, Waldo R.
1938   The Direct-Historical Approach in Pawnee Archaeology. *Smithsonian Miscellaneous Collections* 97(7). Washington, DC.
Whitehouse, Harvey
2004   *Modes of Religiosity: A Cognitive Theory of Religious Transmission.* AltaMira Press, Walnut Creek.
Whitley, David S.
2004   Archaeology of Shamanism. In M. N. Walter and E. J. N. Fridman, editors, pp. 16–21. *Shamanism: An Encyclopedia of World Beliefs, Practices, and Culture, Volume 1.* Santa Barbara, ABC-Clio.
2008   The Archaeology of Religion. In A. Baxter, H. Maschner, and C. Chippindale, editors, *Handbook of Archaeological Theories,* pp. 547–566. AltaMira Press, Lanham, MD.
Winkelman, Michael
1992   *Shamans, Priests, and Witches: A Cross-Cultural Study of Magico-Religious Practicioners.* Anthropological Research Papers No. 44, Arizona State University, Tempe.

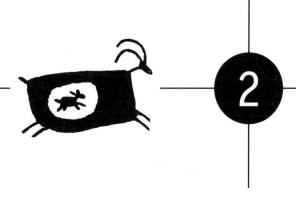

RELIGION AND ARCHAEOLOGY: AN ANALYTICAL, MATERIALIST ACCOUNT

J. David Lewis-Williams

"Religion" is a notorious word. Like many others, people use it freely, but, if asked to define it, they are immediately at a loss—or soon will be. Yet archaeologists employ it frequently to designate certain ancient activities, evidence for which they find during the course of their research. Some are happy to leave it at that, thus confirming the old jest that inexplicable remains may be safely attributed to "religion" or "ritual." Religion is thus a last resort: researchers invoke it only when no rational, probably adaptive explanation can be devised. It is a case of religion by default. Thereby, they create a dichotomy between religion and what they see as more mundane, practical components of life. Here, I present a view of religion that aims to elude the barbed joke by pointing to some fundamental features of religion that are useful in understanding archaeological evidence of both the puzzling and the apparently day-to-day kinds.

In addition to expressing reservations about "religious" explanations, some present-day researchers go further and decry any endeavor to address "origins." They say that every origin must have had its origin and so on in an infinite regression; to speak of discovering "an origin" of religion then is facile. Although there is some truth in this position, it is founded on a misunderstanding of at least some kinds of "origins." As will become clear, when I speak of the origin of religion, I am not referring to a specific time, or a specific event, but rather to a continuing process.

Social or Psychological?

Emile Durkheim (1858–1911), the highly influential French sociologist and anthropologist manqué, advocated a view of religion that is still attractive because it seems (to Westerners) to embody much common sense. He summed up his position in a passage that is worth quoting in full because it encapsulates a number of ideas that are still prominent in archaeologists' minds:

> For the author religion derives from a double source: firstly, the need to understand; and secondly, from sociability. We would say, at the outset, that these factors should be inverted, and that sociability should be made the determining cause of religious sentiment. Men did not begin by imagining gods; it is not because they conceived of them in a given fashion that they became bound to them by social feelings. They began by linking themselves to the things which they made use of, or which they suffered from, in the same way as they linked each of these to the other—without reflection, without the least kind of speculation. The theory only came later, in order to explain and make intelligible to these rudimentary minds the modes of behaviour which had thus been formed. Since these sentiments were quite similar to those which he observed in his relationships with his fellows, man conceived of these natural powers as beings comparable to himself; and since they at the same times differed amongst themselves, he attributed to these exceptional beings distinctive qualities which made them gods. (Durkheim 1972:219)

For many archaeologists, Durkheim's sociological emphasis is attractive because it can be readily brought into line with evolutionary notions of adaptation: religion exists because it is adaptive; it helps people to survive in sometimes hostile environments by providing a foundation for cooperation against the elements. It also chimes well with notions of alliance networks to which archaeologists frequently appeal to provide a social context for their accounts of past behavior. Religion is thus, at base, a means to survival, even if some of its beliefs may seem to us today to be irrational.

"Sociability" and "the need to understand," to place them in his preferred order, are Durkheim's cornerstones (see also Berger 1973). The one he relegates to second place has overtones of psychology: human beings are believed to have an innate desire to explain their environments. Religion is thus essentially etiological, and Durkheim implies the existence of a universal, innate human drive to explain things. There is here an implication of a psychological, or emotional, need to do so. If people cannot explain, say, the regular appearance of the sun in the east, they become psychologically unsettled. Perhaps "intellectualism" would be a better word than "psychological" to describe this point of view because the mental state that demands explanations for everything is a product of Western history. It culminated in the nineteenth century with the offshoots of Darwinism (and, one may add, Durkheim).

If a need to explain is cultural and not hard-wired, what is the defining characteristic of religion? Are sociology and psychology the only two routes to understanding the essence of religion? Let me put it this way: It is sometimes said that baseball is a religion in the United States of America. It has a pantheon of "worshipped" heroes; its practice incorporates elaborate rituals and accoutrements; it is socially cohesive; it even provides emotional catharsis. But to conclude that baseball is therefore a "religion" is surely a distortion; rather, it is like religion in some ways. Baseball may well perform some of the functions of religion, but that does not make baseball a religion. If we claim that it is, we are using the word "religion" metaphorically.

Baseball is, I argue, markedly unlike religion in that all religions have some orientation to unseen realms, beings, and powers; religion posits the existence of supernatural things. For the position that I develop, this is its defining characteristic. The sociological component follows rather than precedes what Durkheim called "imagining gods." The real questions are these: What does "imagining" mean? What leads people everywhere to suspect the existence of an unseen realm?

The Supernatural

The existence of a whole realm inhabited by spirits that is set over and against the material world in which we live is, on the face of it, a highly unlikely proposition. There is no evidence in the material world that there are, for instance, beings living beneath the surface of the land or up beyond the blue of the sky. If, for example, people interpret thunder as the voice of god, they do so because they already have a conception of invisible beings and spirit realms. The same applies to other natural phenomena, such as the shapes of clouds, earth tremors, and reflections in water, all of which are occasionally put forward as triggering religious beliefs.

Neither does death suggest an after-life in another realm, as numerous writers assert. The earliest *Homo sapiens* communities experienced death not only among their own number but also all around them in nature. Death did not set them apart from other animals or even plants; on the contrary, it showed them that they were no different from them. So, while they may well have grieved, there was no evidence before them to suggest that the deceased lived on in another dimension. If people believe in, say, the reincarnation of an animal in human or another animal form, they must a priori believe in spirit realms. Beliefs in life after death could not flow simply from awareness of death. If they came to believe in that other kind of existence, they must have had something other than death itself to differentiate them from animals.

To get at that "something," we go back to one of the founding fathers of anthropology, Sir Edward Burnett Tylor (1832–1917). Unfortunately, his ideas about religion were eclipsed by Durkheim's sociological theory. Tylor believed that death, trances, visions, and especially dreams suggested to early people the existence of a soul or spirit, something immaterial. This is the well-known dream theory of the origin of religion. Early people, so the argument continues, then transferred the notion of a soul to animals and things, and out of this transference was born the supposed primitive belief system now known as "animism," a word coined by Tylor (1871). Eventually animism developed, along with its corollary, magic, into beliefs about gods and, finally, monotheistic religions.

Tylor thus sensibly distinguished between the origin of religion and its subsequent development through the millennia. But in doing so he missed a key point. The origin of religion was not an event that is now lost in the depths of time and that, once it happened, was left far behind. Religion did not evolve as animals evolved, leaving behind them earlier forms. Detached from its economic and political components and taken across the world, it is today not much different from what it was thousands of years ago: there are still people who believe in a spirit-inhabited realm that has the power to influence the weather and other aspects of material life. Indeed, there is no reason to suppose that monotheism is any better or more evolved than polytheism: both demand belief in a spiritual, non-material realm.

Today, Tylor's explanation for the origin of religion is, unlike Durkheim's, largely dismissed. Critics say that it is a "just-so story." The late-nineteenth-century anthropologist thought himself into the minds of baffled early people. How, he asked his Victorian, Darwinian self, would I explain my dreams? His critics say that he came up with an explanation that is in fact unverifiable. They also point out that attitudes to dreams vary greatly in societies around the world. Finally, they ask how it is that religion, merely the result of a primitive illusion, has lasted through millennia and is still part of life. The persistence of religion, I argue, in fact points to the answer to the problem of the origin of religion. Rather than the evolutionary stages of religion, it is the origin, or, as I prefer, origin-as-process, that concerns us now because it is the key to the social and conceptual development of religion—and Tylor was within grasping distance of seeing the difference between origin and process.

Beliefs in a supernatural realm do indeed persist, and however diverse they may be, they are worldwide. They remain an inadequately explained human phenomenon. Neither Durkheim nor Tylor dealt adequately with the universality of religion. Indeed, the universality of religion suggests that beliefs in supernatural realms with huge emotional impact are not merely attempts to make sense of the world, but rather they are in some way "wired" into the human brain. So Tylor had a point.

But the "wiring" is more comprehensive than he knew. As we shall see, features of dreams and some altered states of consciousness that are neurologically wired occur in most religions. These common features suggest that religion is closely related to mental states generated by the electro-chemical functioning of the human brain. Modern research on the ways in which the brain functions to produce the complex experience call consciousness provides a foundation for an understanding of religion that is more nuanced than Tylor's and that unites its social and psychological elements.

A Spectrum of Consciousness

Human beings are not either conscious or unconscious, as may be popularly supposed. Consciousness should rather be thought of as a spectrum (for more on the consciousness spectrum see Lewis-Williams 2002; Lewis-Williams and Pearce 2005).

At one end of the spectrum is alert consciousness—the kind that we use to relate rationally to our environment and to solve the problems that it presents. This is an outward-directed perspective. A little farther along the spectrum are more introverted states in which we solve problems by inward thought. Now sensory input, while not eliminated, is diminished. Relax a little bit more, and you are day-dreaming: mental images come and go at will, unfettered by the material world around you. This state is sometimes known as reverie. Gradually, you slip into sleep. On the threshold between sleep and waking is the hypnagogic state. In it, people experience vivid hallucinations that are principally visual but may also have an aural component. From there, sleepers drift into normal dreaming, a world of changing forms and impossible circumstances. And from there, into deep, dreamless sleep.

What we think of as normal waking consciousness is thus not a discrete, consolidated state. Evidence suggests that our normal day comprises cycles of 90 to 120 minutes of moving between outward-directed attention and inward-directed states (Laughlin et al. 1992:132). Waking consciousness is thus closely linked to dreaming with its fragments of remembrance, bizarre concatenations of events, and transformations. Although the specifics of dreams are cultural and personal, the structure of dreams and the sorts of events that recur in them are neurologically engendered. Dreaming is a human universal created by the electro-chemical functioning of the brain.

Altered States of Consciousness

So far, I have spoken about the mercurial states of consciousness that everyone experiences in the natural course of life. But there is more to human consciousness. In all religions there is an ecstatic component, whether of the introverted (meditative) or the extroverted (frenzied) kind. Human beings are universally intrigued by the "autistic" end of the consciousness spectrum that they inevitably glimpse in dreams. They try to intensify "autistic" consciousness by a wide variety of means, including ingestion of psychotropic substances, hypnagogia, intense rhythmic dancing, auditory driving (e.g., chanting, clapping, drumming), electrical stimulation, flickering light, fatigue, hunger (fasting), sensory deprivation, extreme pain, and intense concentration (meditation). It can also be intensified by natural circumstances, such as near-death experiences, migraine, temporal lobe epilepsy, schizophrenia, and other pathological conditions.

These means, either singly or in combinations, lead to three intergrading stages of what most people think of as "altered states of consciousness" (Clottes and Lewis-Williams 1998, 2001; Lewis-Williams 2001, 2002, 2004a; Lewis-Williams and Dowson 1988; Lewis-Williams and Pearce 2005).

Stage 1

Altered states often start with geometric mental images. Researchers have given these percepts various names: form constants (e.g., Klüver 1966), phosphenes (Oster 1970), endogenous percepts (Dronfield 1995, 1996), and entoptic phenomena (Lewis-Williams and Dowson 1988). I prefer the term "entoptic," which means generated anywhere in the optic system, not necessarily within the eye itself. By and large, six frequently repeated forms can be identified:

1. A basic grid and its development into a lattice and expanding hexagon pattern.
2. Sets of parallel lines.
3. Bright dots and short flecks.
4. Zigzag lines, reported by some subjects as angular, by others as undulating.
5. Nested catenary curves, the outer arc of which comprises flickering zigzags (well known to migraine sufferers as the "fortification illusion").
6. Filigrees, or thin meandering lines.

Because these forms are mercurial, the six categories are not as rigid as this list seems to imply. Moreover, the percepts pulsate, or vibrate, with bright light that is independent of any source in the subject's environment. They rotate, expand, contract, combine, and change one into another. They may be projected onto veridical imagery when the eyes are open; the manner in which they seem to float on walls or ceilings is an important point.

We need to note that, even though all people have the potential to see all the forms, cultural emphases may lead them to value some and to ignore others. People in societies that accord altered states of consciousness important religious status therefore watch for and try to cultivate a restricted range of forms—the ones to which their religion ascribes emotionally charged spiritual meanings. The Tukano people of South America, for instance, take undulating parallel lines (Type 4) to represent "the thought of the Sun-Father." An arc of several multicolored parallel lines (Type 5) is taken, understandably enough, to represent a rainbow, but in some mythological contexts which would be impossible for an outsider to construe, it is said to be the Sun-Father's penis (Reichel-Dolmatoff 1978:32–34). The southern African San, on the other hand, concentrate on brilliant lines (Types 2 and 6) that they believe to be "threads of light" that healers climb, or along which they float, to the Great God in the sky. Similar funicular visions have been reported from Australia. A boy taking part in an initiation ceremony that involved looking at "a large, bright crystal that stole the light from the dawn and dazzled their eyes" sank "into a state of repose that was almost sleep." Then he saw cords that "seemed to rise into the air, and the old fellows climbed hand over hand up them to treetop height" (Rose, in Narby and Huxley 2001:123). The Tukano, the San, and the Australians were all experiencing entoptic phenomena.

Stage 2

When people move into the deeper, second stage of altered consciousness, they begin to try to make sense of the entoptic forms they are seeing by construing them as objects with emotional or religious significance (Horowitz 1964:514, 1975:177, 178, 181), a tendency already described for the Stage 1 visions. In a normal state of consciousness the brain receives a constant stream of sense impressions. A visual image reaching the brain is decoded (as, of course, are other sense impressions) by being matched against a store of experience. If a "fit" can be effected, the image is "recognized." In altered states of consciousness the nervous system itself becomes a "sixth sense" (Heinz 1986) that produces a variety of images including entoptic phenomena. The brain attempts to recognize, or decode, these forms as it does impressions supplied by the nervous system in a normal state of consciousness. Mardi Horowitz links this process of making sense to the disposition of the subject:

> Thus the same ambiguous round shape on initial perceptual representation can be "illusioned" into an orange (if the subject is hungry), a breast (if he is in a state of heightened sexual drive), a cup of water (if he is thirsty), or an anarchist's bomb (if he is hostile or fearful). (Horowitz 1975:177)

Stage 3

In the third (still "deeper") stage, subjects find themselves in a bizarre, ever-changing world of hallucinations. People report somatic hallucin-ations, such as attenuation of limbs and bodies, intense awareness of one's body, polymelia (the sensation of having extra digits and limbs), zoopsia (seeing animals), changing into animals, and other transformations. As long ago as 1880, William James, the American psychologist and phil-osopher and brother of the novelist Henry, recorded the experiences of a friend who had ingested hashish; my observations are in square brackets:

> Directly I lay down upon a sofa there appeared before my eyes several rows of human hands [polyopsia], which oscillated for a moment [pulsat-ing], revolved and then changed into spoons [transformation]. The same motions were repeated, the objects changing to wheels, tin soldiers, lamp-posts, brooms, and countless other absurdities [some of these transform-ations appear to derive from entoptic forms 2 and 3] ... I became aware of the fact that my pulse was beating rapidly ... I could feel each pulsation through my whole system [somatic intensity] ... There were moments of apparent lucidity, when it seemed as if I could see within myself, and watch the pumping of my heart [preternatural sight]. A strange fear came over me, a certainty that I should never recover from the effects [heightened emotions] ... Suddenly there was a roar and a blast of sound and the word "Ismaral" [aural hallucination] ... I thought of a fox, and instantly I was transformed into that animal. I could distinctly feel myself a fox, could see my long ears and bushy tail, and by a sort of introversion felt that my com-plete anatomy was that of a fox [transformation into an animal]. Suddenly, the point of vision changed. My eyes seemed to be located at the back of my mouth; I looked out between parted lips [somatic transformation]. (William James, quoted in Siegel and Jarvik 1975:104–105)

One feature of Stage 3 experiences like these is that the entoptic forms of Stage 1 persist, peripherally or integrated with iconic hallucinations. One subject found that the lattice, or grid form (Type 1), merged with his body:

> He saw fretwork before his eyes, that his arms, hands, and fingers turned into fretwork. There was no difference between the fretwork and himself, between inside and outside. All objects in the room and the walls changed into fretwork and thus became identical with him. While writing, the words turned into fretwork and there was, therefore, an identity of fretwork and handwriting. "The fretwork is I." He also felt, saw, tasted, and smelled tones that became fretwork. He himself was the tone. On the day follow-ing the experiment, there was Nissl (whom he had known in 1914) sitting somewhere in the air, and Nissl was fretwork. (Klüver 1966:71–72)

Here we see further points of interest:

– Hallucinations are experienced in all senses.
– The senses become confused so that one may smell a sound (synesthesia).

– Entoptic forms may be projected onto surfaces and objects in the environment.
– Entoptic forms can become all-pervasive.
– Subjects can themselves become an entoptic form.
– So-called after-images may recur unexpectedly some time after a hallucinatory experience.

There is an interaction between wired experiences that are activated in altered states of consciousness and the culturally specific content that is incorporated into those experiences. Human brains exist in societies.

The Religious Cosmos

Once it is realized that the mind can open up on realms of experience other than those of everyday life, people begin to ask, What sort of world, or two worlds, are we living in? How do we harmonize such diverse experiences? Where do the beings that we see in dreams and visions live?

A cosmology is a culturally constructed view of reality, of the universe. The nature of a community's cosmology is governed by the degree of credence that people give to the introverted end of the consciousness spectrum. Those who emphasize the revelatory nature of dreams and visions have a different cosmology from those who insist on alert observation as the only means to understanding the material world. Here, we are principally concerned with societies that take altered consciousness seriously. One of the remarkable features of the religions of such societies worldwide is that people believe in cosmological levels. At its simplest, the cosmos is believed to have three levels:

A realm above,
inhabited by beings and spirit animals

The daily world
in which people live

An underworld,
where beings and spirit animals dwell

Some societies, especially more complex ones, often believe in more than three tiers, but the layered nature is retained. A tiered cosmos provides a framework not only for the experiences of dreams and visions but also for daily life. It coordinates the diverse experiences of the consciousness spectrum. How can we account for the ubiquity of such beliefs? I argue that they are wired into human consciousness. Two neurologically generated experiences are part of the consciousness spectrum.

Vortex

As subjects move towards Stage 3, they often experience a vortex or tunnel, at the end of which is bright light. On the internal surface of the vortex there is sometimes a grid, in the compartments of which appear the first images of people, animals, monsters, and so forth (Siegel 1977).

Today the vortex, which is discussed frequently, is particularly associated with near-death experiences (e.g., Blackmore 1982; Fox 2003). Examples abound. A child who was grievously ill and was rushed to a hospital later recalled that "I was moving through this ... long dark place. It seemed like a sewer or something" (Moody, quoted in Fox 2003:17). Another person who had been near to death recounted his passing down a passageway: "I floated on down the hall and out of the door onto the screened-in porch ... I floated right straight on through the screen ... and up into this pure crystal light" (ibid.). Less beatific experiences have also been recorded: "It was like being in a cylinder which had no air in it" (ibid., 21).

I wish to dispel the possibility that these experiences may be unique to the Western culture from which these examples come by pointing out that ritual specialists around the world frequently use similar imagery to describe their out-of-body travels to the spirit realm, regardless of the way in which they alter their consciousness. A southern African San healer, for example, spoke of "a big hole in the spirit world" and of following a line "that goes underground" (Keeney 2003:80, 105–108, 127). Similarly, a Sora shaman in India climbs down a huge tree that leads to the underworld: "The path includes dizzying precipices on the descent to the 'murky-sun country, cock-crowlight country'" (Vitebsky 1995:70).

Descent to an underworld is indeed a common shamanistic experience, and Mircea Eliade collated a number of accounts of such journeys in his book *Shamanism: Archaic Techniques of Ecstasy* (1972). For instance, Siberian Yakut shamans' costumes had attached to them symbols known as "Opening into the Earth" or "Hole of the Spirits"; these enabled them to travel to the nether realms (Eliade 1972:234). A Tungus shaman, also in Central Asia, sometimes descends to the underworld, a dangerous undertaking during which "he goes into ecstasy" and "goes down through a narrow hole and crosses three streams before he comes upon the spirits of the infernal regions" (ibid., 240).

Another Siberian shaman told of his initiation. His spirit guide, who was associated with a tree that the young man had cut down, took him to a hole in the earth.

My companion asked: "What hole is this? If your destiny is to make a [shaman's] drum of this tree, find it out!" I replied: "It is through this hole that the shaman receives the spirit of his voice." The hole became larger and larger. We descended through it and arrived at a river with two streams flowing in opposite directions. "Well, find out this one too!" said my companion, "one stream goes from the centre to the north, the other to the south—the sunny side. If you are destined to fall into a trance, find it out!" (Halifax 1979:38)

Such experiences are also associated with pathological conditions. A patient suffering from schizophrenia described his visions this way:

There were small suns and strange twilight worlds of lakes and islands ... An ancient cave, passage, or hollow ladder, seemed to connect new earths; perhaps this was such as Jacob saw, for it was an image of remote antiquity. (Cohen 1964:76–77)

A corollary of the vortex also needs to be mentioned. One of the near-death experiences cited above mentioned the sensation of being in a cylinder "which had no air in it" (Moody, quoted in Fox 2003:21), and the Siberian shaman spoke of "two streams flowing in opposite directions" (Halifax 1979:38). Similarly, a southern African San shaman said that he entered a wide river: "My feet were behind, and my head was in front ... I travelled like this. My sides were pressed by pieces of metal. Metal things fastened my sides" (Biesele 1993:71). The sensations of passing through a constraining vortex, difficulty in breathing, affected vision, a sense of being in another world, and weightlessness are frequently interpreted as being underwater. "Submersion in pools, springs, whirlpools, and rivers provides access to the underworld. The process by which one travels there is akin to drowning" (Sullivan 1988:122). Indeed, many shamans speak of diving into water. Lapp shamans, for instance, refer to altered states as "immersion," and Inuit shamans situate the beyond in the sea (Eliade 1972:235).

In Western reports we read of corridors, trains in tunnels, sewers, and so forth; the ethnographic reports express the same sensations in their own imagery of holes in the ground, trees that link the sky (their foliage) to the underworld (their roots), subaquatic travel, and so forth. Together, all the descriptions I have given show that there must be some common human proclivity to experience passage through a vortex. That commonality is clearly wired into the human nervous system and manifests itself in certain conditions of altered consciousness. That wiring is principally in the functional architecture of the striate cortex (Bressloff et al. 2000).

Flight

The vortex is one means of access to Stage 3 hallucinations. Flight is a sensation frequently experienced in that stage. South American Tapirapé shamans speak of traveling through the cosmos in a canoe. Like the Siberian shaman's horse, a feature of the open steppe, the canoe is clearly related to the riverine life of the Amazon Basin. The Tapirapé also speak of changing into birds and flying through the cosmos, a more widespread trope (Sullivan 1988:412). Other South American people, the Tupinamba of Brazil and the Caribs of Guyana, ingest a hallucinogen that helps "his soul to leave his body and fly" (Narby and Huxley 2001:99).

A recurring shamanistic dream among the South American Bororo is one of soaring very high above the earth like a vulture, accompanied by the soul of some living person, often but not always a shaman. The dreamer sees "a curiously altered but perceptually vivid world, in which 'things are very little and close to one another'" (Crocker 1985:201).

North American Inuits similarly speak of shamanistic transformation from human to bird, and they carve ivory shamanistic bears in a flying posture. (Some researchers believe these may represent a hanging bear skin; Sutherland 2001:138–140). In Siberia, Khanty drum rhythms serve to facilitate shamanistic flight. Shamans "were able to fly faster than a speeding arrow and pierced the sky on drums, flying to the golden residence of the sky god Torum" (Jordan 2001:92). Then, too, in southern Africa, nineteenth-century San spoke of their shamans transforming themselves into birds (Bleek 1935:18).

Eliade recognized the ubiquity of spiritual flight in his survey of world shamanism: "All over the world, indeed, shamans and sorcerers are credited with the power to fly, to cover immense distances in a twinkling, and to become invisible" (Eliade 1972:140). The widespread nature of such flights is indeed striking. Vitebsky (1995:11) comments that "there are astonishing similarities, which are not easy to explain, between shamanistic ideas and practices as far apart as the Arctic, Amazonia and Borneo, even though these societies have probably never had any contact with each other." Worldwide, therefore, there are tiered cosmological levels and passages between them. How can this situation be explained?

I argue that descent into a tunnel and flight to a realm above (or through the real world) are both sensations wired into the human brain that are activated in certain altered states of consciousness (Blanke et al. 2002). Beliefs in magical flight and vortex travel seem to be inextricably linked to beliefs about a tiered cosmos. How else could it be? Both are generated by neurological mechanisms. Neurological processes explain the continuing nature of religious belief in a supernatural dimension and the ways in which beliefs of this kind are coordinated with daily life in a coherent tiered cosmos. Religion and a tiered cosmology are closely related.

Transcendence and Immanence

A difficulty may seem to arise when we recall that, although shamans and other mystics talk of traveling between layers of the cosmos, they also describe the way in which spirit beings and influences are present in this world as well as above and below. Spirits are here, not exclusively there. This widespread belief leads Vitebsky to conclude that space is a metaphor for "the otherness of the spirit realm. If we see spirits around us, then this realm is not geographically removed ... Space is a way of expressing difference and separation, but the shaman's journey expresses the possibility of coming together again" (Vitebsky 1995:15).

The problem of how the spirit realms can be spatially removed and, at the same time immanent in the material world is resolved by a further understanding of human neurology. Flight, to be sure, suggests space, but the sensations of flight are experienced within the brain; that is, inside one's head. Then, too, hallucinations, as we have seen, are frequently projected onto a person's immediate environment—outside of one's head: hallucinations (perhaps of spirit beings and animals) are therefore also part of this world.

That at least some people who experience visions are aware of this duality of transcendence and immanence is evident in an explanation that a Huichol shaman gave to Joan Halifax:

> There is a doorway within our minds that usually remains hidden and secret until the time of death. The Huichol word for it is *nieríka*. *Nieríka* is a cosmic portway or interface between so-called ordinary and nonordinary realities. It is a passageway and at the some time a barrier between worlds (Halifax 1979:1; emphasis added [within our minds]).

In summary, we can say that both neuropsychology and world ethnography show that the near universality of belief in a tiered cosmos and in movement between the levels may be ascribed to the functioning of the human nervous system in a variety of altered states. The vortex leads through a tunnel or some such construal down to a nether level, while flight leads up to a realm in or above the sky. At the same time, the spiritual dimension blends with, or invades, daily life.

This conclusion does not mean that each and every member of a community experiences the full gamut of altered states. Rather, those who do thereby acquire high status and are in a position to "naturalize" their experiences, to proclaim their irrefutable reality. Those who do not experience states at the fully hallucinatory end of the consciousness spectrum manage to glimpse in their dreams something of what the visionaries experience.

Experience, Belief, Practice

The neurologically generated experiences that I have considered must be understood in a shared way for them to become the foundation of a religion. This point brings us to the matter of religious belief.

Religious belief derives, in the first instance, from attempts to codify religious experiences in specific social circumstances. The mental, neurologically engendered experiences that lie at the foundation of religion are common to all people. That is why others understand what they are talking about when they speak about the experiences. Shared beliefs about, rather than idiosyncratic views of, those experiences, become a feature of society: people develop a set of (a) fundamental, shared beliefs about the (neurologically generated) spirit world and (b) a penumbra of debated extensions of those core beliefs.

In this way, the elaboration of religious belief takes on a life of its own within a social structure that has its own tensions and divisions. A belief system discriminates between essential and penumbral beliefs. But a belief system need not, in fact seldom does, refer back in every detail to mental experiences. In literate societies, written scriptures become a canon (established by the most powerful social groups) to which people appeal for support for their own views (Whitehouse 2000). Far from consolidating religious communities, as is generally believed, sacred scriptures become the foundation for struggles far more bitter than any between communities that do not have scriptures. The written codification of verbally shared beliefs is an outcome of dissent and power struggles within a society. Written beliefs are there to facilitate the identification and exclusion of heretics.

On both sides of the divide between what Harvey Whitehouse (2000) calls imagistic and doctrinal religions (those without and those with sacred scriptures) we find people performing acts that are related to their beliefs. Religious practice, as we may call those acts, includes rituals that are designed to plug into religious experience and those that manifest religious beliefs, with or without an experiential component. We must, however, allow that, for example, a requiem mass in St. Peter's, Rome, is not representative of all rituals: the mass is highly formalized, while in many societies outsiders hardly notice some rituals, the ritual functionaries are not easily distinguished by accoutrements, and the place where the ritual is performed is not prepared in any way. It seems to be a matter of degree.

In addition to rituals, religious practice includes socially extensive projects that reproduce and entrench social discriminations, while at the same time providing means for holding different groups together in a single society. Examples include the building of cathedrals and monuments and, sometimes, the waging of crusades and genocidal war. For some, this is an uncomfortable view. Today people therefore often try to separate religious belief from religious practice by claiming that religious wars and persecutions (often triggered by individuals' religious experiences) are not true to the fundamental beliefs and experiences of a given religion (those who wage the wars, of course, claim that they are the genuine fundamentalists, in the strict sense of the word). By contrast, I suggest that what we may see as ethically "acceptable" and "unacceptable" practices can simultaneously flow from religious experience and belief, and that a religion should be judged—I see no reason why religions should not be judged—not only by what its sages or (usually ambiguous) scriptures say its tenets are but also by what adherents practice. The social practice of a religion is inseparable from its systematized beliefs. Experience, belief, and practice are thus an integrated whole.

Seers and Those Who Do Not See

It is now clear that some social relations are intimately bound up with states of consciousness. Every community of people has to come to terms with shifting human consciousness. Every community has to divide up the spectrum of consciousness and to place different values on its components—that is, to make shared sense of the diverse mental states that everyone experiences. It is, for instance, impossible to imagine a society that does not entertain some beliefs about what dreams are and what significance (if any) they have.

Today, in the modern West we value alert consciousness and problem-solving cogitation. We do not value dreams. (Exceptions are, of course, a couple of schools of psychology that believe that dreams have a symbolic content.) It is, by and large, the alert end of the spectrum that people value. The more that individuals cultivate that end of the spectrum, the more they are admired. They are deemed highly intelligent and accorded respect. The luminaries of our pantheon are Galileo, Albert Einstein, Niels Bohr, and others of their ilk. They used the alert end of their consciousness spectrum to explain and control the material world, not the introverted, "spiritual" end. Whatever inspiration may come to scientists in dreams, the answers to their research questions have to be rationally supported by mental activity at the alert end of the spectrum.

We know that this emphasis on rationality is not found in all societies, nor has it always been the case in the West. It is indeed rare. During the Middle Ages, people believed that God could communicate with them in dreams and visions; they did not laugh off their dreams as readily as we do. In the largely unquestioning ethos of pre-Enlightenment Europe the threat of excommunication was sobering. Hell and the Devil lived not only in sermons and wall paintings in churches, but also in the brains and dreams of ordinary people, fed as they were by those sources of terror. No wonder, then, that some witches truly believed themselves to be in league with the devil.

Medieval dreams, visions, and voices could be the foundation for disastrous political and military action, as Joan of Arc amply demonstrated. Similarly, the Medieval abbess Hildegard of Bingen experienced visions in which she believed God revealed to her the structure of the cosmos—where heaven was in relation to the earth and where degrees of angels and other beings resided. Most people of that time did not differentiate between material and spiritual things: the cosmos embraced both. Altered states revealed the nature of materiality. As a result of her visions, Hildegard developed a position of influence and respect.

It is today believed that Hildegard's visions were caused by migraine (Sacks 1970). But, once it is realized that dreams and unsought visions afford glimpses of a realm that is very different from, yet inextricably related to the material world, they become a source of influence and power. It is then that the induction and intensification of the introverted end of the spectrum is deliberately sought in altered states of consciousness. These states provide the most intense religious experiences.

In Medieval Christianity, the more intense forms of meditation and prayer were the preserve of the clergy: it was they who, through extended prayer, solitary meditation, fasting, repetitive ritual, and chanting altered their consciousness, and possibly even induced visions. In doing so, they also maintained their status. The difference between monks and lay brothers in some monasteries was not just one of education: the monks through their chanting, fasting, and incessant prayers were able to reach a mental state that was considered closer to God than any that ordinary people could attain. Those few who could go even beyond euphoria and dissociation and experience vivid visions were more likely to achieve positions of influence in the church and therefore in affairs of state as well. When "outsiders," such as adolescent girls, experienced visions of the Virgin Mary, they occupied an unusual, ambivalent social category and were investigated by the church.

So far I have argued that the types of experience that lead to belief in a supernatural realm and to social discrimination are the foundation of the phenomenon we call religion. Lest it be thought that I argue that altered states of consciousness, as popularly conceived, are the only basis for religion I point to other mental states that many people would not considered "altered."

In some secular circumstances, people understand these experiences not as supernatural in origin but as some sort of aesthetic effulgence— Wordsworth's response to unexpected beauty: "Ne'er saw I, never felt, a calm so deep!" Somewhere between supernatural and aesthetic experiences is the sense of being one with the universe. This state has been termed "absolute unitary being"—AUB. It is often the result of meditation: people in this state feel that boundaries between themselves and others (including the world itself) break down. The neurological foundation of AUB has been studied (d'Aquili and Newberg 1993, 1999; see also Ramachandran and Blakeslee 1998); the sensations of religious exaltation, calm, and AUB are wired into the brain.

Religion and Social Discrimination

The need to accommodate shifting consciousness and the different values placed on segments of the spectrum necessarily mean that religion, long before the Christian era, was the first means of social discrimination that was not founded on age, sex, and strength (Lewis-Williams 2002). New values entered human ethics. How did this come about?

As long ago as the Upper Palaeolithic it was the shifting nature of human consciousness that led people to suppose that there was another realm of existence and that beings in that realm interacted with people in the material world. The more a person, or group of people, inhabited the altered end of the consciousness spectrum the closer they considered themselves to be to that other realm. That closeness distinguished them from other people and was worth defending: access to "spiritual" states was regulated. This regulation was underwritten by religious belief (whether committed to writing or not) and religious practices that repeatedly manifested social differences. Religion and social discrimination always go hand in hand. And social discrimination is the foundation of social change.

Archaeology

Shifting consciousness is universal, and we may assume that the people whom archaeologists study experienced the spectrum as I have described it. But to say that they experienced it is not enough. We need to ask if what we know about consciousness and its links with cosmology explains specific archaeological remains, or at any rate provides a framework for the construction of explanations. I have illustrated the way in which this explanatory process may proceed in an examination of Upper Palaeolithic cave art (Lewis-Williams 2002), the domestication of the aurochs (Lewis-Williams 2004b; Lewis-Williams and Pearce 2005) southern African San religion (Lewis-Williams and Pearce 2004), and surveys of Neolithic megalithic monuments (Lewis-Williams and Dowson 1993; Lewis-Williams and Pearce 2005).

Far from being of peripheral interest to archaeologists, religion in its three dimensions (experience, belief, and practice) was integral to the societies that they study. It was not merely icing on the cake. Rather, religion was often a dynamic and causal factor in the complex web of social and economic change. Moreover, religion is not an intrinsically unrecoverable component of the past (Lewis-Williams 1991, 1997). Its universal neurological foundations and the ways in which those foundations articulate with beliefs and practices make religion, as I have conceived of it in this chapter, a viable and indeed indispensable component of archaeologists' research.

References Cited

Berger, Peter L.
1973   *The Social Reality of Religion*. Penguin, Harmondsworth.

Biesele, Megan
1993   *"Women Like Meat": The Folklore and Foraging Ideology of the Kalahari Ju/'hoansi.* Witwatersrand University Press, Johannesburg.

Blackmore, Susan
1982   *Dying to Live: Science and the Near-Death Experience.* Grafton, London.

Blanke, O., S. Ortigue, T. Landis, and M. Seeck
2002   Stimulating illusory own-body perceptions: the part of the brain that can induce out-of-body experiences has been located. *Nature* 419:269–270.

Bleek, Dorothea F.
1935   Beliefs and Customs of the /Xam Bushmen: Part VII: Sorcerors [*sic*]. *Bantu Studies* 9:1–47.

Bressloff, P. C., J. D. Cowan, M. Golubitsky, P. J. Thomas, and M. C. Wiener
2000   Geometric Visual Hallucinations, Euclidean Symmetry and the Functional Architecture of the Striate Cortex. *Philosophical Transactions of the Royal Society, London*, Series B, 356:299–330.

Cohen, Sidney
1964   *The Beyond Within: The LSD Story.* Atheneum, New York.

Clottes, Jean, and J. David Lewis-Williams
1998   *The Shamans of Prehistory: Trance and Magic in the Painted Caves.* Harry Abrams, New York.

2001   *Les chamanes de la préhistoire: texte intégral, polémique et réponses.* La Maison des Roches, Paris.

Crocker, Jon Christopher
1985   *Vital Souls: Bororo Cosmology, Natural Symbolism, and Shamanism.* University of Arizona Press, Tucson.

d'Aquili, Eugene G., and Andrew B. Newberg
1993   Religious and Mystical States: A Neuropsychological Model. *Zygon* 28:177–199.

1999   *The Mystical Mind: Probing the Biology of Religious Experience.* Fortress Press, Minneapolis.

Dronfield, Jeremy C.
1995   Subjective Vision and the Source of Irish Megalithic Art. *Antiquity* 69:539–549.

1996   Entering Alternative Realities: Cognition, Art and Architecture in Irish Passage-Tombs. *Cambridge Archaeological Journal* 6:37–72.

Durkheim, Emile
1972   *Emile Durkheim: Selected Writings*, edited by Antony Giddens. Cambridge University Press, Cambridge. First published in 1887.

Eliade, Mircea
1972   *Shamanism: Archaic Techniques of Ecstasy.* Routledge and Kegan Paul, New York.

Fox, Mark
2003   *Religion, Spirituality and the Near-Death Experience.* Routledge, London.

Halifax, Joan
1979   *Shamanistic Voices: A Survey of Visionary Narratives.* Penguin, Harmondsworth.

Heinz, R.-I.
1986   More on Mental Imagery and Shamanism. *Current Anthropology* 27:154.

Horowitz, Mardi J.
1964   The Imagery of Visual Hallucinations. *Journal of Nervous and Mental Disease* 138:513–523.

1975   Hallucinations: An Information-Processing Approach. In *Hallucinations: Behaviour, Experience and Theory*, edited by Ronald K. Siegal and Louis J. West, pp. 163–195. John Wiley, New York.

Jordan, Peter
2001   The Materiality of Shamanism As a 'World-View': Praxis, Artefacts and Landscape. In *The Archaeology of Shamanism*, edited by Neil Price, pp. 87–104. Routledge, London.
Keeney, Bradford
2003   *Ropes to God: Experiencing the Bushman Spiritual Universe*. Ringing Rocks, Philadelphia.
Klüver, Heinrich
1966   *Mescal and Mechanisms of Hallucination*. University of Chicago Press, Chicago.
Laughlin, Charles D., John McManus, and Eugene G. d'Aquili
1992   *Brain, Symbol and Experience: Towards a Neurophenomenology of Human Consciousness*. Columbia University Press, New York.
Lewis-Williams, J. David
1991   Wrestling with Analogy: A Methodological Dilemma in Upper Palaeolithic Art Research. *Proceedings of the Prehistoric Society* 57:149–160. Reprinted in *Reader in Archaeological Theory*, edited by David S. Whitley, pp. 157–175. London: Routledge.
1997   Agency, Art and Altered Consciousness: A Motif in French (Quercy) Upper Palaeolithic Parietal Art. *Antiquity* 71:810–830.
2001   Brainstorming Images: Neuropsychology and Rock Art Research. In *Handbook of Rock Art Research*, pp. 332–357. AltaMira Press, Walnut Creek.
2002   *The Mind in the Cave: Consciousness and the Origins of Art*. Thames and Hudson, London.
2004a   Neuropsychology and Upper Palaeolithic Art: Observations on the Progress of Altered States of Consciousness. *Cambridge Archaeological Journal* 14: 107–111.
2004b   Constructing a Cosmos: Architecture, Power and Somestication at Catalhuyuk. Journal of Social Archaeology 4:28–59.
In press *The Mind in the Tomb: Neolithic Cosmology, Religion and Monuments*. Thames and Hudson, London.
Lewis-Williams, J. David, and Thomas A. Dowson
1988   The Signs of All Times: Entoptic Phenomena in Upper Palaeolithic Art. *Current Anthropology* 29:201–245.
1993   On Vision and Power in the Neolithic: Evidence from the Decorated Monuments. *Current Anthropology* 34:55–65.
Lewis-Williams, J. David, and David G. Pearce
2004   *San Spirituality: Roots, Expressions and Social Consequences*. AltaMira Press, Walnut Creek and Double Storey, Cape Town.
Lewis-Williams, J. D., and D. G. Pearce
2005   Inside the Neolithic Mind: Consciousness, Cosmos and the Realm of the Gods, pp. 102–122. Thames and Hudson, London.
Narby, Jeremy, and Francis Huxley (editors)
2001   *Shamans Through Time: 500 Years on the Path to Knowledge*. Thames and Hudson, London.
Oster, G.
1970   Phosphenes. *Scientific American* 222(2):83–87.
Ramachandran, V. S., and S. Blakeslee
1998   *Phantoms in the Brain: Probing the Mysteries of the Human Mind*. (Quill) Harper Collins, New York.
Reichel-Dolmatoff, Geraldo
1978   *Beyond the Milky Way: Hallucinatory Imagery of the Tukano Indians*. UCLA Latin America Center, Los Angeles.
Sacks, Oliver W.
1970   *Migraine: The Evolution of a Common Disorder*. Faber, London.

Siegel, Ronald K.
1977   Hallucinations. *Scientific American* 237:132–140.
Siegel, Ronald K., and Murray E. Jarvik
1975   Drug-Induced Hallucinations in Animals and Man. In *Hallucinations: Behaviour, Experience and Theory*, edited by Ronald K. Siegel and Louis J. West, pp. 81–161. John Wiley, New York.
Sullivan, L. E.
1988   *Icanchu's Drum: An Orientation to Meaning in South American Religions.* Macmillan, New York.
Sutherland, Patricia D.
2001   Shamanism and the Iconography of Palaeo-Eskimo Art. In *The Archaeology of Shamanism*, edited by Neil Price, pp. 135–145. Routledge, London.
Tylor, E. B.
1871   *Primitive Culture: Researches into the Development of Mythology, Philosophy, Religion, Art, and Custom.* John Murray, London.
Vitebsky, Piers
1995   *The Shaman.* Macmillan, London.
Whitehouse, Harvey
2000   *Arguments and Icons: Divergent Modes of Religiosity.* Oxford University Press, Oxford.

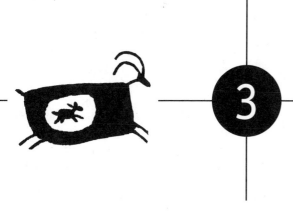

CROSS-CULTURAL AND BIOGENETIC PERSPECTIVES ON THE ORIGINS OF SHAMANISM[1]

Michael Winkelman

The question of whether shamanism is universal has been plagued by definitional problems. Some people define shamanism broadly enough to make it universal and to incorporate almost any spiritual practice, while others define it so narrowly as to specify that only Siberian cultures have shamanism. When shamanism is defined based upon a particular set of assumptions, the question of "what is a shaman" becomes problematic.

I have provided an alternative to the definitional approach by empirically assessing the characteristics associated with magico-religious healers in a cross-cultural sample (Winkelman 1992; see Winkelman and White 1987 for data and methods). This provides an empirical basis for establishing the nature of shamanism and its characteristics, as well as providing etic models for inferences regarding religious practices. Cross-cultural research reveals universals of shamanism worldwide in hunter-gatherer societies, and similar but distinct forms of shamanistic healers (shaman/healers, healers and mediums) in more complex agricultural and politically integrated societies (Winkelman 1992). They have in common the use of altered states of consciousness in community rituals that provide healing through interactions with the spirit world. Shamans also differ in significant ways from the spiritual healers of more complex societies.

The universals of shamanism and shamanistic healers reflect underlying biological structures. Shamanism was originally an ecological adaptation of hunter-gatherer societies to mammalian social bonding rituals elaborated primate healing capacities to address humans' psychosocial bonding and therapeutic needs (Winkelman 2000). This psychobiological foundation involving ritual healing through altered states of consciousness, which met psychosocial needs represented in spirit world beliefs, persisted among the shamanistic healers and transformed shamans that resulted as societies became more complex. Changes in the original forms of core shamanism resulted from the effects of agriculture, political integration, and class structures on personal psychology and consciousness (Winkelman 1992). The innate aspects of human ritual therapeutic processes found in shamanism persisted, however, in these more complex societies. The cross-cultural similarities in hunter-gatherer shamans and their differences from the shamanistic healers of more complex societies provide etic models that can be used as ethnological analogies for inference about religious practices in archaic societies.

Universals of Shamans

My cross-cultural study based on societies from around the world (Winkelman 1990, 1992) revealed similarities in the characteristics associated with the healing practitioners of hunter-gatherer societies—customarily called shamans. In addition to the characteristics emphasized by Eliade (1964)—ecstasy (altered state of consciousness or ASC), spirit world interaction, and community relations—the cross-cultural research (Winkelman 1992) reveals that shamans share a number of other characteristics:

– involvement of the entire community in overnight rituals
– the use of chanting and music
– dancing and enactment
– an ASC experience known as soul journey or soul flight
– training through deliberately induced ASC, particularly vision quests
– an initiatory experience involving death and rebirth
– therapeutic processes focused on soul loss and recovery
– disease caused by attacks by spirits and sorcerers, and the intrusion of foreign entities
– abilities in divination, diagnosis, and prophecy
– charismatic leadership
– malevolent acts, or sorcery
– animal relations, including control of animal spirits, transformation into animals, and hunting magic.

I have also characterized the aspects of humans' innate psychology in relationship to the principal elements of shamanism as follows:

– the phylogenetic basis of collective ritual and charismatic group leadership manifested in communal dances generally carried out overnight, and involving the use of chanting, music, drumming, and dancing

– the "ecstasy" and soul flight of shamanism as manifestations of altered states of consciousness that constitute forms of cognitive integration and perspectives that free consciousness from the body
– the spirit world as reflecting functions and structures of consciousness that play a role in psychosocial formation and personal transformation, exemplified in vision quests and initiatory death-and-rebirth experiences and animal spirits as a primary source of personal power.

Mithen (1996) has shown how the psychologist's concept of innate processing modules helps to explain the evolution of human cognitive capacities. Humans have a variety of evolved specialized capacities for tasks that affect survival and reproduction (such as animacy detection, animal species recognition, self-awareness, mental inference programs, social intelligence, social recognition mechanisms, self-recognition, and language). Many innate human processing modules are reflected in the core characteristics of shamanism (Winkelman 2002, 2004); these provide the basis for many of the shamans' professional characteristics, such as their special relations to animals, charismatic leadership abilities, and conceptual abilities for diagnosis, divination, and psychological healing. Shamanic concepts such as spirits, animal spirits, totemic clans, out-of-body experiences, and visionary spirit worlds reflect the elicitation of associated innate processing modules related to animals, visual symbolism, self, and social others (Winkelman 2000).

Shamanic Universals as an Evolved Psychology

Shamanic universals have direct relationships to the basic principles of brain operation and innate structures of the brain (Winkelman 2002, 2004). Biological bases are exemplified in the foundations of shamanism emphasized by Eliade (1964)—the spirit world, community, and ecstasy (ASC)—as well as other universal characteristics of shamanism (e.g., death and rebirth, soul journey, music, dance). "Spirits" reflect the adaptive consequences of a hyperactive agency detection device (see Atran 2006), coupled with the tendency to attribute inferred characteristics to social others as a form of incorporating the expectations of the social other into the formation of self. The representation of the spirit world involves the use of innate representation modules for understanding self, social others, and their mental capacities. Shamanic universals of animism, animal spirits, guardian spirits, and soul flight involve manipulation of these modules in understanding nature, and in the formation of personal and social identities. "Community" represents the importance of social others and their roles in synchronizing human psychobiological functions. Ecstasy, or an altered state of consciousness (ASC), involves a mode of consciousness; these physiological conditions induce the relaxation response, brain integration and synchronization, and other neurological processes directly related to healing. These expand mammalian and primate caring capacities (Fabrega 1997) into a large complex of healing rituals capable of addressing physical and psychological problems. Shamanic healing manipulates the paleomammalian brain structures to produce emotional healing by evoking socio-emotional and psychodynamic processes, strengthening social identity, and eliciting the body's opioid and immunological systems.

Biogenetic Structural Foundations of Shamanism in Animal Ritual

Theoretical frameworks for understanding the adaptive origins and biological bases of shamanic rituals are provided in *The Spectrum of Ritual* (d'Aquili et al. 1979). The biogenetic structuralist approach illustrates homologies of shamanic ritual behaviors with prior adaptations in other species, providing a basis for examining adaptive functions and biological foundations of religion (see Winkelman and Baker 2007). Ritual is integral to vertebrate nature providing mechanisms for communication that are basic to social coordination. Ritual uses behaviors or actions that signal readiness for social behaviors (d'Aquili et al. 1979). Animal rituals are formalized behaviors and displays that have communication and social signaling functions. These genetically based behaviors provide information that facilitates intraspecies interactions, coordinating the behaviors of individuals and contributing to cooperative behaviors by making internal dispositions publicly available. Animal rituals generally precede and contribute to cooperative behaviors by facilitating the flow of information, synchronizing individual behaviors into socially coordinated patterns. Laughlin and d'Aquili (1974:40–41) characterize ritual as "an evolutionary, ancient channel of communication that operates by virtue of homologous biological functions (i.e., synchronization, integration, tuning, etc.) in man and other vertebrates."

Music and Mimesis

While the use of song and chanting is a universal aspect of shamanic healing rituals, reflecting a uniquely human capability for music based in innate brain modules (Molino 2000), music also has evolutionarily earlier roots found in other animal vocalizations such as calls and hoots as a group expressive system. These affective displays use vocalizations during states of high arousal to communicate about affective states and alarm; to provide information for maintaining social contact and spacing; for mate attraction, pair bonding, and band territorial advertisement; for inter-individual and intergroup communication, particularly location, spacing, food sources, and danger; to have motivational effects on other members of the group; and to enhance group cohesion and unity (Geissmann 2000).

Group singing, chanting, and dancing are not only core to shaman-ism but are a key aspect of religious rituals found throughout the world because they have deep evolutionary roots in the functions of rituals found in primates. Activities found among chimpanzees indicate that our hom-inid ancestors had developed social adaptations involving excited synchron-ous singing and dancing among members of a territorial group. Songs and vocalizations of gibbons and chimpanzees share functional common-alities as affective displays made during conditions of high arousal that are used for social contact and interpersonal spacing. Structural and behav-ioral similarities indicate that loud calls are communicative precursors of human singing and musical abilities. Calls are emotive vocalizations that communicate to other members of the species, and have motiv-ational effects upon them. Music plays a similar function in human groups in fight songs, warriors' battle songs, and national anthems, as well as babies' lullabies, children's medleys, and love songs. Group and inter-personal *non-verbal* expressive performances are a basic form of inter-personal integration that forms in-groups of kin, biological as well as those upon whom kinship is socially imprinted.

Music is part of a larger group of cultural activities such as chanting, singing, poetry, dancing, and play that share origins in common modules that provide rhythm, affective semantics, and melody (Molino 2000:165, 173; also see Donald 1991 on mimesis). This rhythmic module of the brain provided an expressive system that predated language. Freeman (2000) suggests that music and dance co-evolved to enhance social bond-ing and communication of internal states, contributing a technology for inducing ASC and breaking down existing habits and thought patterns. Music's adaptive roles include its ability to promote group cohesion and coordination, enhancing synchrony and cooperation among group mem-bers through mutual cognitive and emotional expression, and coordinat-ing the behavior of individuals into synchronized performances (Brown 2000; Merker 2000).

The close linkage of musical expression with movement and dance reflects the operation of an innate brain device known as the "mimetic controller," which provides the unique human ability to entrain the body to external rhythms (Donald 1991). Group ritual dances and vocal imita-tions of animals were among the first human mimetic activities, providing an ability to represent through imitation, using gestural and facial systems. Mimesis provides a basis for metaphorical symbolism: representing through enacting. The shaman's use of dance, imitation, and drumming reflects the utilization of this innate mimetic controller. This communication system of the body involves "*rhythmo-affective semantics*," which express the fundamental emotions (Molino 2000). This mimetic ability expressed through imitation and ritual produced a mythic ethos that was enacted early in human evolution in activities involving collective participation.

Drumming and Alpha Male Displays

Ritual activities involving drumming are universal aspects of shamanism that have deep evolutionary roots in mammalian species as intra- and interspecies signaling mechanisms.

> An amazing variety of mammals produce seismic vibrations by drumming a part of their body on a substrate. The drumming can communicate multiple messages to conspecifics about territorial ownership, competitive superiority, submission, readiness to mate, or presence of predators. Drumming also functions in interspecies communication when prey animals drum to communicate to predators that they are too alert for a successful ambush. (Randall 2001:1)

Drumming is a widespread mammalian adaptation, a communication mechanism conveying information about predators to nearby kin. Drumming manifests vigilance, fitness, and a readiness to act. A so-called costly signaling mechanism, it displays fitness in a way that both prepares for and reduces the need for action.

In an effort to protect their territory against other groups, Bonobo chimpanzees engage in group shouting, vocalizations, and aggressive displays with fast and loud "drumming" produced by beating and jumping up and down on tree buttresses (De Waal 1997). Chimpanzees incorporate a variety of acoustic signals into their aggressive charging displays, including pant hooting (a loud call) and drumming, both of which are typically performed by males. These drumming activities are accompanied by pant hoots that provide a system of long-distance communication. Striking their hands and feet against the ground and trees, they generate low-frequency sounds audible up to one kilometer distances in the human auditory range. These drumming activities are carried out during travel and in communicative exchanges between individuals who are outside of visual contact. Drumming, like vocalizations, provides an auditory signal that allows dispersed foraging groups to remain in contact with one another as they forage in separate areas. Drumming helps maintain group contact, with distinctive individual patterns of drumming allowing for identification of specific individuals. Acoustic exchanges provide signaling mechanisms to call upon other members of the groups who can provide support in confrontations with chimpanzees from other communities (Arcadi et al. 1998).

Among chimpanzees, call episodes are often accompanied by aggressive displays, such as bipedal charges and the shaking of branches. Gorilla calls are often terminated with chest-beating, running through the foliage, and breaking branches. Among chimpanzees, males predominantly perform loud calls, with the pant hooting peak phase followed by charging displays. The typical aggressive displays of chimpanzees involve charging around, uprooting small trees, and slapping the ground. There are also commonalities among the great apes in their locomotor displays: they kick, stomp, shake branches, and beat on the chest, ground, or vegetation, as well as jumping and running (Geissmann 2000). This is part of the dominance drive, the need to exhibit a superior power and receive deference from subordinates. This is an integrating mechanism that is at the basis of some of the most dramatic chimpanzee displays. These occur in the evening as the dispersed subgroups of the troop group together at a specific tree. The loud vocalizations as they gather in the protective branches of a tree and the dramatic charging displays provide an auditory beacon for those still distant from the gathering site. The aggressive displays into the settling darkness provide both intimidations to "others" in the darkness and solidifying mechanisms as other chimpanzees subordinately observe the dominant displays of their alpha males. The dramatic ritual expression provides a fundamental tool for the integration of a dispersed society into a single group.

Community Relations as a Psychobiological Therapy

Eliade (1964) emphasized that shamanic healing was performed on behalf of the community, and shamanistic healing occurs in the context of the local community. Community presence produces therapeutic effects derived from both psychosocial influences (positive expectation and social support) and psychobiological effects. Collective rituals strengthen group identity and community cohesion not only through social processes, but through their effects upon human psychobiology (see Whitley, this volume). Communal activities reinforce attachment needs in the mammalian biosocial system (Kirkpatrick 2005) and elicit psychosociophysiological mechanisms that release endogenous opiates (Frecska and Kulcsar 1989). The attachment and affectional bonds that evolved in mammals to maintain proximity with infants provide a secure basis for the self in the feelings of protection from powerful figures.

Hayden (2003) characterizes the biological aspects of shamanism as having derived from the key role it played in adaptations to inhospitable environments several million years ago. Early hominid adaptations to these hostile environments involved selective pressures for the ability to forge close emotional bonds with members of other groups who could provide them with essential resources like food and physical protection when needed. Rituals producing altered states of consciousness strengthened emotional bonds between individuals. In addition, these ecstatic states fostered alliances over time and brought about an expanded sense of community. Hayden (2003) suggests that these ecstatic states of consciousness made it possible for early humans to overcome the "natural" tendency of distinguishing their own social group from that of outsiders, and instead experiencing deep bonds of connection with others.

These affectional bonds are used in shamanistic rituals, which reinforce these innate mechanisms for attachment with the symbols and processes of shamanic healing. Frecska and Kulcsar (1989) have reviewed the evidence that shamanic rituals elicit psychobiologically mediated attachment processes that are based in the body's opioid mechanisms. Shamanic rituals use cultural symbols that have been cross-conditioned with patterns of attachment and their physiological and emotional responses. The emotionally charged cultural symbols that were associated with physiological systems during early attachment relations and socialization processes provide a basis for elicitation of the opioid system in shamanistic ritual. The ritual use of symbols that have been repeatedly associated with certain physiological reactions enables shamanic ritual to manipulate physiology, just as the Christian churchgoer finds comfort in returning to the places, prayers, and songs that have been associated with uplifting emotions, hope, and community bonding.

The release of endogenous opioids is also provoked by a variety of physical activities associated with shamanic ritual (see Prince 1982; Winkelman 1997). Shamanic activities that stimulate the release of the body's own opioid system include exhaustive rhythmic physical activities (e.g., dancing and clapping), exposure to temperature extremes (e.g., cold or sweat lodges), and austerities such as prolonged water deprivation and fasting, flagellation, and self-inflicted wounds. Opioids are also elicited by emotional manipulations that involve fear and positive expectations, as well as the night-time activities typical of shamanic ritual, when endogenous opioids are naturally highest.

The release of natural opioids stimulates physiological processes, including the immunological system (Frecska and Kulcsar 1989). Activation of the opioid system also produces a sense of euphoria, certainty, and belongingness. These processes enhance coping skills and the maintenance of bodily homeostasis (Valle and Prince 1989). Endogenous opioids reduce pain, enhance tolerance of stress, facilitate environmental adaptation, and enhance psychobiological synchronization within the group. These processes enhance group solidarity in a sense of *communitas*—the experience of the essential bonds among group members. Enhancement of community identity promotes the dissolution of self-boundaries and enhances the sense of identification with others. This reinforces individual commitment to the group and promotes the development of an integrated sense of self.

Shamanic ASC

The conditions of ecstasy, trance, or ASC central to shamanic training and practice are induced by a variety of procedures that have the same basic overall physiological effects (Winkelman 2000). Shamanic ASCs typically involve singing, chanting, drumming, and dancing, followed by a phase of collapse and apparent unconsciousness. The overall physiological dynamics involve an activation of the autonomic nervous system until exhaustion and collapse, inducing the body's relaxation response. This relaxation response is associated with a number of other systemic physiological features that constitute a natural feature of the nervous system. These procedures have the further common effects of stimulating the production of higher coherent theta wave patterns across the different areas of the brain.

The natural and biological basis of the integrative mode of consciousness is attested to by the presence in all cultures of procedures for accessing ASC, reflecting the brain's normal response to diverse stimuli. These responses induce synchronized brain wave patterns, typically in the theta (3–6 cycles per second) and slow alpha (6–8 cps) range. These brain wave patterns are produced by patterns of activity in the limbic system, also referred to as the emotional brain and the paleomammalian brain. These discharges first establish linkages between the limbic system and the lower brain structures, integrating emotions and memory with information from the whole organism. These strong theta wave patterns are produced by the action of the neurotransmitter serotonin and the connections between the emotional and lower brain structures (Mandell 1980). These synchronous discharges generate powerful synchronous brain wave discharges upward into the frontal cortex, where they replace the normal fast and desynchronized brain wave activity with the coherent slow wave discharges in the alpha and theta range (Mandell 1980; Winkelman 1992, 2000). The overall effect of the shamanic ASC is to dominate the frontal part of the brain with information from the emotional and behavioral brains. This integrates the information and processes of these preverbal brain structures into the personal and cultural systems mediated by language and the frontal cortex.

Dreams in Shamanic Scenario Building

The overnight shamanic rituals engage the dream processes, a capacity found throughout mammalian species that provides an adaptation for learning by producing memory associations during sleep through use of the "off-line" frontal cortex for information consolidation (Winson 1985). The centrality of these cognitive processes in shamanism is reflected in widespread references in shamanism to "dream time" and practices of dream incubation. Shamanic activities incorporate normal dream processes through overnight rituals and other dream incubation activities that deliberately blend waking and dream processes, reducing barriers between dream awareness and consciousness. Dreams are the closest engagement of ego awareness with the operational structures of the unconsciousness (Laughlin et al. 1992), reflecting an "unconscious personality" (Winson 1985), which shamanism manages through ritual.

Brereton (2000) has analyzed the adaptive aspects of dreaming that explain their utilization in shamanic practices. He characterizes dreams as a representation of self in emotionally salient space, a process of "virtual scenario construction" that provides processes for risk-free construction and examination of options. This dream capacity is elicited in visionary states, an adaptation to the importance of social manipulation skills through the ability for "social intellectual play." These scenario-building processes engage model construction processes related to social adaptation, using this visual symbolic modality as a workspace to exploring different scenarios. Non-verbal, body-based aspects of dreaming reflect connections with the body-self at a pre-egoic and prelinguistic level. Dream research suggests a "replaying" of previous scenarios, emotionally marked memories that have not been effectively resolved and incorporated into behavior patterns.

Shamanic visionary experiences engage the self-representation capacity based in the same systems that underlie dream experiences (Hunt 1995). This is a symbolic capacity distinct from representational symbolism of words, instead based in imagestic information. This is a symbolic capacity that predates the emergence of spoken language, as illustrated by its manifestations across mammalian species.

Images as Presentational Symbolism

Visionary experiences engage a presentational symbolism (Hunt 1995) involving symbolic imagery and engaging brain structures associated with processing perceptual information (Baars 1997) and dreaming. Images are a preverbal symbol system that has the capacity to recruit and coordinate muscle systems to achieve goals, arousing autonomic responses and engaging unconscious muscle control centers (Baars 1997). Images engage psychobiological communication processes that mediate across different levels of information processing, integrating unconscious, non-volitional, affective, and psychophysiological information at cognitive levels. This visual information system links domains of experience, integrating somatic, psychological, and cognitive levels through visual images and analogical processes (Winkelman 2000). These visual symbol systems provide advantages in engaging an analogic system of analysis, synthesis, and planning through visual images.

Soul Journey: Self in Presentational Symbolism

Shamanic ASC also produces forms of self-awareness that transcend the embeddedness of biologically based body consciousness. The shaman's ASC is characterized as a "soul journey" or "soul flight"—the experience of leaving one's body and traveling to other worlds. The basic structure of soul flights or journeys is also found in many other experiences reported cross-culturally (e.g., astral projection, out-of-body-experiences, near-death experiences). The similarities with shamanic flight reflect an innate basis in psychophysiological structures. The experience of flight and the vision associated with the soul journey is a natural response of the human nervous system. Hunt (1995) proposes that the experience of soul flight can be seen as a representation of oneself from another point of view, the "other's" perspective. Soul journeying involves the prototype of "taking the role of the other," seeing oneself from another's perspective. In the soul journey, this perspective is represented in the visual spatial modality, involving what Hunt refers to as a presentational symbolism. This is a symbolic system that operates independently of language, providing a medium for an externalized self-representation. These experiences provide a new form of self-awareness not tied to one's ordinary self and body, and create the shaman's transcendence of ordinary awareness and identity.

The Holistic Imperative and Shamanic Healing: Integrating the Triune Brain

Shamanism integrates a mammalian caring heritage into community ritual practices that provide healing and survival through physiological effects of community rituals and ritually induced ASC, elicit the parasympathetic response and the opioid and serotonergic neurotransmitter systems, eliciting the visionary and psychosomatic capacities of hypnotic susceptibility, social therapies engaging community participation, social symbol systems engaging self-development and the mammalian attachment dynamics, psychological and self-therapies engaging spirits as psychocultural systems and representations of innate psychological dynamics of the self represented in animal spirits, and symbolic-psychophysiological dynamics from ritual manipulation of emotions, self-structures, and the nervous system (see Winkelman 2000 for details).

Therapeutic and Adaptive Qualities of ASC

A central effect of shamanic healing derives from the ASC induction of alpha and theta brain wave discharge patterns, reflecting a shift in the autonomic nervous system to parasympathetic dominance. This reduces stress hormone levels and activates the serotonergic nervous system. The central roles of serotonin are to integrate emotional and motivational processes and to synthesize information across the functional levels of the brain. This serotonergic action is exemplified in the effects on the brain by meditation (Walton and Levitsky 1994) and psychointegrators (hallucinogens; Winkelman 2001). Shamanistic ASCs integrate information from the lower levels of the brain, particularly the emotional and behavioral preverbal brain structures, into the language-mediated activities of the frontal cortex. This is why ASCs are often experienced as providing understanding, enlightenment, a sense of unity and oneness with the universe, feelings of connection with others, and personal integration.

The neurological mechanisms of the therapeutic effects of shamanistic ASC are suggested by research on transcendental meditation (TM; Walton and Levitsky 1994). ASC in general addresses physiological dispositions associated with anxiety, stress, and depression by modifying the imbalance in serotonergic systems, reducing stress, and enhancing serotonin functioning through inducing relaxed states. Walton and Levitsky propose that TM acts on the locus coeruleus, increasing serotonin availability and producing an inhibitory action that parallels the effects of sedatives and opiates. Increases in serotonin levels reduce cortisol levels, indirectly reducing stimulation of limbic anger and fear centers. The serotonin-enhancing effects of TM affect the activity of the hypothalamic pituitary adrenal axis and chronic stress, reversing the serotonin depletion effects that result from the release of cortisol. TM-induced increases in serotonin availability mirror Mandell's (1980) model of the serotonergic mechanisms of "transcendent states," suggesting a generic role of enhanced serotonin availability in ASC. Shamanic rituals exploit the ancient role of ritual to enhance serotonergic production and to produce the special forms of awareness that integrate waking and dreaming.

Hypnosis as a Ritual Healing Capacity

McClenon (2002) illustrates how an inheritable quality manifested in hypnosis was a central factor in our evolved psychology and propensity for religious healing. Hypnosis induces the same overall general physiological changes associated with ASC. Hypnotizability contributes to ritual healing through the induction of relaxation, ASC, and an engagement of attention and imagination. McClenon (2002) has reviewed the evidence for the presence of hypnotic capacities in other primates, illustrating that it is an ancient primate adaptation for reducing social stress and engaging the relaxation response. Rituals among animals involve the kinds of repetitive movements that facilitate hypnotic induction in humans and produce relaxation, thereby reducing aggression. In humans, rituals' repetitive and stereotyped behaviors produce both an alteration of consciousness and a sense of intragroup cohesion, experienced as "union" or "oneness," which are classic aspects of religious and mystical experiences.

The hypnotic capacity provides enhanced innovation derived from access to the unconscious mind. Hypnotizability involves focused attention, reduced peripheral awareness, and an abeyance of critical mentation that facilitates a focus upon internal imagetic representations and enhanced belief and expectation. Shamanism exploits the co-occurrence of hypnotizability, dissociation, fantasy proneness, temporal lobe lability, and thin cognitive boundaries, all involving enhanced connections between the unconscious and conscious aspects of the mind. Highly hypnotizable people have thin cognitive boundaries, which enable greater access to the unconscious and the flow of information from the unconscious to the conscious, providing survival advantages by facilitating the development of creative strategies.

McClenon (2002) points out how the tendency to suggestibility involved in hypnotic capacities contributed to a biological capacity for recovery from disease. This capacity of suggestibility enhances symbolically induced physiological changes and psychophysiological responses that facilitate healing. Shamanic practices appear successful in treating the same kinds of conditions for which hypnosis has been shown to have significant clinical effects: somatization, mild psychiatric disorders, simple gynecological conditions, gastrointestinal and respiratory disorders, self-limiting diseases, chronic pain, neurotic and hysterical conditions, and interpersonal, psychosocial, and cultural problems (see McClenon 2002 for review).

Shamanism as Psychointegration of the Triune and Modular Brain

All societies have shamanistic religious practices derived from the biologically based roots of shamanism and manifested in community rituals involving the use of ASC for healing through contact with the spirit world. These universals are expanded by many other features of human psychology manifested in shamanism. Human evolution selected for shamanic potentials because they were adaptive in enhancing social cohesion, mediating stress responses, and producing personal integration. In mammalian rituals, the aggressive archaic emotions of the lower brain structures, called the R-complex or "reptilian complex" by neurobiologist Paul MacLean (1990, 1993), are suppressed and sublimated. Human ritual also gives these aggressive tendencies a controlled expression and release in rituals that subordinate these reptilian and mammalian tendencies with symbolic healing processes.

Human evolution produced a fragmentation of consciousness due to the modular structure of the brain (Mithen 1996), the diversification of personal and social identities, and the automization of brain processes (Laughlin et al. 1992). This produced a need for integrative brain processes—what Laughlin et al. (1992) refer to as the *holistic imperative*, the drive towards the expansion and integration of consciousness at higher levels. Shamanistic activities produce psychological, social, and cognitive integration, managing relationships among behavioral, emotional, and cognitive processes, and between physiological and mental levels of the organism. Shamanistic activities use intuitive body metaphors, visual symbols, and the physiological effects of ASC and group rituals to integrate the operations of various brain systems and their functions.

One aspect of this shamanic integration involves linkages across the evolutionary strata of the brain. MacLean (1990, 1993) proposes that the brain involves three anatomically distinct yet interconnected systems—the reptilian, paleomammalian, and neomammalian brains—which provide the basis for behavioral, emotional, and informational functions. MacLean (1993:39) uses the terms protomentation, emotiomentation, and ratiomentation, respectively. These communication systems have been referred to as "subsymbolic" (Ashbrook 1993) and presentational symbolism (Hunt 1995). Interactions across levels of the brain are primarily mediated not through verbal language, but through nonverbal forms of mentation that utilize social, affective, and presentational (visual symbolic) information.

The hierarchical management of behavior, emotions, and reason is mediated both physiologically and symbolically. The relationships among innate drives, social attachment, and cultural demands create many different kinds of health problems—chronic anxiety and fears, behavioral disorders, conflicts, excessive emotionality or desires, obsessions and compulsions, dissociations, and repression. The paleomammalian brain mediates many of these processes to promote an integration of the self and the community. The paleomammalian brain's emotiomentation processes provide a major basis for shamanic healing, based on integrating its own subjective evaluative influences and self-reference with the instinctual responses of the reptilian brain and the cognitive processes of the neomammalian brain.

These integrative processes are elicited by key aspects of shamanism—the ASC, the physiological and psychological effects of community rituals, and the representations of person and social processes in spirits. Shamanic traditions produce an integration of consciousness through rituals that stimulate physiologically based psychological integration, metaphoric cognitive processes, and community bonding rituals. Shamanic therapies involve a variety of mechanisms for the transformation of the patient's health, eliciting physiological responses and social support and enhancing symbolically mediated placebo and other psychosomatic effects (Winkelman 2000). A physiological basis of shamanistic healing involves ASCs that produce systemic brain integration, a coordination and increased coherence of the potentials of many parts of the brain. Altered states of consciousness impose the paleomammalian brain's analogical processes and material of an emotional, social, and personal nature onto the self-conscious processes of the frontal cortex. Physiological aspects of ASC—parasympathetic dominance, inter-hemispheric synchronization, and limbic-frontal integration—have inherent therapeutic effects, counteracting excessive activity of the sympathetic nervous system. Shamanistic rituals provide adaptations through the assurances of hope, counteracting emotional distress and anxiety and their deleterious physiological effects.

The basis of shamanism is in the rituals that bond groups together, rituals that involve the displays of dominant males. These aggressive stances against the unknown other, a potentially superior being, provide an attitudinal stance characteristic of shamans.

ASC and ritual effects have the ability to elicit emotional memories and reduce the ego-centeredness that inhibits the experience of community connectedness and support that meets the need for belonging, comfort, and bonding with others. Shamanic ritual management of behavior, emotions, and reason is mediated physiologically and symbolically within the paleomammalian brain, where social signaling and bonding promote subjective evaluations that play a vital role in integrating the instinctual responses of the ancient brains with the cognitive processes of the neo-mammalian brain. Shamanic ritual evolved as a system for managing the relationships among innate drives and needs, social bonding processes, and cultural representational systems, providing a system for managing health problems derived from anxiety, fears, conflicts, excessive emotionality, obsessions, and compulsions.

Spirit Assumptions as Adaptive Mechanisms

Atran (2006) points out that the social functions of religion did not predict the following cognitive characteristics of religion specifically: the predominance of agent concepts, the cultural universality of supernatural agents, the specific features of supernatural agents, the validation of supernatural agent concepts in ways that are immune to logical and factual scrutiny, and the compulsion of religious moral orders that keeps people from defecting. The inability of functional arguments to account for the universal features of spirit beliefs indicate "that social functions are not phylogenetically responsible for the cognitive structure and cultural recurrence of religion" (Atran 2006:185).

Atran points out that there is good evidence that religious beliefs in practice have the ability to alleviate this functional stress and anxiety and to foster the maintenance of social cohesion in the face of conflict. Atran reviews a range of findings that suggest that religion is not an evolutionary adaptation but a cultural byproduct of humans' evolved cognitive, emotional, and social qualities.

> Religion exploits ordinary cognitive processes to passionately display costly devotion to counterintuitive world governed by supernatural agents. (Atran 2006:185)
> Religion has endured in nearly all cultures and most individuals because humans are faced with problems they can't solve. As people routinely interact, they naturally tend to exploit various mundane cognitive faculties in special ways to solve an array of inescapable, existential problems that have no apparent worldly solution. (ibid., 187)

Atran's perspective is that religion does not have any evolutionary functions, but that religious beliefs survive because they play a central role in addressing some of the elements of the human condition. The persistence of religion is due to its ability to accommodate these cognitive elements, and to address our susceptibility to specific innate modularized conceptual processes, including our folk psychology which interprets the supernatural within the functions of minds and social groups. The focus of religion on supernatural agent concepts provides a general source of agent concepts as central constructs in a pan-human "folk psychology" or "theory of mind." Atran proposes that the highly evolved tendency to attribute agency is a consequence of our adaptation to intelligent predators. The concept of agency reflects an "innate releasing mechanism" that evolved to respond to significant ambiguities and objects in the environment, and was extended to account for all sorts of phenomena, particularly those involving complex designs of unknown origins.

But spirit concepts involve more than mundane agents. Our evolved agency detection devices may account for the perception of intentional agents, but may not work as well for other qualities of the supernatural, such as functioning as self-directed actors with a variety of social characteristics, as well as a variety of nonintuitive properties. Do these other spirit qualities reflect adaptations that contributed to human evolution, or are they exaptations, where a feature or trait that first originated to serve one purpose (e.g., feathers as insulation for warmth) was later used (exapted) for a different function (i.e., assisting in flight)?

Wildman address the key issues in distinguishing the concept of adaptation from the concepts of "by-products" of evolution called exaptations (and spandrels; also see Winkelman and Baker, 2008). As Wildman (2006:255) states, "adaptations just are adapted traits. Exaptations are side effects tightly linked to genes, with the side effect possibly co-occurring in the original selection context though never the cause of the fixing of the trait." Both adaptations and exaptations involve biological traits and provide adaptive functions, but they have different origins. Wildman (2006:252) contends that the crucial question is whether the "secondary adaptive functions of traits having religious beliefs and behaviors as their side effects [were] evident from the beginning [adaptations], even in the original selection context, or did those secondary adaptive functions only appear later, in changed environments [exaptations]?"

These perspectives can be applied to assessing the evolutionary significance of the nonintuitive properties of spirit entities that are "contradictions," not conforming to human limitations, but rather having an expanded set of behavioral capacities (supernatural abilities). The origins of many of the social qualities of the supernatural are found in other adaptive assumptions, derived from the fact that other humans constitute the most intelligent predators to whom we need to adapt. The unknown is presumed to be as dangerous as we are. But is there something prior in human evolution that provided the basis for spirit's counterintuitive properties, constituting the basis for a later exaptation of the superhuman capabilities attributed to spirits? What was exapted from prior human evolution to provide the counterintuitive properties ascribed to the supernatural? The lack of an apparent answer to these questions suggests that the supernatural assumption may provide an adaptation in those aspects of the supernatural premise involving the nonintuitive, contradictory, and superhuman capabilities.

Atran proposes instead that "as people routinely interact, they naturally tend to exploit various mundane cognitive faculties in special ways to solve an array of inescapable, existential problems that have no apparent worldly solution" (2006:187). But his subsequent contentions tend to support the notion that the adaptations provided by supernatural agent concepts are intrinsically religious adaptations. He points out that supernatural agent concepts are particularly effective at triggering the powerful emotions associated with evolutionary survival templates, making them memorable and compelling. While many aspects of our innate cognitive processes may make the supernatural concept particularly memorable and functional, this does not negate that there are fundamental adaptations provided by the supernatural concept: "survival of religious beliefs in the supernatural are, in part, due to success in accommodating these elements" (Atran 2006:188).

What is it about religion that makes it particularly well suited for providing a collective process for engaging with our existential needs for security and our inevitable anxieties such as fear of death? What was it that religion exapted from our prior capabilities in order to meet human needs? Or did religion and the supernatural premise constitute an adaptation that was obviously effective in managing human emotional and cognitive dilemmas? These questions pose a challenge to the view that religion is merely an evolutionary byproduct (e.g., exaptation). The byproduct arguments would require establishing that the religious behavior was based solely on the prior adaptations designed to meet other needs.

It is undoubtedly true, as Atran claims, that "supernatural agents are readily conjured up perhaps because natural selection has trip wire cognitive schemata for agency detection in the face of uncertainty" (Atran 2006:190). But this does not explain the counterintuitive qualities that are universals of supernatural agents. As Atran points out, a "minimally counterintuitive world allowed supernatural agents to resolve existential dilemmas" (ibid., 190). These counterintuitive agents have particular adaptive value because they are "cognitively optimal," optimally managing memory, communication, and transmission. The counterintuitive properties of religious beliefs are adaptive in spite of their contradictions with factual knowledge, because they provide possibilities not found in our innate capabilities and modules.

Atran tries to sidestep this conclusion by suggesting that we don't "bypass our hardwiring to form counterintuitive religious beliefs [because] ... we don't entirely bypass common sense understanding but conceptually parasitize it to transcend it. This occurs through the cognitive process of metarepresentation" (2006:194). Metarepresentation is exemplified by symbolic processes that allow us to think about and represent one thing in terms of another.

Supernatural ideas always remain metarepresentational. (Atran 2006:195)

In brief, human metarepresentational abilities, which are intimately bound to fully developed cognitions of agency and intention, also allow people to entertain, recognize and evaluate the differences between true and false beliefs. Given the ever-present menace of enemies within and without, concealment, deception, and the ability to both generate and recognize false beliefs in others would favor survival. (ibid., 196)

The natural landscape of humans' evolution of religious beliefs includes a variety of social, emotional, and cognitive capabilities that provide a range of pre-adaptations for modern religiosity. The extent to which these provide a foundation for religion as an exaptation depends on the extent to which these cognitive mechanisms perform exactly the same functions in religiosity. Religion might instead be viewed as an adaptation to the extent that religiosity provides a unique set of adaptive capabilities beyond those provided by our cognitive pre-adaptations. "Invoking supernatural agents who may have true beliefs that people ordinarily lack creates the irrational conditions for people to steadfastly commit to one another in a moral order that goes beyond apparent reason and self-conscious interest" (Atran 2006:197).

Insofar as the supernatural premise enables humans to deal effectively with existential anxieties (such as death) not addressed by previous cognitive adaptations, the supernatural premise constitutes an adaptation. To the extent that religiosity enables us to expand our kin of based preferences to include others, producing larger social groups, religion is an adaptation. To the extent that the omniscient properties of the supernatural engage possibilities beyond that of our innate modular structures, religious thought provides an adaptation. Without doubt, religiosity is based on many pre-adaptations; complex modern human behaviors depend upon many pre-adaptations. The extent to which religiosity provides cognitive and social functions not met by those prior pre-adaptations illustrates the ways in which religion may be viewed as an evolutionarily acquired adaptation. For instance, our ability to relate to supernatural beings exapts a variety of social and cognitive skills designed to enable us to function effectively in complex social groups.

The question of the role of religion as an adaptation must be assessed in terms of how it facilitates the long-term survival of individuals and groups. These solutions to cooperative living have their roots in the role of ritual in maintaining cooperation and reducing conflict in animal society. These ancient phylogenetic origins of religion and ritual have been expanded as humans have acquired other needs and capacity as the members of larger and more complex social groups.

While the dominant approaches in evolutionary biology have emphasized individual selection in terms of the acquisition of innate characteristics and dispositions, individual selection takes place in a group context in which powerful collective forces shaped the individual's success and reproduction. These collective forces select for individuals that are well suited for integration in a collectivity, a capacity for holding the individual into a range of collectively shared patterns and dispositions. We must address the questions of how participation in religious groups enhances individual survival and reproduction. What does religion provide collectively and individually that enhances adaptation, survival, and successful reproduction?

The elements of a supreme deity provide an important mechanism for forming connections between individual and collective psychology. A common "significant other" provides a basis for expansive group identity, particularly exceeding the innate capacities to prefer closed kin alone in engaging in reciprocal altruism. The evolution of religious behavior must be understood in the context of a variety of factors that have contributed to the evolution of the human propensity to help other humans. These patterns of cooperation among humans have posed a challenge to evolutionary theory and understandings of the processes of natural selection. The cooperation manifested in religion can be understood as part of a broader set of altruistic behaviors involved in helping others, perhaps at one's own expense. "Perhaps" because while it may appear that one sacrifices for the benefit of others, there may be a variety of reasons why one might personally benefit from those sacrifices. While it might appear that helping others incurs some reproductive costs, decreasing the resources for one's own offspring and exposing one to an increased risk of death, the behaviors may nonetheless benefit one's own offspring, or contribute to social support from others in the long run—a concept referred to as reciprocal altruism. The benefit that altruistic acts have for relatives can be personally beneficial since one's kin share many of one's own genes. The concept of inclusive fitness also considers the reproductive effects that are accrued by one's own descendants and relatives as a consequence of one's altruistic behavior.

Once there is a basis for altruism within a population, there will be additional selective forces favoring it. Behavioral mechanisms that increase reciprocity include what are called kin recognition mechanisms that involve both a disposition to identify kin and a behavioral tendency to engage in favorable actions based on those recognition cues. Kin recognition mechanisms that are based upon a direct association are expanded in what is referred to as a phenotype mechanism where a broader template is used to recognize unfamiliar kin. These mechanisms involve environmentally acquired cues. Among humans and other highly social animals the kin of selection altruism biases are acquired through intermediary individuals, a "socially mediated nepotism" that is found in many social animals. Religion is a central mechanism for expanding kin recognition mechanisms to others, god the father, earth mothers, and the brothers and sisters of the religious community.

Conclusions

The models of the biological nature of shamanism provided by the integration of ethnological research with biogenetic approaches to ritual and human evolutionary psychology have great power for the interpretation of prehistoric religious behaviors. Shamanism was a central feature of the emergence of modern human culture in the middle Upper Paleolithic transition (see Clottes and Lewis-Williams 1998; Ryan 1999; Whitley

1998; Winkelman 2002). This recognition, combined with ethnological research on the features of shamanism, provides a rationale for the reconstruction of shamanistic religious healing practices in extinct cultures. The cross-cultural model provided by Winkelman (1992) can also be used to interpret the nature of other forms of religious developments in prehistory; for example, see Hayden's (2003) discussion of the emergence of priestly religions prior to the Neolithic. Religion reflects many universal and socially induced aspects of human nature. These neurobiological models provide an evolutionary basis for religion and a justification for inferences regarding many aspects of the religiosity of the past. Interpretations of the religions of the past will benefit from the increasing research carried out on the biological bases of religion (e.g., d'Aquili and Newburg 1999; McNamara 2006; Rayburn and Richmond 2002; Winkelman and Baker 2008).

Note

1. Material discussed here has been published elsewhere, including Winkelman 2000, 2002, 2004, 2006a, and 2006b.

References Cited

Arcadi, A., D. Robert, and C. Boesch
1998   Buttress Drumming by Wild Chimpanzees: Temporal Patterning, Phrase Integration into Loud Calls, and Preliminary Evidence for Individual Distinctiveness. *Primates* 39(4):505–518.
Ashbrook, J.
1993   The Human Brain and Human Destiny: A Pattern for Old Brain Empathy with the Emergence of Mind. In *Brain, Culture and the Human Spirit: Essays from an Emergent Evolutionary Perspective*, edited by James Ashbrook, pp. 183–210. University Press of America, Lanham.
Atran, S.
2006   The Cognitive and Evolutionary Roots of Religion. In *Where God and Science Meet: How Brain and Evolutionary Studies Alter Our Understanding of Religion. Volume 1, Evolution, Genes, and the Religious Brain*, edited by Patrick McNamara, pp. 181–207. Praeger, Westport, Connecticut.
Baars, B.
1997   *In the Theater of Consciousness*. Oxford University Press, New York.
Brereton, D.
2000   Dreaming, Adaptation, and Consciousness: The Social Mapping Hypothesis. *Ethos* 28(3):379–100.
Brown, S.
2000   The "Musilanguage" Model of Music. In *The Origins of Music*, edited by N. Wallin, B. Merker, and S. Brown, pp. 271–300. MIT Press, Cambridge.
Clottes, J., and D. Lewis-Williams
1998   *The Shamans of Prehistory: Trance and Magic in the Painted Caves*. Harry Abrams, New York.

d'Aquili, E., and A. Newburg
1999   *The Mystical Mind*. Fortress, Minneapolis.
d'Aquili, E., C. Laughlin, and J. McManus (editors)
1979   *The Spectrum of Ritual*. Columbia University Press, New York.
De Waal, Frans
1997   *Bonobo The Forgotten Ape*. University of California Press, Berkeley.
Donald, Merlin
1991   *Origins of the Modern Mind*. Harvard University Press, Cambridge.
Eliade, M.
1964   *Shamanism: Archaic Techniques of Ecstasy*. Pantheon Books, New York.
Fabrega, H.
1997   *Evolution of Sickness and Healing*. University of California Press, Berkeley.
Frecska, E., and Z. Kulcsar
1989   Social Bonding in the Modulation of the Physiology of Ritual Trance. *Ethos* 17(1):70–87.
Freeman, W.
2000   A Neurobiological Role of Music in Social Bonding. In *The Origins of Music*, edited by N. Wallin, B. Merker, and S. Brown, pp. 411–424. MIT Press, Cambridge.
Geissmann, T.
2000   Gibbon Songs and Human Music from an Evolutionary Perspective. In *The Origins of Music*, edited by N. Wallin, B. Merker, and S. Brown, pp. 103–123. MIT Press, Cambridge.
Hayden, Brian
2003   *Shamans, Sorcerers, and Saints: A Prehistory of Religion*. Smithsonian Books, Washington, DC.
Hunt, H.
1995   *On the Nature of Consciousness*. Yale University Press, New Haven and London.
Kirkpatrick, Lee
2005   *Attachment, Evolution, and the Psychology of Religion*. Guilford Press, New York.
Laughlin, C., and E. d'Aquili
1974   *Biogenetic Structuralism*. Columbia University Press, New York.
Laughlin, C., J. McManus, and E. d'Aquili
1992   *Brain, Symbol and Experience toward a Neurophenomenology of Consciousness*. Shambhala, Boston, and Shaftesbury. Reprinted by Columbia University Press.
McClenon, J.
2002   *Wondrous Healing Shamanism, Human Evolution and the Origin of Religion*. Northern Illinois University Press, DeKalb.
MacLean, P.
1990   *The Triune Brain in Evolution*. Plenum, New York.
1993   On the Evolution of Three Mentalities. In *Brain, Culture and the Human Spirit: Essays from an Emergent Evolutionary Perspective*, edited by J. Ashbrook, pp. 15–44. University Press of America, Lanham.
McNamara, P. (editor)
2006   *Where God and Science Meet*, vols. 1–3. Praeger, Westport, Connecticut.
Mandell, A.
1980   Toward a Psychobiology of Transcendence: God in the Brain. In *The Psychobiology of Consciousness*, edited by D. Davidson and R. Davidson, pp. 379–464. Plenum, New York.
Merker, B.
2000   Synchronous Chorusing and Human Origins. In *The Origins of Music*, edited by N. Wallin, B. Merker, and S. Brown, pp. 315–327. MIT Press, Cambridge.
Mithen, S.
1996   *The Prehistory of the Mind: A Search for the Origins of Art, Religion and Science*. Thames and Hudson, London.

Molino, J.
2000   Toward an Evolutionary Theory of Music. In *The Origins of Music*, edited by N. Wallin, B. Merker, and S. Brown, pp. 165–176. MIT Press, Cambridge.
Prince, R.
1982   The Endorphins: A Review for Psychological Anthropologists. *Ethos* 10(4):299–302.
Randall, Jan
2001   Evolution and Function of Drumming As Communication in Mammals. *American Zoologist* 41(5):1143–1156. Retrived from www.bioone.org on 4/29/2005.
Rayburn, C., and L. Richmond (editors)
2002   Special Issue. Theobiology: Interfacing Theology, Biology and the Other Sciences for Deeper Understanding, *American Behavioral Scientist* 45(120).
Ryan, R.
1999   *The Strong Eye of Shamanism: A Journey into the Caves of Consciousness.* Inner Traditions, Rochester.
Valle, J., and R. Prince
1989   Religious Experiences As Self-healing Mechanisms. In *Altered States of Consciousness and Mental Health: A Cross-cultural Perspective*, edited by C. Ward, pp. 149–166. Sage, Newbury Park.
Wallin, Nils, B. Merker, and S. Brown (editors)
2000   *The Origins of Music.* MIT Press, Cambridge.
Walton, K., and D. Levitsky
1994   A Neuroendocrine Mechanism for the Reduction of Drug Use and Addictions by Transcendental Meditation. In *Self-recovery: Treating Addictions Using Transcendental Meditation and Maharishi Ayur-Veda*, edited by D. O'Connell and C. Alexander, pp. 89–117. Hayworth Press, New York.
Whitley, D.
1998   Cognitive Neuroscience, Shamanism, and the Rock Art of Native California. *Anthropology of Consciousness* 9(1):22–37.
Wildman, Wesley
2006   The Significance of the Evolution of Religious Beliefs and Behavior for Religious Studies and Theology. In *Where God and Science Meet: How Brain and Evolutionary Studies Alter Our Understanding of Religion.* vol. 1, edited by Patrick McNamara, pp. 227–272. Praeger, Westport, Connecticut.
Winkelman, M.
1990   Shaman and Other "Magico-religious" Healers: A Cross-cultural Study of their Origins, Nature and Social Transformations. *Ethos* 18(3):308–352.
1992   Shamans, Priests and Witches: A Cross-cultural Study of Magico-religious Practitioners. *Anthropological Research Papers* No. 44. Arizona State University, Tempe.
1997   Altered States of Consciousness and Religious Behavior. In *Anthropology of Religion: A Handbook of Method and Theory*, edited by S. Glazier, pp. 393–428. Greenwood, Westport, Connecticut.
2000   *Shamanism: The Neural Ecology of Consciousness and Healing.* Bergin and Garvey, Westport, Connecticut.
2001   Psychointegrators: Multidisciplinary Perspectives on the Therapeutic Effects of Hallucinogens. *Complementary Health Practice Review* 6(3):219–237.
2002   Shamanism and Cognitive Evolution. *Cambridge Archaeological Journal* 12(1):71–101.
2004   Shamanism As the Original Neurotheology. *Zygon: Journal of Religion and Science* 39(1):193–217.
2006a   Cross-cultural Assessments of Shamanism As a Biogenetic Foundation for Religion. In *Where God and Science Meet: How Brain and Evolutionary Studies Alter Our Understanding of Religion*, edited by Patrick McNamara, pp. 139–159. Praeger, Westport, Connecticut.

2006b   Shamanism: A Biogenetic Perspective. In *Science, Religion, and Society: An Encyclopedia of History, Culture, and Controversy*, edited by A. Eisen and G. Laderman, pp. 139–159. ME Sharp, Armonk, New York.

Winkelman, M., and J. Baker

2008   *Supernatural As Natural: A Biocultural Theory of Religion*. Prentice Hall, Upper Saddle River, New Jersey.

Winkelman, M., and D. White

1987   A Cross-cultural Study of Magico-religious Practitioners and Trance States: Data Base. In *Human Relations Area Files: Research Series in Quantitative Cross-cultural Data*, vol. 3, edited by David Levinson and Roy Wagner. HRAF Press, New Haven.

Winson, J.

1985   *Brain and Psyche: The Biology of the Unconscious*. Anchor Press/Doubleday, Garden City.

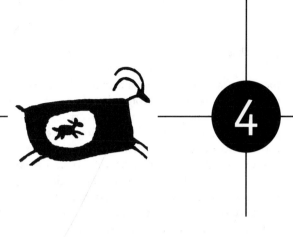

SUPERNATURAL METAPHORS AND BELIEF IN THE PAST: DEFINING AN ARCHAEOLOGY OF RELIGION

Elisabeth V. Culley

In 1871, E. B. Tylor defined religion as the "belief in spiritual beings" that develops from otherwise inexplicable sensory and psychological phenomena. This simple definition initiated anthropology's ongoing concern with the origin, qualities, and functions of religion, as well as with specific religious traditions. Archaeologists must also grapple with belief in the supernatural; we must reconstruct and understand prehistoric religions from the material remains of past behaviors. Yet as archaeology came of age in the 1950s and 60s, researchers maintained a commitment to traditional scientific methods and directed attention to prehistoric adaptations that could be studied empirically, effectively excluding the interpretation of ideas and values from archaeological research (e.g., Binford 1972:195–199, 1987; Dunnell 1971; Hawkes 1954; see also Renfrew 1994a:3), and leaving our understanding of prehistoric ideation, including religious beliefs, markedly underdeveloped.

Cognitive archaeology is now attempting to reconstruct prehistoric religion in terms of the neurological phenomena that support and limit religious beliefs. The approach holds that religion is a way of understanding the world, or a type of reasoning, that may be constrained by systematic and knowable cognitive processes. Most important, the material evidence of systematic processes should be discernible in the archaeological record (Renfrew 1985, 1994a, 1994b; Renfrew and Bahn 1991; see also Hinde 1998; Mithen 1998; Van der Leeuw 1994; Zubrow 1994a, 1994b).

Colin Renfrew (1985, 1994b; Renfrew and Bahn 1991; see also Whitehouse 1996), in particular, argues that formalized ritual, specialized locations, and specialized material culture constitute patterned ways of processing and storing information. Renfrew further claims that it is essentially only through these phenomena that we may identify prehistoric religion. But as Renfrew readily acknowledges (1994b:47–51), prioritizing formal ritual and ceremonial items while de-emphasizing informal praxis may exclude many religious ideas and behaviors from analysis. For example, we may overlook the construction of religious identities through seemingly inconsequential body adornments while attending to the dramatic accoutrements of organized prayer. It is even possible that formalized activity will cause us to overlook the sacred orientation of ostensibly secular acts, resulting in the misrepresentation of belief systems (Lee 2005; Spiro 1996).

Anthropological research indicates that the formalization, centralization, and control of religious behaviors vary relative to social complexity (Alcorts and Sosis 2005; Bourguignon 1973; Rappaport 1999; Wallace 1966; see also Roes and Raymond 2003). While formal ritual exists in most if not all religions, informal behavior embedded within the larger sociocultural matrix may account for most religious activity in small-scale societies. Belief in and action toward the supernatural will cross-cut and thus integrate various social domains, with religiosity ultimately supporting and being supported by non-religious ideas and behaviors. For archaeology to adequately represent prehistoric religions, Renfrew's approach must be expanded.

An archaeology of religion should continue to research the ceremonial contexts and materials that constitute the most abundant and direct evidence of religious beliefs. Yet researchers must address prehistoric belief as a set of behaviors and better specify the cognitive constraints of both formal and informal religious expression. We must identify the cognitive processes through which these formal and informal expressions articulate with one another and with the larger sociocultural matrix to constitute belief *systems*, and we must learn to recognize these cognitive processes throughout the archaeological record. Here, I direct attention to conceptual metaphor as a form of reasoning that may structure if not source religious thought and behavior and as a systematic and knowable cognitive process that grants access to prehistoric beliefs and practices. An analysis of the ethnographic and archaeological records of Numic speakers from the Western United States illustrates the role of metaphorical reasoning in Numic religiosity and helps develop analytical parameters and expectations for a broadly applicable archaeology of belief.

Conceptual Metaphor Theory

Conceptual metaphor theory integrates the research of various scholars from the cognitive sciences and from cognitive linguistics. Workers have assigned different names to the model (e.g., contemporary metaphor theory, the Embodied Mind Hypothesis, and Lakoff and Johnson's metaphor theory), but to be most consistent with other archaeological applications and to encourage consistency across disciplines, I will use "conceptual metaphor theory."

Conceptual metaphor theory draws on linguistic data and experiments in neural modeling to argue that metaphor is a form of reasoning that structures our ideas about and responses to the world, including religious beliefs and practices (Fauconnier 1997; Gibbs 1994; Gibbs and Franks 2002; Johnson 1987, 1993; Lakoff 1987, 1993, 1997; Lakoff and Johnson 1980, 1999; see also Culley 2000, 2003, 2006; Ortman 2000, 2008; Strauss and Quinn 1997). The following summary of conceptual metaphor theory emphasizes and describes principles that are particularly relevant to understanding and identifying religiosity in prehistory.

Metaphor as Experiential

The nature of language allows for an infinite number of metaphorical expressions, yet our speech suggests that metaphors are systematically structured by our physical experience. For example, the statements "I *see* what you mean" and "Your point is *clear*" use the experience of seeing to define and represent knowledge and understanding. Seeing is an experiential source domain that has been borrowed or "mapped" onto the target domain—knowing. Many statements illustrate the relationship between knowing and seeing: "a point of *view*," "a new *perspective*," and "love is *blind*." Linguistic data indicate that our spoken metaphors often verbalize conceptual metaphors, or permanent relationships between source and target domains.

Conceptual metaphor theory argues that during early childhood development, we do not differentiate between our sensorimotor and subjective experiences[1]. Furthermore, if we repeatedly experience particular sensorimotor and subjective phenomena as the same, the association may become "hardwired." From a neurological perspective, conceptual metaphors are the repeated coactivation of neurophysiological mechanisms that support sensorimotor and subjective experiences, such that their coactivation is permanent. Thus, a child who continually gains knowledge of the world through observation will equate the act of knowing with the act of seeing and will form the permanent association KNOWING IS SEEING[2].

Conceptual metaphors are gestalt perceptions, or whole concepts that we perceive without intellectual processing, that consequently structure verbal, material, and kinesthetic discourse (Johnson 1987:41–64; Lakoff and Johnson 1980:71, 77–82, 1999)

Metaphor and Coherence

When metaphors have the same or very similar sensorimotor experiences as part of their internal structure, they are "coherent" (Lakoff and Johnson 1980:22–23). For example, MORE IS UP and BETTER IS UP use the same sense of direction to define different concepts and are conceptually coherent. We can also combine metaphors like building blocks to structure increasingly complex ideas. If different complex metaphors use some of the same simple metaphors as building blocks, then the complex metaphors will also be conceptually coherent.

As coherent metaphors find expression in social practice, their shared sensorimotor domains implicitly reference each other, linking the expressions and their respective social contexts. Conceptual metaphors thereby constitute a perceptual system that defines and integrates various socially meaningful concepts and experiences in a coherent matrix (Lakoff and Johnson 1980:22–24, 77–105, 1999:60–73).

Metaphor as Cultural Logic

The sheer ubiquity of metaphorical discourse suggests the potential importance of conceptual metaphors in human reasoning. George Lakoff and Mark Johnson (Johnson 1987, 1993; Lakoff 1993, 1997; Lakoff and Johnson 1980, 1999) argue that conceptual metaphor is both epistemological and ontological—a way of knowing and a theory of being that provides us with an everyday metaphysic.

For example, TIME IS MONEY is central to Western thought and behavior: we speak about time as if it were money and actually punch time clocks for money. And consider the ontological status of KNOWING IS SEEING as evidenced in the judicial value we grant eyewitness accounts (Lakoff and Johnson 1980:25–29, 1999:137–234). Indeed, we typically accept conceptual metaphors as self-evident and as *literally* true. Conceptual metaphor is "metaphor that is meant"—and with very real consequences (following Bateson 1985:135; Lakoff 1997:9; Lakoff and Johnson 1980:25–29, 1999:137–234).

Metaphor is also meant differently in different cultures. There are widely shared sensorimotor and subjective experiences that generate widely shared conceptual metaphors. However, culturally specific experiences will generate culturally specific metaphors. As communities uniquely prioritize, combine, and express metaphors sourced in both universal and culturally bound experiences, metaphorical reasoning creates distinct perceptual systems, or cultural logics, and the perception and construction of unique worlds (Lakoff and Johnson 1980:22–25, 82–86, 1999).

Metaphor and the Supernatural World

Lakoff and Johnson (1980, 1999; Lakoff 1987) have identified a suite of metaphorical conceptualizations that may structure our sense of self and that entail human religiosity. For example, they explain that our experiences with containers, of being in containers (cars, rooms), and of ourselves as containers are the sensorimotor ground for the BODY IS A CONTAINER metaphor. Concomitantly, our experiences with "inner lives" provide the source domain for the SUBJECT-SELF metaphor. These metaphors specify a Subject or "inner self" that is contained in the physical body and that is the locus of consciousness, reason, and will. The Subject may also be our "essential self," or "soul," or this essential self may be a second Subject within the body. The physical Self consists of our public personae: our bodies, social roles, and histories (Lakoff and Johnson 1980:58–59, 1999:31–32, 267–289)[3].

The BODY IS A CONTAINER and SUBJECT-SELF metaphors structure the statements *"I'm beside myself* with anger" and *"I* must be *out* of *my mind*!" These statements illustrate conceptualizations of a Self ("myself" and "my mind") that are distinct from and that normally contain the Subject, "I." Expressions of the BODY IS A CONTAINER and SUBJECT-SELF are really very common—*"I* just can't *contain myself,"* *"I* had to force *myself* to do it," *"I* am so mad at *myself,"* and *"I'm* not *myself* today." These two metaphors may also combine with other conceptual metaphors. The statements "I'm *beside* myself with anger" and "I must be *out* of my mind!" actually express BODY IS A CONTAINER, SUBJECT-SELF, and STATES ARE LOCATIONS. These metaphors structure multiple identities and correlate the Subject's location in or out of the body with particular states of being or emotion.

This suite of metaphors may also source and thus make sensical concepts of the soul or spirit, "out of body" experience, and the Christian after-life. Indeed, implicit in otherself is otherworld and otherworld phenomena—the supernatural (Lakoff and Johnson 1999:267–289, 561–564).

It is through empathetic projection, another form of metaphorical reasoning that uses one concept to define another, that we may map human qualities and behaviors onto supernatural beings or map the entire self to become a supernatural being. In this way, metaphorical reasoning allows us to construct multidimensional and numinous worlds (Lakoff and Johnson 1999:269, 564–568).

Conceptual metaphor theory thus defines religiosity as an entailment and expression of metaphorical conceptualizations of self. It is only one aspect of metaphorical reasoning and the resulting cultural logics; the metaphors that structure religious beliefs will necessarily also structure and integrate other sociocultural expression. Metaphorical values that are foundational to religious beliefs should thus be accessible throughout the archaeological record.

The Metaphorical Numa

The Numa comprise a linguistic family that includes the Northern and Southern Paiute and Shoshone peoples who occupy the Great Basin and surrounding regions (Figure 4.1). Anthropologists began studying the Numa in the late 1800s, providing a rich ethnographic record in which to examine conceptual metaphors that structured historically known beliefs and practices. The linguistic and cultural continuity among Numic speakers through time also allows archaeologists to use the ethnographic record to identify conceptual metaphors once structuring prehistoric Numic culture[4].

The ethnographic Numa practiced shamanism (Chalfant 1922; Driver 1937; Fowler and Fowler 1971; Kelly 1939; Kroeber 1925; Lowie 1909; Park 1938; Steward 1933, 1934), loosely defined here as the belief in and practice of effecting change through supernatural interaction. Numic shamans traveled to otherworlds to receive knowledge and power from the supernatural realm in "vision quests" or trance states. If these practices are understood as reification of the inner self and otherworld experience, Numic shamanism implicitly expresses a suite of conceptual metaphors: BODY IS A CONTAINER, SUBJECT-SELF, STATES ARE LOCATIONS, and KNOWING IS SEEING.

For example, the Numa defined disease as soul loss from the body or object/ghost intrusion into the body. During healing ceremonies, a shaman would enter a trance and solicit the aide of his spirit helper. He would then have the power to retrieve the patient's soul or to suck out the object

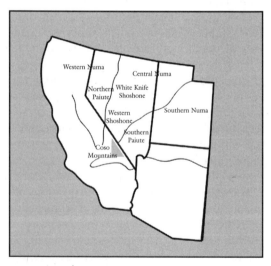

Figure 4.1 Map of the Great Basin showing the major divisions and geographic distribution of Numic speakers.

causing illness. Upon his success, the shaman might exhibit the offending object to show his power, but certainly he would destroy it (Chalfant 1922:30; Fowler and Fowler 1971:53–60, 243–246; Kelly 1939:152–163, 166–167; Lowie 1909:228; Park 1938:37–43, 122–124, 135–139, 146). The patient's recovery indicates the shaman's ability to engage and transform his inner self, to manifest the powers of his spirit helper, and to negotiate otherworlds and the supernatural. The ritual itself reifies a conceptualization of multiple selves, visionary knowledge, and a correlation between states of being and the soul's location.

The Numa defined those who used supernatural powers to cause illness or otherwise inflict misfortune as "witch doctors," and it was not unusual for communities to murder them, or even murder unsuccessful shamans (Chalfant 1922:27–29; Fowler and Fowler 1971:218, 246; Steward 1934:423). This practice implies that the Numa accepted metaphorical conceptualizations of shamans' inner selves, otherworlds, and visionary knowledge as *real*.

The Numa's storytelling traditions also indicate that conceptual metaphor structure shamanic identity and practice. In Numic mythology, Coyote and Wolf are strongly associated with witch doctors and shamans, and several myths differentiate between their physical and inner selves. In one story, Coyote is punished for his trickery and is physically decapitated, yet he survives until his heart, or soul, is removed (Fowler and Fowler 1971:223–224). In a similar myth, Wolf is scalped but then reborn when Coyote retrieves his soul (ibid., 299). Another story evidences KNOWING IS SEEING when Coyote's visions forewarn him of danger and ensure the successful creation of the Numic people (Culley 2000; Steward 1943:262–263).

Coyote and Wolf stories detail the multiple identities of shamans and witch doctors and the appropriate use of supernatural power. However, Numic semantic fields indicate that the metaphorical values that structure shamanic identity and experience also structure identity and experience for all Numa: both a physical and inner self and their respective experiences are recognized throughout the Numic languages (Fowler and Fowler 1971:242–244, 269–270; Harris 1940:65–66; Kelly 1939:155; Park 1938:37–43; Steward 1933:307).

The Northern Paiute, for example, speak of the *Numü cunamin*, or "Spirit of the Head." It is the *Numü cunamin* that leaves the body during illness and shamanic trance. Similarly, the Northern Paiute define sleepiness as the *cunamin* wishing to visit someone, and dreaming as the *cunamin* wandering from the body. Insanity is the displacement of the *cunamin* by a very "bad spirit" (Fowler and Fowler 1971:242–244).

Metaphorical conceptualizations of self and the supernatural seem central to Numic identity and to a range of experiences. In his autobiography,

Jack Stewart (Steward 1934:423–432) speaks of his many visionary experiences and of an active relationship with his inner self. Stewart's soul often "confessed," "admitted," or "told" information that aided him in hunting, in illness, when in danger, and with women. Stewart heeded this advice and earned great status among the Paiute. Yet Stewart was not a shaman, and his experiences illustrate the prevalence and coherence of metaphorical reasoning throughout Numic lifeways.

The ethnographic record indicates that metaphorical values structure and link diverse phenomena, including explicitly religious and ostensibly secular praxis, to collectively constitute Numic religiosity. We see Numic shamanism not as distinct from other phenomena, but as expressions of a coherent logic, fully embedded within the sociocultural matrix.

There are certainly behavioral differences between formal shamanic practice and informal religious expression. One definitive component of shamanic practice is public accountability. Numic healing rituals, for example, typically involve both an audience and the materialization of the expelled "bad medicine" to evidence the shaman's power. Shamans also distinguish themselves, their spirit helpers, and their personal powers through highly visible headdresses, staffs, and other material objects (Driver 1937; Kelly 1932, 1939; Steward 1941; see also Whitley 2003:98–99; Whitley et al. 1999:Table 5). Most significant, Numic shamanism involves the solicitation of the supernatural on behalf of community members and thus entails public accountability. Shamans exhibiting the successful and accountable use of power were rewarded with political status, and religion and politics were intertwined (Whitley, personal communication 2007). The shaman's inner self and otherworld experiences are thus brought forth, valued, and reified in the public domain, such that the shaman *is* his *cunamin* aspect (Culley 2000:33–35).

In contrast, Jack Stewart's otherworld travels and visionary knowledge were personal and for personal benefit. Stewart actually rejected shamanic power on two occasions because he foresaw failure and severe public retribution (Steward 1934:428). Other Numa's inner self and otherworld experiences, such as sleepiness, dreams, and insanity, are similarly private.

Numic religiosity is thus founded in and structured by metaphorical reasoning, but Numic shamanism also illustrates a so far unrecognized permutation of the SUBJECT-SELF metaphor. As has been noted, Lakoff and Johnson (1999:268) define the SUBJECT-SELF metaphor as flexible and its expression highly variable. Nonetheless, they specify that the inner self (selves), or Subject, is "always conceptualized as a person," and that the physical "Self is that part of a person that is not picked out by the Subject. This includes the body, social roles, past states, and actions in the world.... [The] Self is conceptualized metaphorically as either a person, object, or a location" (Lakoff and Johnson 1999:269).

We know, however, that the Numa did not distinguish between a shaman and his spirit helper and that spirit helpers were often animals, objects, or locations (Whitley 1998a:30, 1998b:13, 16–18, 23, 1998c:95–97; Whitley et al. 1999:Table 5). It is the shaman's inner self/spirit helper who is brought forth, reified, and socially valued—it is a social identity. Material reference to and publication of the shaman's inner self reverses the Subject and Self and thus distinguishes the shaman from other Numa.

The distinction between shamanic and non-shamanic Subject and Self identities may have significant implications for archaeological research. If shamanism is the publication and reversal of the Subject as the Self, shamans' inner selves should be explicitly and materially referenced in order to be socially present. These material expressions should also differ from non-shamanic material expressions that are structured by a traditional SUBJECT-SELF conceptualization. More generally, it is evident metaphorical reasoning will use the same fundamental values to structure a range of sociocultural phenomena. Researchers may then identify specific cultural logics—with or without recourse to formal ceremonial contexts—to help reconstruct prehistoric belief systems.

A Supernatural Landscape: Conceptual Metaphors in Prehistory

The Coso Mountains rise near the western boundary of the Numic territories and host the largest concentration of petroglyphs in North America (Grant et al. 1968:12; Whitley 1998a:23:Figure 1). The ethnographic literature associates the thousands of images that dot the landscape with Numic shamans (Driver 1937; Kelly 1932; Park 1938; see also Grant et al. 1968; Whitley 2003:95–97; Whitley et al. 1999), thereby placing the rock art within the Numa's discourse on self and the supernatural.

The ethnography indicates that rain shamans traveled throughout the region to conduct rituals and to depict their trance experiences in rock art (Driver 1937; Kelly 1939; see also Whitley 2003:95–97; Whitley et al. 1999). The rain shaman's spirit helper is the bighorn sheep, and the tendency for Numic shamans to publicize the inner self predicts and makes sense of the bighorn sheep imagery found throughout the Coso Range.

Bighorn sheep imagery is ubiquitous in the Cosos, and appears in various styles (Grant et al. 1968:Table 5; Whitley 1998c:115, Table 1). Nonetheless, there are two relatively rare bighorn motifs that have received little attention from researchers. The first depicts bighorn sheep with "windowpane" bodies framing or containing smaller sheep (Figures 4.2 and 4.3). The images are commonly referred to as "pregnant bighorns," yet this is unquestionably a misnomer—the larger of the two animals inevitably has the incurving horns of a fully developed male. The second and

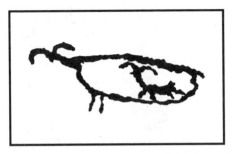

Figure 4.2 The incurving horns of adult *male* bighorn sheep indicate the sheep containing a smaller sheep is not pregnant (Digital tracing of Grant et al. 1968:102).

Figure 4.3 The "pregnant bighorn" motif may reflect the Numa's understanding of the body as a container, and specifically as containing an inner self (Modified from Grant et al. 1968:21n).

particularly enigmatic motif represents bighorn sheep with an additional head in place of a tail (Figures 4.4 and 4.5).

Conceptual metaphor theory defines both motifs as expressions of metaphorical reasoning and specifically as depictions of the shaman's multiple selves. As material representations of the shaman's spirit helper, the images suggest the shamanic variant of the SUBJECT-SELF metaphor that sources and structures the reification of the inner self. The "pregnant bighorns" also appear to be literal representations of the BODY IS A CONTAINER. As shamanic rock art, both motifs implicitly evidence metaphorical conceptualizations of self, knowledge, and states of being.

This interpretation is consistent with David Whitley's (1998a:31, 1998b:23, 1998c:158–159; Whitley et al. 1999:23–24) understanding of images depicting humans hunting bighorn sheep (Figures 4.6 and 4.7). Whitley notes that sensations of dying often accompany trance and that death and dying are common metaphors for trance experience. He interprets the hunting motif as the rain shaman killing his own spirit helper, or an auto-sacrifice to induce trance for rain-making ceremonies.

Figure 4.4　The two-headed sheep motif found on the lower left may represent the Numa's multiple identities (Photograph: Rupestrian Cyberservices).

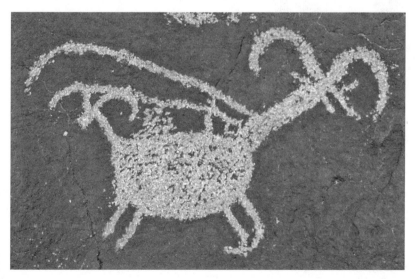

Figure 4.5　This motif may depict rain shamans' inner selves (Photograph: Rupestrian Cyberservices).

Figure 4.6 Scenes with anthropomorphs hunting bighorn sheep suggest metaphorical representations of rain shamans' "auto-sacrifice," or entrance into trance states (Photograph: David Whitley).

Figure 4.7 The hunting motif may juxtapose the rain shamans' physical and inner selves (Photograph: David Whitley).

The hunting scenes visually juxtapose and define the shaman's physical and inner selves, further evidencing BODY IS A CONTAINER, SUBJECT-SELF, STATES ARE LOCATIONS, and KNOWING IS SEEING. The motif also suggests a reversal of the SUBJECT-SELF metaphor as it explicitly brings forth and materializes the inner self within the social domain.

There is, however, a potentially important distinction between the expression of the SUBJECT-SELF metaphor apparent in the "pregnant" and "two-headed bighorns" and the expression apparent in the hunting scenes. The first two motifs depict two identities as bighorn spirit helpers. This seems inconsistent with Numic semantic fields that clearly distinguish the physical and inner selves and that define otherworld experiences in terms of the inner self's location. However, although Numic languages define both a physical and inner self, many Numa also recognize multiple inner selves. The Northern Paiute speak of the *Numa cunamin* and the *Numa mugoa*. It is the *Numa mugoa* that resides in the heart and that leaves the body at death. This distinction further clarifies the myth in which Coyote survives until his heart is removed. In fact, the myth explains that because his heart could not be burned, Coyote remains on Numic lands (Fowler and Fowler 1971:223–224).

It is possible then that different expressions of the SUBJECT-SELF metaphor in Numic imagery reflect rock art production by different Numic peoples. Identifying imagery as specific to a Numic band may also account for the different frequencies in bighorn sheep motifs (see Grant et al. 1968:Table 5, for numeric counts). It is certainly likely that shamans' use of the Cosos varied across bands.

Conclusions

The identification of metaphorical reasoning underlying Numic traditions hints at the analytical potential of operationalizing conceptual metaphor theory as an archaeology of belief. The analysis illustrates how metaphors that structure religious beliefs and practices constitute a systematic cultural logic that actually cross-cuts and integrates diverse sociocultural phenomena. It is then possible to anticipate, recognize, and better understand religiosity in a range of behavioral contexts and material forms. Here, recognizing patterned variation in the SUBJECT-SELF metaphor in both religious and non-religious expression increases our understanding of Numic shamanism and refines interpretations of prehistoric rock art. The analysis also facilitates cross-cultural comparisons that should refine understandings of shamanism and our consequent expectations of the archaeological record, more generally.

Operationalizing conceptual metaphor theory, then, operationalizes the tenets of Renfrew's cognitive archaeology while promising access to systems of beliefs and behaviors that constitute religiosity. Indeed, operationalizing conceptual metaphor theory promises a mechanism through which prehistorians can move toward a broadly applicable archaeology of religion and access belief in the past.

Acknowledgments

I would like to thank Evelyn Billo, Bob Mark, and David Whitley for use of the images in this paper. I am especially indebted to David and to Kelley Hays-Gilpin for improvements to this paper and for including my work in their efforts to access belief in the past.

Notes

1. The terms "subjective" and "sensorimotor" experience distinguish cognitive and physical phenomena without implying one is more or less basic, important, or objective than the other (following Lakoff and Johnson 1980:59).
2. This paper adopts the convention of cognitive linguistics and demarcates conceptual metaphors in capital letters. The linguistic metaphors that conceptual metaphors structure appear in quotation marks as regular verbal statements.
3. Lakoff and Johnson's discussion of the SUBJECT-SELF metaphor describes a very complex and flexible metaphor that may source markedly different conceptualizations of self. The number, qualities, and relationships of the Subjects and Self may all vary. There are also cultures that do not seem to recognize multiple selves. Discussing all permutations of the metaphor is far beyond the scope of this paper. Future researchers might take a cross-cultural approach to better clarify how widespread or variable the SUBJECT-SELF metaphor actually is.
4. For more extensive discussions of metaphors in Numic myths, languages, and rock art, see Culley 2000, 2003, 2006.

References Cited

Alcorts, Candace S., and Richard Sosis
2005   Ritual, Emotion, and Sacred Symbols: The Evolution of Religion As an Adaptive Complex. *Human Nature* 16(4):323–359.
Bateson, Gregory
1985   A Theory of Play and Fantasy. In *Semiotics: An Introductory Anthology*, edited by Robert E. Innis, pp. 131–144. Indiana University Press, Bloomington.
Binford, Lewis R. (editor)
1972   Archaeological Perspectives. In *An Archaeological Perspective*, pp. 78–104. Seminar Press, New York.
Binford, Lewis R.
1987   Data, Relativism, and Archaeological Science. *Man* 22:391–404.
Bourguignon, Erika (editor)
1973   *Religion, Altered States of Consciousness, and Social Change.* Ohio State University Press, Columbus.

Chalfant, W. A.
1922   *The Story of Inyo*. Hammond Press, Chicago.
Culley, Elisabeth V.
2000   The Shaman's Inner Self: A Non-Literal Ontology Manifest in Coso Range Rock Art. Unpublished undergraduate honors thesis, Department of Anthropology, University of Colorado, Boulder.
2003   Examining Metaphorical Reasoning in Rock Art Production: Conceptualizations of Self in Coso Range Imagery. *American Indian Rock Art* 29:69–82.
Culley, Elisabeth V.
2006   The Meaning of Metaphor: A Cognitive Approach to Prehistoric Ideation. Unpublished Master's thesis, Department of Anthropology, Northern Arizona University.
Driver, Harold E.
1937   Culture Elements Distribution: VI, Southern Sierra Nevada. *Anthropological Records* 1(2):53–154. University of California Press, Berkeley.
Dunnell, Robert C.
1971   *Systematics in Prehistory*. Free Press, New York.
Fauconnier, Gilles
1997   *Mappings in Thought and Language*. Cambridge University Press, Cambridge.
Fowler, Donald D., and Catherine S. Fowler (editors)
1971   *Anthropology of the Numa: John Wesley Powell's Manuscripts on the Numic Peoples of Western North America, 1868–1880*. Smithsonian Contributions to Anthropology No. 14. Smithsonian Institution Press, Washington, DC.
Gibbs, Raymond W., Jr.
1994   *The Poetics of Mind: Figurative Thought, Language, and Understanding*. Cambridge University Press, Cambridge.
Gibbs, Raymond W., Jr., and Heather Franks
2002   Embodied Metaphor in Women's Narratives About Their Experiences with Cancer. *Health Communication* 14(2):139–165.
Grant, Campbell, James W. Baird, and J. Kenneth Pringle
1968   *Rock Drawings of the Coso Range*. Maturango Museum Publication 4. Maturango Press, China Lake, California.
Harris, Jack
1940   The White Knife Shoshoni of Nevada. In *Acculturation in Seven American Indian Tribes*, edited by R. Linton, pp. 39–116. Appleton-Century-Crofts, New York.
Hawkes, Charles Francis
1954   Archaeological Method and Theory: Some Suggestions from the Old World. *American Anthropologist* 56:155–168.
Hinde, Robert A.
1998   Mind and Artefact: A Dialectical Perspective. In *Cognition and Material Culture: The Archaeology of Symbolic Storage*. McDonald Institute Monograph Series, edited by Colin Renfrew and Chris Scarre, pp. 175–179. McDonald Institute, Cambridge.
Johnson, Mark
1987   *The Body in the Mind: The Bodily Basis of Meaning, Imagination, and Reason*. University of Chicago Press, Chicago.
1993   Conceptual Metaphor and Embodied Structures of Meaning. *Philosophical Psychology* 6(4):413–422.
Kelly, Isabel T.
1932   Ethnography of the Surprise Valley Paiutes. *University of California Publications in American Archaeology and Ethnography* 31(3):67–210. University of California Press, Berkeley.
1939   Southern Paiute Shamanism. *Anthropological Records* 2(4):151–167. University of California Press, Berkeley.

Kroeber, Alfred L.
1925 Handbook of the Indians of California. *Bureau of American Ethnology Bulletin* 78. Smithsonian Institution Press, Washington.

Lakoff, George
1987 *Women, Fire, and Dangerous Things: What Categories Reveal About the Mind.* University of Chicago Press, Chicago.
1993 The Contemporary Theory of Metaphor. In *Metaphor and Thought*, edited by Andrew Ortony, pp. 202–251. 2nd ed. Cambridge University Press, Cambridge.
1997 How Unconscious Metaphorical Thought Shapes Dreams. In *Cognitive Science and the Unconscious*, edited by D. J. Stein. American Psychiatric Press.

Lakoff, George, and Mark Johnson
1980 *Metaphors We Live By.* University of Chicago Press, Chicago.
1999 *Philosophy In the Flesh: The Embodied Mind and Its Challenge to Western Thought.* Basic Books, New York.

Lee, Dorothy
2005 Religious Perspectives in Anthropology. In *Magic, Witchcraft, and Religion: An Anthropological Study of the Supernatural*, edited by Arthur C. Lehmann, James E. Myers, and Pamela A. Moro, pp. 19–25. McGraw-Hill, New York.

Lowie, Robert H.
1909 *The Northern Shoshone.* Anthropological Papers of the American Museum of Natural History 2(2):165–306. The Smithsonian Institution, Washington, DC.

Mithen, Steven
1998 The Supernatural Beings of Prehistory and the External Storage of Ideas. In *Cognition and Material Culture: The Archaeology of Symbolic Storage.* McDonald Institute Monograph Series, edited by Colin Renfrew and Chris Scarre, pp. 97–106. McDonald Institute, Cambridge.

Ortman, Scott G.
2000 Conceptual Metaphor in the Archaeological Record: Methods and an Example from the American Southwest. *American Antiquity* 65(4):613–645.
2008 Archaeology Without Borders: Contact, Commerce, and Change in the U.S. Southwest and Northwestern Mexico (Southwest Symposium Series), edited by Laurie D. Webster, Maxine A. Mcbrinn, and Eduardo Gamboa Carrera, in press, University Press of Colorado, Boulder.

Park, Willard Z.
1938 *Shamanism in Western North America: A Study in Cultural Relationships.* Northwestern University Studies in the Social Sciences No. 2. Northwestern University Press, Evanston.

Rappaport, Roy A.
1999 *Ritual and Religion in the Making of Humanity.* Cambridge University Press, Cambridge.

Renfrew, Colin
1985 *The Archaeology of Cult.* Thames and Hudson, London.
1994a Towards a Cognitive Archaeology. In *The Ancient Mind: Elements of Cognitive Archaeology*, edited by Colin Renfrew and Ezra B. W. Zubrow, pp. 3–12. Cambridge University Press, Cambridge.
1994b The Archaeology of Religion. In *The Ancient Mind: Elements of Cognitive Archaeology*, edited by Colin Renfrew and Ezra B. W. Zubrow, pp. 47–54. Cambridge University Press, Cambridge.

Renfrew, Colin, and Paul Bahn
1991 *Archaeology, Theories, Methods and Practice.* Thames and Hudson, London.

Roes, Frans L., and Michel Raymond
2003 Belief in Moralizing Gods. *Evolution and Human Behavior* 24(2):126–135.

Spiro, Melford E.
1996   Religion: Problems of Definition and Explanation. In *Anthropological Approaches to the Study of Religion*, edited by Michael Banton. Tavistock, London.
Steward, Julian H.
1933   Ethnography of the Owens Valley Paiute. *University of California Publications in American Archaeology and Ethnography* 33(3):233–350. University of California Press, Berkeley.
1934   Two Paiute Autobiographies. *University of California Publications in American Archaeology and Ethnography* 33(5):423–438. University of California Press, Berkeley.
1941   Culture Elements Distribution: XIII, Nevada Shoshoni. *Anthropological Records* 4(2):209–359. University of California Press, Berkeley.
1943   Some Western Shoshoni Myths. *Bureau of American Ethnology Bulletin* 136: 249–299. Smithsonian Institution Press, Washington, DC.
Strauss, Claudia, and Naomi Quinn
1997   *A Cognitive Theory of Cultural Meaning.* Cambridge University Press, Cambridge.
Tilley, Christopher
1999   *Metaphor and Material Culture.* Blackwell, London.
Tylor, Edward B.
1871   *Primitive Culture: Researches into the Development of Mythology, Philosophy, Religion, Art, and Custom.* 2 vols. John Murray, London.
Van der Leeuw, Sandra
1994   The Archaeology of Religion. In *The Ancient Mind: Elements of Cognitive Archaeology*, edited by Colin Renfrew and Ezra B. W. Zubrow, pp. 47–54. Cambridge University Press, Cambridge.
Wallace, Anthony F. C.
1966   *Religion: An Anthropological View.* Random House, New York.
Whitehouse, Ruth
1996   Ritual Objects. Archaeological Joke or Neglected Evidence? In *Approaches to the Study of Ritual: Italy and the Ancient Mediterranean*, edited by John B. Wilkin, pp. 9–30. Accordia Research Center, London.
Whitley, David S.
1998a   Cognitive Neuroscience, Shamanism and the Rock Art of Native California. *Anthropology of Consciousness* 9(1):22–37.
1998b   Finding Rain in the Desert: Landscape, Gender and Far Western North American Rock Art. In *The Archaeology of Rock Art*, edited by Christopher Chippindale and Paul S. C. Taçon, pp. 11–29. Cambridge University Press, Cambridge.
1998c   Meaning and Metaphor in the Coso Petroglyphs: Understanding Great Basin Rock Art. In *Coso Rock Art: A New Perspective*, Maturango Museum Publication 12, edited by Elva Younkin, pp. 109–174. Maturango Press, Ridgecrest, California.
2003   What Is Hedges Arguing About? *American Indian Rock Art* 29:83–104.
Whitley, David S., J. M. Simon, and Ronald J. Dorn
1999   The Vision Quest in the Coso Range. *American Indian Rock Art* 25:1–31.
Zubrow, Ezra B. W.
1994a   Cognitive Archaeology Reconsidered. In *The Ancient Mind: Elements of Cognitive Archaeology*, edited by Colin Renfrew and Ezra B. W. Zubrow, pp. 187–190. Cambridge University Press, Cambridge.
1994b   Knowledge Representation and Archaeology: A Cognitive Example Using GIS. In *The Ancient Mind: Elements of Cognitive Archaeology*, edited by Colin Renfrew and Ezra B. W. Zubrow, pp. 107–118. Cambridge University Press, Cambridge.

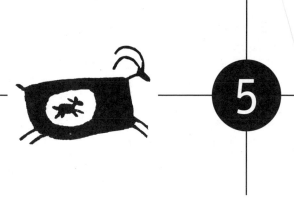

COGNITION, EMOTION, AND BELIEF: FIRST STEPS IN AN ARCHAEOLOGY OF RELIGION

David S. Whitley

"Why, given the empirical inadequacies of magic and the flagrant lack of consensus regarding religious 'truth,' are both magical and religious behaviors so fervent, ubiquitous, and persistent among all the peoples of the earth?"

—Weston La Barre, *Culture in Context*, p. 269

Science is bedeviled by history as much as by method or by philosophy. For even as we contest evidence, debate method, and battle over paradigms, we often overlook a significant fact: we are all part of a shared Western intellectual tradition which is itself a reflection of our common European culture. As moral philosopher Mary Midgley (e.g., 2001, 2002, 2003) has repeatedly shown, this means that we all hold deeply embedded—historical—views of our intellectual tasks, despite apparent and sometimes rancorous differences of opinion about specifics. And what we accept unthinkingly as a given—the received knowledge of our Western intellectual background—is often a product of Enlightenment agendas and thought. This historical fact is more than merely anecdotal, however, because many of these are problematic, once recognized, regardless of whether we espouse processualism, support post-modernism, or practice post-positivism. Science as practiced in this sense is partly defined by its own history, despite its claim to be divorced from it.

One important topic involved in any discussion of what science should or cannot properly study is of course religion, and for (at least) two reasons. One is that religion (as La Barre notes above) is a cross-cultural universal. For this obvious reason, it is nonsensical to insist that a social phenomenon shared by all known human groups is somehow beyond the scientific purview. (If so, what then is the use of science?) The second is the *historical* fact that moral indignation against Christian churches, and perceived competition with Christian thought, were tacit motivations of the Enlightenment scientific program (e.g., Midgley 2003:40).

While these aspects of Enlightenment science were useful in their time, their utility has expired. Partly this is because the Christian churches are no longer a threat, intellectually or politically: the intellectual revolution of the Enlightenment was also accompanied by a political one, and it now seems safe to say that in the West we are freed from the shackles of religious thought and authority. But it is also because the concept of a competition between science and Western religion no longer has much currency. As Midgley has stated,

> the functions of science and religion within a society are too different for this idea of a competition between [them] to make much sense once one begins to consider it seriously. Rivalry here only looks plausible when both elements are stated in a crude form (which of course they often are). (2003:18)

While science partly developed as a reaction against and an antidote to religion, the anti-religion agenda had been satisfied by the mid-nineteenth century (Morris 1987:88). Continued scientific work even partly informed by this Enlightenment motivation, to be sure, seems silly in the twenty-first century. Despite this circumstance, it is no news to any Western scientist that religion is still a marginalized research topic. This is partly, I suspect, because the science versus religion debate continues to be fought in the minds of many academics, most of whom never stop to realize that the other side long ago left the battlefield[1]. But it is also partly because religion, perceived as a subjective experience, is likewise thought scientifically unstudiable. This attitude reflects another inheritance from our Enlightenment past.

To look towards a scientific study of prehistoric religion, then, from a cognitive perspective, I start with some comments on epiphenomenalism and the related topic of emotions and their relationship to reason and evolution. This leads me to cognitive neurosciences research on the nature of religious experience, and to religion in terms of social theory, focusing on the implications of consciousness and emotion, and how the control and manipulation of these play in socio-cultural terms.

Epiphenomena and "Objective Facts About Subjective Experiences"

The Western sciences, including archaeology, have long considered religion to be epiphenomenal (Flannery and Marcus 1993:261). Midgley calls this the "steam-whistle theory of mind,"

> which says that what happens in our consciousness does not affect the behaviour of our bodies. Subjectivity is then a causal dead end. Our experience is just an *epiphenomenon*, which means idle froth on the surface, a mere side-effect of physical causes. Consciousness is thus an example—surely a unique one?—of one-way causation, an effect which does not itself cause anything further to happen. (2001:107)

There are a series of reasons why epiphenomenalism as an intellectual doctrine is simply wrong. Perhaps the most important of these involves its fundamental internal contradiction: if thought and intellectual activities are of no consequence, then where do theories come from, and why do academic theorists—including especially those who view cognition as epiphenomenal—measure their own personal success exactly in terms of their own intellectual contributions? (Midgley 2001:107–112, 2003:34–40; Whitley 1998a:303; see also Whitley et al. 1999:221). Epiphenomenalism as an intellectual theory defeats itself (much like relativism) because if it were valid, it would be at the same time also equally invalid, due to academic practice, and this makes no sense whatsoever. That I wrote this paper, and that you are reading it, demonstrates the very relevance of cognitive phenomena that archaeology traditionally has dismissed, despite the importance that archaeology places on writing and reading about research.

The important point then is the following: this scientific myth is a historical product of Rene Descartes' separation of mind and body (Damasio 1994), which also served to distance cognition in general terms and emotion specifically from the things that (putatively) matter to science. Descartes apparently emphasized this separation due to his enthusiasm for and the primacy he ascribed to physics and his resulting view that physics should be the model for all sciences, despite the fact that this position contradicted his own metaphysical beliefs (Midgley 2003).

The opposition established by Descartes between physical/mental (and thus body/mind), and the importance he placed on the former, established a materialist (as opposed to idealist) approach to science. This reached its logical extreme in Skinnerian behaviorism which attributed all human action to stimulus/response reactions to an external environment. As Christopher Peebles (1992) and I have both noted (Whitley 1992, 1998a), behaviorism is an implicit but fundamental presupposition of processual archaeology, and even outside of the strictures of narrow processualism it continues to hold sway as the putative "common-sense" view of human action (Homans 1987). But regardless of specific manifestation, epiphenomenalism is simply an expression of a metaphysical belief, not a scientific fact (Midgley 2003:38).

In practical terms the issue of epiphenomenalism devolves methodologically to questions of what can or cannot be studied scientifically. Eminent neurologist V. S. Ramachandran has described the traditional distinction usefully by reference to figures of speech (Ramachandran and Blakeslee 1999). He notes (only partly metaphorically) that anything expressed in terms of third-person observations has traditionally been taken as somehow tacitly "objective" and reliable (e.g., "the patient was seen to have a contusion on her left knee"). First-person narratives, in contrast, are taken as "subjective" and therefore intrinsically unreliable (e.g., "I fell down and scraped my left knee"). As a practicing physician, Ramachandran finds this distinction insupportable because, among other things, his patients often are the best qualified to comment on their own physical or mental status.

The traditional distinction between subjective experience (epiphenomena) versus external observation (empirical fact) is then based on a fallacy of equivocation that conflates external with objective, accurate, and reliable, and internal and cognitive with unreliable and inaccurate. But as we all now know, all observations are theoretically informed and biased, not just "subjective" personal ones. The traditional distinction between what can or cannot be science, in other words, is based on attitudes about form, not substance. Midgley says it most clearly by noting simply that "there can be objective facts about subjective experiences" (2003:34).

Emotion, Evolution, and Religious Experience

The idea among social scientists that cognition and its by-products can be studied scientifically has benefited greatly from recent developments in the cognitive neurosciences, including the elimination of Freudian and Jungian theories of mind (and the psycho-babble that accompanied them). One area of this recent research that is especially relevant to an understanding of religion involves emotions (e.g., Damasio 1994, 2003; Gibbs 2006; Hinton 1999; Hobson 1994; LeDoux 1996). Emotions and feelings are typically the furthest removed from behaviorist views of science and they are still seen by most social scientists with suspicion (Hobson 1994). In fact this is a mistake, as Charles Darwin (1965) was quick to recognize. Not only are emotions critical to rational thought, but they played a key role in human evolution.

This is because emotions and feelings are not epiphenomenal, first, but instead are powerful expressions of drives and, especially, "instincts" (Damasio 1994:115). Perhaps the most obvious and strongest of the emotions involves the so-called fight-or-flight response which, to be sure, is directly linked to adaptive behavior. This response is controlled in the hypothalamus, the "brain" of our "archaic" limbic system, along with two other behaviors: feeding and sex (Ramachandran and Blakeslee 1999:177–178). But the hypothalamus also controls a series of somatic and somatosensory responses, through the autonomic nervous system. Indeed, because of its control of emotional response and its regulation of corresponding bodily activities, the hypothalamus has been called the body's "survival center" (ibid., 177–178).

Emotions, in other words, have measurable and obvious physical effects and are therefore anything but epiphenomenal—a fact that Darwin (1965) may have been the first to recognize. Regardless of intellectual primacy, he emphasized this fact by the very title of his landmark 1872 study: *The Expression of Emotions in Man and Animals*. Indeed, Darwin defined the term "expression"—used in the sense of a facial expression—as "the language of the emotions" (1965:366). Modern physiology of course gives us a slightly more detailed read on the somatic effects of emotions than Darwin had at his disposal. In the case of the fight-or-flight response, for example, these include increased blood-flow to the muscles and heart, and elevated blood pressure and respiratory rates. But the idea that emotions have somatic effects is now an established fact. It is well expressed by our use of the term "feelings," used to express the awareness of our emotions. That our English word for this state of emotional awareness is based on a tactile metaphor is far from accidental.

Second, emotion and reason evolved together, and both are required for rational thought (Damasio 1994, 2003; Midgley 2003:102). While "primary" or innate emotions are centered in the limbic system, emotions are not entirely restricted to this primitive, ancestral "reptilian" brain. Secondary or learned emotions, in particular, occur in the ventro-medial pre-frontal cortices, along with reason. Lesions in this area, as a result, diminish both reasoning *and* emotional response, and sociopaths with brain damage in this area typically display a decline in rationality along with feeling (Damasio 1994). Emotion and reason in other words are neuroanatomically and functionally linked.

Emotion in this sense is implicated in any comprehensive theory of cognition or human evolution. Religious experience is also implicated with these concerns due to the now established fact that such experiences are neither ethereal nor epiphenomenal, but instead are localized neurochemical reactions in the temporal lobe and limbic system. (This is an empirical fact which has no bearing on the potential supernatural or numinous importance of these experiences. The neuropsychology of religious experience can be used equally to argue for or against the sacral validity of religion.) Indeed, "religious" experiences can be artificially induced electromagnetically using a transcranial magnetic stimulator, as Michael Persinger (e.g., 2001) has shown. More commonly, however, clinical evidence concerning the generation of intense religious experiences derives from studies of left temporal lobe (TL) epilepsy: 38 percent of TL epileptics report having mystical experiences (Ramachandran and Blakeslee 1999:175, 285), whereas other neurological pathologies, involving different neural circuitry, yield no such reactions.

Four points are important here. The first is that permanent alterations of an individual's personality can result from these brief "temporal lobe storms" (Ramachandran and Blakeslee 1999:179). The effects of religious experience in this sense are not transitory but may instead be life-changing, resulting in what is known as "Temporal Lobe Personality." This involves heightened emotions, the tendency to find cosmic significance in everyday events, humorlessness, self-importance, and reduced sexual drive. It also can result in hypergraphia, which is the tendency to maintain detailed and elaborate diaries about everyday events (ibid., 180).

Second, while I have emphasized the importance of TL epilepsy in the generation of religious experience, there are some important details about this fact that require emphasis. Gross neurochemical and neuroanatomical similarities exist between TL epilepsy and shamanistic ASC, and in this sense TL storms provide us with a useful general neuropsychological model for religious experiences, even when detached from pathology. But while the focal seizures of the TL epileptic do result in a kind of ASC that is grossly similar to the shaman in trance, there are other varieties of altered states that also yield mystical experiences. These differ partly in terms of which aspects of the limbic system are involved, and partly in terms of their resulting somatosensory expression. According to Wright (1989), for example, meditative and possession trances differ psychologically and physiologically from shamanistic trance. Possession (or mediumistic) trances are closest to the TL ASC, with amnesia, convulsions, and spontaneous onset some of the characteristics that set them apart from shamanistic or meditative trances. Although the differing nature of these states is still far from fully understood, one implication is already clear: an altered state of consciousness or trance is not a single phenomenon but instead represents a neuropsychological spectrum, and this spectrum has implications for ritual practice and behavior (Lewis-Williams, this volume). That is, "religious experience" itself—even though rooted in neuroanatomical architecture and driven by neurochemical changes—is variable in nature, intensity, and outcome.

Third, in a wide-ranging study Michael Winkelman (1989, 1992, and this volume), has demonstrated that regular cross-cultural differences exist between characteristic trance/religious experiences and social complexity. In general terms Winkelman has found that as societies become more complex, the trance-based practices of the shaman shift towards possession-trance mediums. The implication here, likewise, is clear: cultures and societies of different types use states of consciousness in different ways (or, perhaps better, different states of consciousness are accessed by different kinds of social groups.)

Fourth, humans evolved specialized neural circuitry to mediate religious experiences (Ramachandran and Blakeslee 1999:183). Indeed, even our so-called reptilian limbic system has enlarged and evolved, creating more complex neural interconnections with the cortex and thereby better integrating the cognitive/cultural and emotional systems (Armstrong 1999). Whether there is then a gene for religion is not yet clear, and likewise it is uncertain whether there is a "God module" in our brains: these characteristics may have emerged from other changes, and the idea of a modular brain itself is controversial. Still, it is certain that religion is part of (though not necessarily entirely based on) our biological—which is to say evolutionary—make-up.

Emotion and Ritual

The specific relevance of emotion to the prehistory of religion concerns ritual, and it can be seen at two levels. The first involves shamanistic and transcendental religions directly, where altered states of consciousness (ASC) play a central ritual role. One typically ignored outcome of ASC is the generation of intense emotions (Whitley 1998b). Indeed, while ASC experiences can be partly understood as one aspect of the spectrum of human consciousness (Lewis-Williams 2002), more than altered consciousness alone is involved in altered states. Equally, ASC need be recognized as altered emotional states or conditions, with the well-known "ecstatic trance" only one of a variety of potential emotional reactions. We can, in fact, correlate different ASC-inducing psychoactive drugs with particular emotional states. PCP, the large-animal tranquilizer known as the street hallucinogen "angel dust," for example, notoriously and commonly leads to rage and violence; *Datura*, in contrast, is said to be an aphrodisiac and in this sense generates lust (Whitley 1994). Similarly, as Hobson (1994) has shown, the "natural" neurochemical analog to drug- and meditation-induced trance, REM dreaming, yields a complete range of emotional reactions of which anxiety is the most common, reflecting the fact that (to use my teenage daughter's term) humans are inherently *angsty*.

That various of these emotional conditions—and the physical feelings that they engender—are very highly desired by humans almost goes without saying. But it does need saying because of its important implication: humans commonly seek ASC not because of any desire to alter their consciousness—ultimately, an intellectual proposition—but instead, as any teenager could tell you, because of the way ASC make you *feel*. And this is altered emotion, and all this implies, writ large. As Weil (1972) first noted, the human desire for ASC is then analogous to our drives for food and sex. Noll (1985), in a parallel fashion, has outlined the innateness of the "pleasure principle," and in the process emphasized the implications of the universal ability of humans to achieve ASC. While drug or alcohol addiction ultimately then may be physiologically based, humans no more become addicts due to this fact than (as the old evolutionary adage goes) do birds fly because they have wings. In both cases this would confuse consequence with cause: humans become addicts because they like the ASC effects of their preferred mind-altering substance, not because these substances are addictive.

We talk then of shamanistic and transcendental religions in terms of ASC: altered states of *consciousness*. I would like to suggest that this emphasis is only partly a function of empirical reality because, equally, it reflects our Western puritanical valuation of the mental and intellectual over the emotional. (On the conceptual scale that runs from entirely "concrete" to wholly "touchy-feely," emotion is at the bottom rung.) Certainly, trance states do result in changed consciousness, but also much more. As Ramachandran notes:

> I find it ironic that this sense of [religious] enlightenment, this absolute conviction that the Truth is revealed at last, should derive from the limbic structures concerned with emotions rather than from the thinking, rational parts of the brain that take so much pride in their ability to discern truth and falsehood. (Ramachandran and Blakeslee 1999:179)

When we discuss ASC perhaps we could as accurately phrase this in terms of AES: altered emotional states. Regardless, that ASC is central to shamanistic and transcendental religions, that these states result in abundant emotional feelings, and that humans desire and actively seek these emotional reactions are all well-established empirical facts. There is, in this sense, at least one innate and real neurobiological drive or motivation to participate in ASC-oriented rituals (and there almost certainly are others, some of which are cultural).

But religion itself, even if partly grounded in neurobiology and evolution, is also mediated by culture, and ASCs are not central to all religions. That is, while La Barre (1980:51) notes that all religions originate in one individual's "revelation," and thus that ASCs of some kind are a common denominator of all religions, access to sanctioned altered states of consciousness is socially restricted in many, perhaps most, religions (cf. Lewis-Williams 2002, and this volume).

The second level at which emotions are potentially implicated in ritual, and therefore may be relevant to the prehistory of religion, concerns this second group of religions. This involves non-shamanistic/transcendental religions in the general sense, as well as public/group rituals that themselves do not normally lead to ASC for the participants. The relationship of emotion and consciousness to this class of religions and rituals is less studied or understood. And admittedly, my argument about these rituals, which is simplistic, is still hypothetical. But it goes as follows:

1. Group rituals themselves are public performances that, if successful, are designed to generate and manipulate emotional reactions in participants,
2. While these emotional reactions are not necessarily as strong as those released during the various forms of an ASC, they are nonetheless real, measurable, and significant in effect,
3. They may in part be promoted by mirror neurons (Fogassi et al. 2005; Nakahara and Miyashita 2005) that promote person-to-person understandings of intentional acts and, potentially, empathy, and
4. Humans likewise desire and seek the altered emotional states generated by these kinds of group rituals, and are probably again hard-wired to do so.

Note, not incidentally, that there is evidence supporting the idea that the participation in a physical activity that is associated with an emotion may cause the individual to feel that same emotion (Damasio 2003). This obviously is a variation on the old but related general idea that the ultimate appeal of religion is "psychological" (or, as it is sometimes expressed by anthropologists, tied to "sentiment"). While Durkheim (1965) placed primary cause for religion in social structure, for example, he also pointed to the importance of emotion in religious ceremony—emphasizing it so much, in fact, that he was heavily criticized by Evans-Pritchard for biological reductionism. While I raise this aspect of Durkheim's work again below, it is worth quoting Evans-Pritchard's reaction to it:

> No amount of juggling with words like intensity and effervescence can hide the fact that [Durkheim] derives totemic religion ... from the emotional excitement of individuals brought together in a small crowd, from what is a sort of crowd hysteria. (1965:68)

Evans-Pritchard's objection here of course ultimately lies in the Enlightenment commitment to all-or-nothing explanations: nature or culture, then, but not somehow a mix of the two, as Durkheim implied. But perhaps Durkheim was simply right on this point. Certainly, some categories of public ritual, such as mortuary practices, are intensely emotional (see Metcalf and Huntington 1991:43–61; Price, this volume). Indeed, there is empirical evidence for the importance of emotional stimulation in many (though not all) rituals (e.g., McCauley and Lawson 2002; Whitehouse

1995, 2000). These recent studies are ultimately concerned with larger issues (such as explaining the variation in religious systems rather than my narrower interest here: the casual factors in the universality of religious practice). Still, they demonstrate the importance of emotional arousal in many kinds of rituals, especially rare or episodic group ceremonies accompanied by elaborate pageantry[2].

One motivation for individual participation in group rituals, then, is elevated emotions. This has the potential to operate at the individual level, in the sense of emotional excitement and catharsis, but also at the group level. In this last case neurochemical changes (e.g., in serotonin levels) generated by emotional reactions can have social implications, such as the reduction of aggression, resulting in enhanced group socialization, as has been observed in groups of monkeys (e.g., Raleigh and Brummer 1993).

Brain-Mind States and Social Theory

I have so far partly emphasized certain historical aspects of our Western intellectual tradition: one of Enlightenment science's original agendas as an antidote to religion, the separation of the physical from the mental due to Descartes' obsession with physics, and so on. The reason for this emphasis is more than simply pedagogical because the implications are quite significant: even in cases where the connections may not immediately be obvious—indeed, especially where they have been deeply implicit—our Western academic tradition has followed certain intellectual threads that, when exposed to the light of contemporary critical thinking and existing empirical knowledge, simply cannot be sustained. This should be comforting to archaeologists because it demonstrates clearly that understanding the (intellectual) past matters. But it is also disquieting in the sense that the foundations for many of the ideas that we take as givens are not simply shaky, but they rest on the dramatically crumbling ground of ancient (and disproven) prejudice and bias.

Midgley has spent a career describing the origin of many of our most cherished intellectual beliefs and exposing them for what they really are: scientific myths. Two of these are pertinent to the current discussion. The first is the idea that there should only ever be a single comprehensive thought system—ultimately stemming from the fact that Descartes placed physics alone as central to all knowledge: the world is either materialist, or it is idealist, but it cannot, somehow, be a combination of both. As she notes apropos to this point,

> Enlightenment concepts ... tend to be particularly simple and sweeping. Dramatic simplicity tends to be one of their chief attractions and is also their chronic weakness. (Midgley 2003:5)

The irony here is that both materialists and idealists share this all-or-nothing view of the world. But there is nothing in rationality that requires commitment to this extreme and one-sided view.

The second but related concern involves scientific reductivism: the conviction that one fundamental form (or process or theory) underlies everything (ibid., 27). Reductiveness is problematic partly because, despite the attractiveness of parsimony, it is empirically unrealistic (cf. Newton-Smith 1981); in fact, the world and human social processes are complicated phenomena. It is for this reason unlikely that something akin to the mythic unified field theory of the physical sciences (long sought but still undiscovered in physics) will ever be defined in the social sciences—the current inflated claims of neo-Darwinism notwithstanding. Reductivism is also sometimes objectionable because it

> is never value-neutral, never just aimed at simplicity … it is always part of some positive propaganda campaign. (Midgley 2003:32)

Why do these two points, combined with those in the sections above, matter? The answer is relatively simple: our existing social theories are products of nineteenth and twentieth century thinking which, in each case, entailed implicit and tacit commitments to certain of the biases, confusions, and outright errors that accompanied Enlightenment agendas and presuppositions. Not the least of these is their failure to adequately incorporate cognition, emotion and thus mind in their consideration of human social structure and process[3].

Now it is far beyond this paper to propose a new cognitive social theory. One reason for this is the fact that such an undertaking is a lifetime of work. A second stems from the fact that the relatively new discipline of cognitive neuroscience itself has yet to establish a fully confident theory of the brain-mind—how it evolved, functions, and affects human behavior. Still, there are snippets of information that already appear reliable. These allow first steps towards a cognitive theory of society which must necessarily include some explication of the place of religion.

Two components of such a theory can be proposed here, as a start. The first, recently suggested by Lewis-Williams (2002), involves consciousness: specifically that societies control states of consciousness. Because these states of consciousness are implicated in religious belief and practices, it follows that religion at least in part serves this end.

In fact, Lewis-Williams is not the first to broach this broad idea. An earlier expression of this same general concept was raised by Michel Foucault in his first major work, *Madness and Civilization: A History of Insanity in the Age of Reason* (1988; first published in France in 1961). Foucault shows in his analysis how the definition of insanity, its putative relationship to reason, and European society's treatment of the insane changed between Medieval, Renaissance, and then "Classical" (i.e., Enlightenment) times. *Madness and Civilization* can be seen as an outgrowth of Foucault's 1950s historical analyses of psychiatry, but with an important distinction: in *Madness* he argued beyond changes in scientific methods and intellectual theories, linking shifts in the perception and treatment of the insane instead to changing *epistemes*—the metaphysical underpinnings of culture. The important implication then is that our understanding of insanity, a mental condition, and therefore also reason (because insanity is always reason's foil), is not a "natural" given but is socially and culturally constituted, and controlled. And this is no small thing for, as Foucault puts it,

> the Reason-Madness nexus constitutes for Western culture one of the dimensions of its originality. (1988:xi)

Although insanity and consciousness are of course not the same thing, they are both manifestations of cognitive processes. Conceptually, at least, it is a short step from recognizing the implications of the cultural construction of one of these to the cultural construction of the other.

Anthropologists have also been aware of the differing implications of states of consciousness for different cultures. One such researcher was Weston La Barre, due to his work on revivalistic cults (especially the Ghost Dance and the Native American Church) and hallucinogens. He stated that:

> great cultural variety [exists] in concepts and social contexts regarding certain mental states. (1980:37)

La Barre went on to contrast how Christian Europe has traditionally been hostile to hallucinogens but open to alcohol, whereas Muslim societies have reacted in exactly the opposite fashion (1980:64–65). He pointed to the fact that the use of hallucinogenic plants by Native American societies was widespread and quite pervasive, but that their use was reserved exclusively for religious purposes, differing sharply with the Western recreational use of these same botanical hallucinogens (La Barre 1980:66). Moreover, despite the near-pervasive use of hallucinogens in the Americas, La Barre also cited the fact that certain Pueblo Indian priesthoods largely resisted both tobacco and *Datura*, despite their use by surrounding tribal groups (ibid., 82).

The implications of these facts and circumstances are, I believe, straightforward:

1. The definition of acceptable versus inappropriate mental states and states of consciousness is culturally, not biologically, determined, even though the states themselves are neuropsychologically based.
2. Humans have a strong innate drive to alter their state of consciousness.

3. Yet, societies regulate how and when this can be done, and by whom.
4. Because the most dramatic change in states of consciousness involves so-called religious experiences, religion is centrally involved in their social regulation.

A good and recent even if anecdotal example of aspects of this circumstance in action is provided by the history of the Mormon Church. Mormonism was founded in the United States by Joseph Smith during the nineteenth century, and for this reason its history is particularly well documented. Like all religions, its origins lie in revelations, which is to say visionary experiences or ASC. While the initial revelations occurred to Smith, as Krakauer (2003) has outlined, during Mormonism's initial development anyone could have and report on revelations, and based on this experience anyone could in this fashion influence church doctrine and practice. But predictably, given that this was an "organized church" with a quickly solidifying hierarchy (with Smith at the top), individual revelation as a component of church practice did not last beyond the first generation. When the power of individual revelation became impractical for effective leadership and social control, doctrine changed, shifting (almost all) powers of revelation to the church head or "prophet"[4].

The second component of a cognitive social theory that adequately treats religion is, as implied above, emotion. Three points are important. The first, already discussed in some detail, is that there is an innate, evolutionarily based human drive to generate certain kinds of intense emotions. The second is the anthropological fact that, while emotions are at base neuropsychologically driven, specific emotional reactions and appropriate kinds and degrees of reactions and expressions, in different contexts, are culturally determined[5]. In part this follows from the fact that differing kinds of ASC lead to different emotional reactions and, since states of consciousness are culturally controlled, so too then are emotions (albeit, admittedly, to a much lesser degree). But it is also simply true that some cultures make distinctions in emotional reactions or recognize emotions that Westerners do not. The Ifaluk, for example, have words for "justifiable anger" (*song*) and compassion/love/sadness (*fago*) which have no straightforward linguistic—or affective—equivalent in English (Lutz 1988). Emotional reactions are for all of us innate; but how these reactions are understood and used, how intensely they may be felt and when they are appropriate is, at least in part, cultural.

Third, it is also clear that group rituals can serve to manipulate specific emotional responses. A good example of this fact is provided by Metcalf and Huntington in their discussion of Durkheim's analysis of Australian aboriginal mortuary rites:

It has been suggested that Durkheim bridged the gap between individual and society with a crude use of crowd psychology. But the funeral material, as Talcott Parsons (1968:437) noted, provides a crucial demonstration that crowd psychology was not what Durkheim intended. The power of crowd behavior derives from the fact that the crowd is an unorganized, ad hoc assemblage. The rituals that Durkheim describes are, by contrast, minutely organized. Intense emotion and tight organization go hand in hand even in these funerals, where the obligations of slashing one's thighs or burning one's abdomen are precisely determined by kinship. (1991:51)

It is not necessary to agree with Durkheim's overriding conclusion about the relationship of structure and mind/emotion to see the implication of this circumstance[6]. Group rituals can manipulate emotions in quite specific ways, far beyond their use of dominant or key symbols (Ortner 1973; Turner 1967) and the emotive power that these symbols maintain.

Ritual of course does many things or (put another way) has a series of potential social functions. These include inculcating values and norms, masking and/or supporting social inequalities, promoting group solidarity and integration, and/or serving in cultural transmission. But each of these possible purposes (and there are more) raises the functionalist conundrum: what is in it for the participants, at the ritual moment? Surely, and real as these functions may or may not be in specific cases, these are outcomes of, not explanations for, ritual behavior. The answer to the question, I suggest, lies in the real and intense emotional experience of group ritual, and the neuropsychological effects these engender. Sometimes, and in certain contexts, this goes as far as true religious experience: the ASC of the TL epileptic and similar conditions, including shamanistic, meditative, and mediumistic ASCs. But, importantly, it need not go so far in order to have significant effects.

Rituals "work," in this sense, not because they guarantee some outcome in the afterlife[7], nor because they actually have demonstrable positive worldly outcomes (like healing). As we know, the empirical truth of religious doctrine is unverifiable at best, and, where potentially testable, it tends to be an abject failure. Religions "work" instead because of the way rituals make people feel.

Conclusions

Two final points can be made by way of conclusion. The first is an important qualification: I do not claim that all group rituals work because they serve as emotional triggers, nor necessarily (and in a parallel fashion) that the control of consciousness is central to all religions and societies. Following Mary Midgley's lead, as I have emphasized a number of times above, there is no a priori justification for assuming that all human social actions must work in the same way, follow the same set of rules, or always engage equivalent processes. My point is that the variables that

I emphasize here are implicated in a significant number of group rituals and, in this sense, help us understand some, but probably not all ritual action and religious behavior.

Second, and somewhat peripherally, it is worth noting that archaeologists have largely conflated ritual and symbolism. The two are obviously related, in part because ritual action involves the use and manipulation of symbols, and in part because ritual acts themselves may constitute symbolic performances. That said, it is analytically useful to keep the phenomena distinct for one important reason: Bloch's (1986, 1992) studies imply that the rates of change for ritual uses of symbols versus changes in the symbols themselves may differ significantly. In fact, we should expect ritual to change more rapidly than symbolism. Iconography alone, in this sense, is inadequate for any complete study of prehistoric religion.

Notes

1. A subtext of this comment, and this paper more generally, is that cognitive archaeological research on religion confronts two different even if related intellectual biases: the first against the study of cognitive phenomena in general terms, and the second against religion. The relevance of this last point is, I believe, well illustrated by the research published in the 1980s and early 1990s under the guise of both post-processual and cognitive archaeology. This explicitly considered cognitive topics, including especially symbolism, but religion was rarely if ever mentioned despite the fact that it was exactly religious symbolism that was usually the focus of analysis. Many archaeologists (myself included) in this sense "crept up on" the topic of prehistoric religion slowly, before being explicit about what we have been studying. I suspect that this resulted from the continuing disdain that most academics hold for religion and our implicit reaction to this fact, including unease over whether religion is a respectable topic of research.

2. McCauley and Lawson (2002) usefully distinguish between episodic, significant rituals marked by ceremonial pageantry (such as marriage), where emotional arousal plays a part, and quotidian rituals, such as a priest's quick blessing, given in passing, to which neither celebrant nor participant pays much real heed. Rituals in this sense can be contrasted as either excitement filled or boring. In a very rough sense these correspond to group versus personal rituals. My concern here is with the first kind of ritual, because of their heightened social implications.

3. Marx's historical-materialism and its concern with ideology suggests an implicitly psychological/cognitive function for religion. Certain implications of historical-materialism's view of religion are, because of this fact, probably correct, although (I suspect) for the wrong reasons. (When Marx said that religion is the "opiate of the people," I believe that he was onto something valid, but due to the undeveloped understanding of pharmacology, psychology, and neurology available at that time, it is anybody's guess as to the real intended meaning of this oft-repeated phrase.) The difficulty with Marx's view of religion then is (somewhat ironically) ideological: because he viewed religion as always allied with exploitative systems (Bloch 1983), he disdained religion and expressed hostility towards it (Morris 1987). Historical-materialism then represents the anti-religion agenda of Enlightenment science in its most naked form.

   Historical-materialist analysis of religion in this sense reduces concern with function—which has been a major interpretive topic since Durkheim and then Radcliffe-Brown—into a game of "gotcha," wherein the only goal is to prove that religion is socially pernicious. This may or may not be correct, in specific empirical circumstances, but as an analytical (and therefore cross-culturally universal) given, it is hardly a circumstance that breeds confidence in the objectivity or fairness of the resulting interpretation. (A parallel argument can be made about religious function in contract theories of society, of course, where "all roads lead to solidarity.") But more to the point, the emphasis on religion as an expression of ideology, given historical-materialism's undeveloped treatment of cognition, ultimately reduces human thought to the level of sheep: everyone (except, somehow, historical-materialists) believes whatever they are told. This implies a distinction in kind between the cognition of the intellectual elite and that of the masses (cf. Fuller 1999). I do not know what neurobiological evidence could be cited to support this implied distinction.

Giddens's (1984) Structuration comes closest to articulating social process with an explicit theory of cognition. It does this because it recognizes the importance of culture in human action—culture here as defined in cognitive terms—although this is effectively implicit in his overtly sociological theory.

But Giddens's model was developed before the recent major advances in cognitive neurosciences—the 1990s and the "official" decade of the brain—rendering his views on cognition somewhat anachronistic. For example, his tiered stratification model, relating cognition to personal action, has three "levels" of consciousness: discursive consciousness, practical consciousness, and unconscious motives. It is difficult to reconcile this model with any contemporary understanding of cognition and the brain-mind. "Unconscious," for example, is a term that describes a medical condition—"knocked-out"—not cognition nor a brain-mind state. The brain-mind, in fact, has only two cognitive states: conscious and nonconscious (Hobson 1994:207). While there may be a range of variation within these two states, there is no nonconscious cause for the information content of consciousness (ibid., 217–218). Giddens's use of cognition in this sense appears to be implicitly derived from Freud's discredited speculations about the "subconscious mind." The point here ultimately is the same one that I emphasize above: plausible social theory requires accommodation of human cognitive processes, yet cognitive theory itself is far from mature. This means that we are all still some distance from the finishing gate.

4. Mormon males can still assert to a woman that God has revealed that they are to be that man's wife. In conservative communities this is sometimes taken as a true command from God, giving women no effective choice in marriage. Moreover, the early emphasis in Mormon Church scripture on individual revelation continues to plague the organized church, due to the frequent appearance of self-proclaimed prophets whose pronouncements are often at odds with official church doctrine, as Krakauer's (2003) account makes clear.

5. Just as in the mind-matter and nature-culture debates, emotion theory is also sometimes framed oppositionally in entirely biologically reductionist or socially constructivist terms. As is clear, emotions have both a biological and a cultural side, and certain recent researchers, recognizing this fact, have quite usefully argued for a "biocultural" approach, accommodating both aspects (e.g., Hinton 1999).

6. Durkheim's attempt to assign causal primacy to structure at the expense of mind/emotion, I believe, reflects not so much an empirical error as his false idea of causality. In particular, Durkheim appears to have been confused over the fact that there are different levels of causality, the most obvious of which are proximal versus ultimate. Among other things, there is a difference between the linear sequence or series of discrete events (with the first event triggering the next, and so on, down the line, reflecting proximal causality) and the complex fashion in which a social behavior such as this sequence of events might initially evolve (ultimate causality). Durkheim was in fact concerned with the origin of religion, and so his interest really was ultimate causality, but the explanation he proposed in fact did not rise above the level of proximal causation.

7. "Wish-fulfilment" implied by the promise of an afterlife is the common folk-explanation for the function of religion. The problem with this claim is that there are religions (e.g., traditional Judaism and Taoism) that have no such doctrine (Midgley 2003; Morris 1987).

References Cited

Armstrong, Este
1999   Making Symbols Meaningful: Human Emotions and the Limbic System. In *Biocultural Approaches to the Emotions*, edited by A. L. Hinton, pp. 256–273. Cambridge University Press, Cambridge.
Bloch, Maurice
1983   *Marxism and Anthropology*. Clarendon Press, Oxford.
1986   *From Blessing to Violence: History and Ideology in the Circumcision Ritual of the Merina of Madagascar*. Cambridge University Press, Cambridge.
1992   *Prey into Hunter: The Politics of Religious Experience*. Cambridge University Press, Cambridge.
Damasio, Antonio R.
1994   *Descartes' Error: Emotion, Reason and the Human Brain*. G. P. Putnam's Sons, New York.
2003   *Looking for Spinoza: Joy, Sorrow, and the Feeling Brain*. Harcourt, Orlando.
Darwin, Charles
1965   *The Expression of Emotions in Man and Animals*. University of Chicago Press, Chicago. Originally published in 1872.
Durkheim, Emile
1965   *The Elementary Forms of Religious Life*. Translated by J. W. Swain. Free Press, New York. Originally published in 1912.
Evans-Pritchard, E. E.
1965   *Theories of Primitive Religion*. Clarendon Press, Oxford.
Flannery, K. V., and J. Marcus
1993   Cognitive Archaeology. *Cambridge Archaeological Journal* 3:260–270.
Fogassi, L., P. F. Ferrari, B. Gesierich, S. Rozzi, F. Chersi, and G. Rizzolatti
2005   Parietal Lobe: From Action Organization to Intention Understanding. *Science* 308:662–667.
Foucault, Michel
1988   *Madness and Civilization: A History of Insanity in the Age of Reason*. Revised 2nd ed. Vintage Books, New York.
Fuller, Steve
1999   *Thomas Kuhn: A Philosophical History of Our Times*. University of Chicago Press, Chicago.
Gibbs, Raymond W., Jr.
2006   *Embodiment and Cognitive Science*. Cambridge University Press, Cambridge.
Giddens, Antony
1984   *The Constitution of Society*. University of California Press, Berkeley.
Hinton, A. L.
1999   Introduction: Developing a Biocultural Approach to the Emotions. In *Biocultural Approaches to the Emotions*, edited by A. L. Hinton, pp. 1–38. Cambridge University Press, Cambridge.
Hobson, J. Allan
1994   *The Chemistry of Conscious States: Toward a Unified Model of the Brain and the Mind*. Little, Brown, Boston.
Homans, G. C.
1987   Behaviorism and After. In *Social Theory Today*, edited by A. Giddens and J. H. Turner, pp. 58–81. Stanford University Press, Palo Alto.

Krakauer, Jon
2003   *Under the Banner of Heaven: A Story of Violent Faith.* Doubleday, New York.
La Barre, Weston
1980   *Culture in Context: Selected Writings of Weston LaBarre.* Duke University Press, Durham, North Carolina.
LeDoux, Joseph
1996   *The Emotional Brain: The Mysterious Underpinnings of Emotional Life.* Touchstone Books, New York.
Lewis-Williams, J. David
2002   *The Mind in the Cave: Consciousness and the Origins of Art.* Thames and Hudson, London.
Lutz, Catherine A.
1988   *Unnatural Emotions: Everyday Sentiments on a Micronesian Atoll and their Challenge to Western Theory.* University of Chicago Press, Chicago.
McCauley, Robert N., and E. Thomas Lawson
2002   *Bringing Ritual to Mind: Psychological Foundations of Cultural Forms.* Cambridge University Press, Cambridge.
Metcalf, Peter, and Richard Huntington
1991   *Celebrations of Death: The Anthropology of Mortuary Ritual.* Revised 2nd ed. Cambridge University Press, Cambridge.
Midgley, Mary
2001   *Science and Poetry.* Routledge, London.
2002   *Evolution as a Religion: Strange Hopes and Stranger Fears.* Revised 2nd ed. Routledge, London.
2003   *The Myths We Live By.* Routledge, London.
Morris, Brian
1987   *Anthropological Studies of Religion: An Introductory Text.* Cambridge University Press, Cambridge.
Nakahara, K., and Y. Miyashita
2005   Understanding Intentions: Through the Looking Glass. *Science* 308:644–645.
Newton-Smith, W.
1981   *The Rationality of Science.* Routledge and Kegan Paul, London.
Noll, Richard
1985   Mental Imagery Cultivation As a Cultural Phenomenon: The Role of Visions in Shamanism. *Current Anthropology* 26:443–451.
Ortner, Sherry
1973   On Key Symbols. *American Anthropologist* 75:1338–1346.
Parsons, Talcott
1968   *The Structure of Social Action.* Free Press, New York.
Peebles, Christopher
1992   Rooting Out Latent Behaviorism in Prehistory. In *Representations in Archaeology*, edited by J.-C. Gardin and C. S. Peebles, pp. 357–384. Indiana University, Bloomington.
Persinger, Michael
2001   The Neuropsychiatry of Paranormal Experiences. *Journal of Neuropsychiatry and Clinical Neurosciences* 15(4):515–524.
Raleigh, M. J., and G. L. Brummer
1993   Individual Differences in Serotonin-2 Receptors and Social Behavior in Monkeys. *Society for Neuroscience Abstracts* 19:592.
Ramachandran, V. S., and Sandra Blakeslee
1999   *Phantoms in the Brain: Probing the Mysteries of the Human Mind.* Quill, New York.

Turner, Victor
1967   *The Forest of Symbols: Aspects of Ndembu Ritual.* Cornell University Press, Ithaca, New York.
Weil, A.
1972   *The Natural Mind: A New Way of Looking at Drugs and the Higher Consciousness.* Houghton Mifflin, Boston.
Whitehouse, H.
1995   *Inside the Cult: Religious Innovation and Transmission in Papua New Guinea.* Clarendon Press, Oxford.
2000   *Arguments and Icons: Divergent Modes of Religiosity.* Oxford University Press, Oxford.
Whitley, David S.
1992   Prehistory and Post-Positivist Science: A Prolegomenon to Cognitive Archaeology. *Archaeological Method and Theory* 4(4):57–100.
1994   Shamanism, Natural Modeling and the Rock Art of Far Western North American Hunter-Gatherers. In *Shamanism and Rock Art in North American*, edited by S. Turpin, pp. 1–43. Special Publication 1, Rock Art Foundation, San Antonio.
1998a   (editor) *Reader in Archaeological Theory: Post-Processual and Cognitive Approaches.* Routledge, London.
1998b   Cognitive Neuroscience, Shamanism and the Rock Art of Native California. *Anthropology of Consciousness* 9:22–37.
Whitley, D. S., R. I. Dorn, J. M. Simon, R. Rechtman, and T. K. Whitley
1999   Sally's Rockshelter and the Archaeology of the Vision Quest. *Cambridge Archaeological Journal* 9:221–247.
Winkelman, Michael
1989   A Cross-cultural Study of Shamanistic Healers. *Journal of Psychoactive Drugs* 21:17–20.
1992   *Shamans, Priest and Witches: A Cross-Cultural Study of Magico-Religious Practitioners.* Anthropological Research Papers No. 14. Arizona State University, Tempe.
Wright, P. A.
1989   The Nature of the Shamanistic State of Consciousness: A Review. *Journal of Psychoactive Drugs* 21:25–33.

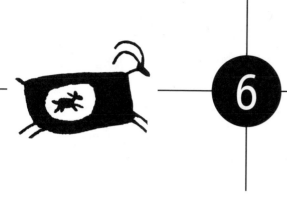

CENTERING HISTORICAL-ARCHAEOLOGICAL DISCOURSE: THE PREHISTORY OF CENTRAL ASIAN/SOUTH SIBERIAN SHAMANISM

Andrzej Rozwadowski

Shamanism in Central Asia and Siberia, though commonly believed to be the key component of regional cultures, is still not fully understood in the archaeological record. It is common knowledge that the very term "shaman" came out of Siberia and today is widely applied by anthropologist and ethnographers to similar cultural phenomena in different parts of the globe. Usually it is accompanied by the supposition that "classic shamanism" appeared (and originated) in Siberia. Hence Siberia is often perceived as a rather monolithic entity, and consequently so-called Siberian shamanism is considered a homogeneous phenomenon. A closer examination of this seemingly simple phenomenon, however, reveals a greater variety of hues in the monochrome picture of Siberian shamanism, and this circumstance is amplified by considering the geographically and culturally related region of Central Asia.

The presence of shamanism in different cultural traditions of Asia has led to the inference that its roots extend into antiquity and it once constituted the most archaic pan-Siberian religion. It is true that shamanism is found among numerous peoples from the Urals to Kamchatka and it undoubtedly crosses many ethnic borders: it is shared by Uralic, Turkic, Mongolian, Tungus, and paleo-Asiatic peoples in Siberia and by Turkic peoples, Tajiks, and Mongols in Central Asia. However, an analysis of the entire Asian shamanic complex is not my aim here. Instead my intention is to focus upon key elements from Central Asia and southern Siberia that offer important insights into the prehistory of Asian shamanism, and the archaeology of religion itself.

Central Asian and southern Siberian traditions today contrast due to different processes and different cultural influences since early times. To begin with, Central Asia in the second millennium BC fell within the sphere of Indo-European migrations. Here the Indo-Iranians gave rise to the great civilizations of this region: Persia and Aryan India. Later, in the seventh century AD, Arabic peoples invaded the lands between the Amu-Daria and Syr-Daria and the new credo of the prophet Muhammad began to sweep through the Central Asian steppe. In contrast, Siberia for many centuries had lived by its own rhythm, until the Russian conquest which began in the sixteenth century AD. Despite these diverse historical dynamics, both areas have in common the steppe environment: vast grass-lands stretching for hundreds of kilometers, which have united Central Asia and southern Siberia since ancient times. What does this environmental factor contribute towards our understanding of Central Asian and Siberian shamanism? I will first examine Asian shamanism's historical origins, then examine its prehistory using the evidence of rock art.

History

Despite the fact that there is no one common word describing a "shaman" amongst the different Asian peoples, the practices, costumes, and characteristic elements of the shamanic ceremony share many features. The Yakuts (Sakha) of East Siberia refer to their shamans as *oyun*, while the Turkic Altaian peoples of southern Siberia call them *kam*. The Turkic word *kam* appears for the first time in the Uygur text Kudatku Bilik, which was written in AD 1069 (Chadwick and Zhirmunsky 1969:235). Another important early source, however, comes from Chinese chronicles during the Tang dynasty (AD 618–906) in which *kam* refers to the name of a shaman belonging to the Yenisei Kirghiz people (Potapov 1978:13). Towards the end of the first millennium BC the Chinese chronicles also refer to *wu* ("shamans") amongst a group of the Huns (Potapov 1978:9).

The Mongols call their shamans *böge* (male) and *niduyan* (female) (Heissig 1980:10). Historic sources dated to the seventh and eighth centuries AD demonstrate that Mongols worshiped *ongons* (material representations of shamanic helping spirits) and venerated Tengri, the highest god/power of Heaven, whose cult has played a crucial role in the traditional religion of Turkic-Mongolian peoples into the present (Boyle 1972; Heissig 1980:6–7).

In the Central Asian countries of Uzbekistan and Tajikistan the shamans are called *parikhon* and *pholbin*, words of Iranian origin. The term *parikhon/porkhan* is also used by the Turkmens of Turkmenistan and the Karakalpaks of northwest Uzbekistan. Moreover, amongst the Kazakhs,

Kirghiz, Uygurs, and Uzbeks a shaman is known as *baksy* or *bakshy*, the Kazakh term for "shamanic initiation" is then baksylyk. Various etymological of this word have been proposed that indicate a derivation from old Turkic *bak* (*bakmak*) "to look carefully," "to watch." Alternatively, it could come from the Chinese word *boshi* (*bag-ši*), "teacher," which was introduced into the Turkic languages via the Mongolian language. An Indian genesis cannot be excluded, however, and this word could possibly derive from the Sanskrit term for Buddhist monk, *bhikshu* (Żerańska-Kominek and Lebeuf 1997:39).

The Indian connection also potentially offers some insight into the genesis of the classic term "shaman." It comes from the Tungus word *saman* which was first recorded in the seventeenth century by Russian Cossacks, however its position in this Siberian tongue is not fully understood. As early as the eighteenth century it has been suggested that *saman* was an Indian word derived from the Sanskrit *śramana* (Shirokogoroff 1935:270). Shirokogoroff argues that this term passed to eastern Asia from India through Central Asia along with the spread of Buddhism. Recent studies lend support to this "Indian path" and extend the time of possible borrowing back to 2000 years ago. Furthermore, Sidorov (1997) suggests that the transfer took place at the time of the eastward movement of the Indo-Europeans, whose main migrating waves reached India and Iran in the mid second millennium BC.

(Pre)History

Written records thus enable us to assert that shamanism has been practiced in this part of Asia for more than 2000 years. To progress deeper into the prehistory of shamanism requires archaeology. This route has some obvious limits as the preservation of shamanic materials in the archaeological record is subject to different processes, especially the deliberate destruction of artifacts at the time of the shaman's death, which has been recorded among the Yakuts in historical times (Kośko 2002). Furthermore, the chance of finding shamans' graves is rather small as they are usually situated in hidden places (deep in the forest, as in the case of the Yakuts), separated from society. In contrast, rock art images have proved to be more durable data as they have survived the centuries after being exposed to natural processes in the environment. Therefore, the permanence of rock art potentially provides a valuable record of shamanistic symbolism. Let us now examine its importance to the archaeology of shamanism.

Shamanistic connections with rock art imagery created in recent times are numerous and easily recognizable. The most significant symbol is, of course, the drum, which is represented as a single image or held by human figures. Such images can be found on rocks, stones, or stelae of south Siberia (Figure 6.1; see, for example, Devlet 2001; Kubarev 2002;

Figure 6.1 The stele at Barbugaza, Altai, with pecked images of humans with shamanic drums (photo by A. Rozwadowski).

Okladnikova 1988). Sometimes these images appear in more complex compositions with animals, which also have shamanic connotations. One can find in petroglyph scenes camels, goats, or deer—animals that appear in other forms of shamanic art, like drum paintings. These were frequently placed on the shamanic drums, especially in the Altai region where the tradition of drum painting is particularly strong.

According to ethnographic accounts from the Altai, shamans did not paint drum images themselves, although the shaman decided what kinds of images the painters should create. Thus, the act of "decorating" the drum directs us to the social context connected with the ceremony of "enlivening" the drum (drum animation; Potapov 1947). This was an important social event that brought together the entire community. The ceremony was also the only time in the drum's "life" when it could be touched and played by any person. After the ceremony was completed, the drum became solely the shaman's property; only the shaman was allowed to use it and had the power to play it. We do not have information about whether rock art was also made during this ceremony.

Some petroglyphs suggest a depiction of the ceremony of enlivening the drum. In the Kuyliu cave in the Altai Mountains, for example, we find a drum motif surrounded by animals, including rams, deer, and the bear (Figure 6.2)—animals sacred to Altaic shamanism (Matochkin 1998). In this rock art scene the drum is "touched" with a deer's hoof, which seems

10 CM

Figure 6.2 Scene with rock images (note the drum in the center of composition) in the Kuyliu cave in Altai (after Matochkin 1998, courtesy of Evgeniy P. Matochkin).

to emphasize the intimate connection between the two symbols. It could relate to the drum animation ceremony, as the drumhead was made of the skin of an animal into which the drum was then symbolically transformed, or rather into which the drum was incarnated. In the Kuyliu cave is another phallic or tailed shaman figure with a drum that deserves our attention because tailed humans frequently appear in second millennium BC rock art from both southern Siberia and Central Asia. The shamanic context of the Kuyliu petroglyphs also points to other images of animals, like the bear, which in the tradition of Altaic shamanism symbolizes the shaman while shamanizing. Three goats surrounding the Kuyliu cave shaman may relate once again to the process of enlivening the drum: during the ceremony the shaman was believed to receive three helping spirits in the form of horned animals.

The drum, however, is not the only ritual attribute that indicates shamanic practice. Equally important is the shamanic staff, which among Turkic tribes is commonly known as the *tayak*. From ethnographic research we know that staffs were often used in curing ceremonies by both Turkic and Mongolian peoples. Shamanic staffs have also been used by the Evenks and Kets who dwell in adjacent Siberian regions. The latter are of an enigmatic ethnic affiliation. It is believed that they moved into their current area of habitation, the middle Yenisei, from the Sayan-Altai, possibly 2000 years ago. If the genesis of the shamanic staff lay in ancient Turkic-Mongolian culture then its dissemination among the Evenks could be explained by close territorial relations between this group and Turks and Mongols in southern Siberia. The hypothesis concerning the Turkic-Mongolian origins of the shamanic staff is supported by the fact that on the symbolic level it is identified with the horse, although the Kets perceive the staff instead as a legendary shamanic tree.

Correspondences between the staff and drum are particularly interesting from the perspective of their shared symbolism. Just like the drum, the staff was subjected to the process of animation, and after a special ceremony the staff became a horse. In the tradition of Mongolian shamanism the ceremony was known as *amilkha*. Here the staff gained life and was transformed into the living horse that helped the shaman to contact the invisible world of spirits. The staff, like the shamanic drum, was enlivened and became a draught animal on which the shaman traveled to other worlds. Furthermore, staffs were also decorated, similar to the drums, in this case by the use of different pendants. Some Buriat shamans named their staff and drum by a single term, *khese* (Dyakonova 1981:152). Moreover, the common Turkic name for drum, *dyungyur/tyungyur/tyuyur*, recalls the word

Figure 6.3 Petroglyph scene in the Arpauzen Valley, south Kazakhstan (note the human figure holding possible drum and hitting it with a drumstick). Traced by author.

tyur, "staff"; other meanings also include "sacred tree" or "sacral pillar" (Prokofeva 1961:449).

Turkic speakers associate the staff with the horse, and likewise many Siberian nations, including the Yakuts, Tuvinians, Khakass, and Buriats, interpret the drum in the same manner. Some groups of Altaians (Teleuts and Shors) call it *ak-chagal*, "sacred spotted horse" (Sagalaev 1984:19). Sometimes the drum is thought of as horse or deer by peoples such as the Khakass and Tuvinians (Potapov 1969:75). Some cultures also have specific drum names reserved solely for shamanizing. The Altaians, for example, called the drum during the ceremony *ak-adan*, "white/sacred camel" (also *er-bodan* "young male camel" and *ergi-adan* "one humped camel"; Sagalaev 1984:19). During the ritual the drum was thus transformed into a camel on which the shaman traveled to the spirit world; while shamanizing the shaman was called *adanyg*, meaning "driving the camel." The camel therefore becomes a symbolic substitute for the horse.

The camel's shamanic associations, however, are not limited exclusively to southern Siberia. In Central Asia the key shamanic musical instrument is the *kobyz*, a two-stringed instrument. According to tradition its resonant box should be covered by camel leather. Furthermore, it is called *nar-kobyz*, "camel-kobyz" (Basilov 1989:158), which reflects a similarity to the Altaic drums.

The above historic and linguistic data allow us to draw some important conclusions. First, it appears that the drum motif has spatial and chronological limits. The drum is noted mainly in southern Siberia while in Central Asia it appears sporadically and in a different form. Here we are dealing with circular motifs held by human figures, like a (possible) drum shown at Arpauzen in Kazakhstan (Figure 6.3). This petroglyph is pertinent to our discussion because the human holding a drum is associated with camels (as noted above, a significant animal in southern Siberian shamanism). Second, rock art images of drums, which vividly resemble historical Siberian drums, come from more recent times. Numerous scholars have already suggested that the drum is a relatively late element in Siberian shamanism and the evidence of rock art seems to support this hypothesis. It was argued that in prehistoric times shamans used other items, like the bow, which may have also played the role of a musical instrument (Devlet 1998:207; Sagalaev 1984:23).

The late introduction and the limited geographic distribution of the drum emphasize the valuable insights that the examination of rock art brings to the archaeology of shamanism, suggesting that "classic Siberian shamanism" was a late rather than a truly archaic phenomenon.

Let us briefly look next at the case of the extraordinary painted and engraved burial chambers discovered at Karakol in Altai Mountains, dated to the second millennium BC (Kubarev 1988, 2002). The Karakol images are characterized by anthropo-zoomorphic figures whose heads are masked or replaced by animals' heads.

Their heads are often distinguished by feather decorations superficially resembling North American Plains Indian plumes (Figure 6.4a). Other anthropomorphic figures clearly represent scenes of metamorphoses, with paws instead of feet. Depictions of flying birds are present in close proximity to these humans (Figures 6.4b and 6.5). These anthropomorphic figures deserve special attention because their bodies are covered by protrusions that resemble the characteristic *bakhroma* decorations of historical shamanic cloaks. The latter, as we know from ethnographic accounts, symbolize birds or are rich in elements of ornithomorphic symbolism (Pavlinskaya 1994). There can be little doubt that bird symbolism plays a crucial role in Siberian shamanism and the Karakol rock art appears to suggest that this symbolism was equally important 4000 years ago. Overall, the iconography of this ancient Altaic art is characterized by features typical of local shamanism, with one exception: it lacks the drum. Instead of this motif we note an object held by a human figure that resembles a bow (Figure 6.4c).

Another important case study involves the rich imagery of staffs found in the Bronze Age rock art of the Altai (second millennium BC). These images occur more widely than drums and they also appear in Central Asia. Staffs are often depicted in shamanistic scenes involving human figures, like at the petroglyph sites of Arpauzen (Kadyrbaev and Maryashev 1977) or Tamgaly (Rozwadowski 2001, 2003, 2004; Samashev 2002) in Kazakhstan (Figure 6.6). "Shamanic" rock art from the Central Asian Bronze Age is important for our discussion because

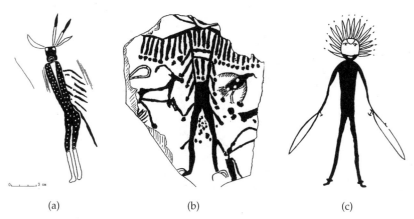

(a)   (b)   (c)

Figure 6.4 Painted (A, C) and engraved (B) humans from the grave slabs discovered in Karakol village in Altai (after Kubarev 2002, courtesy of Vladimir Kubarev). For color photographs see Rozwadowski 2004.

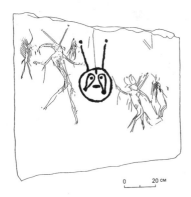

Figure 6.5 Engraved "human-bird" figures on the grave slab from the Tas-khazaa, south Siberia (after Leontev, Kapelenko, Esin 2006). Newly traced by Yuriy N. Esin, by courtesy of Yuriy N. Esin; for old copy see Lipskiy (1961).

it does not have distinct images of drums and it resembles Bronze Age rock art from southern Siberia. Moreover, the prehistoric rock art of these two regions is characterized by some common features which are of special value to the question of the prehistory of shamanism in this part of Asia: human figures in garments that resemble historic costumes of shamans; humans that appear in association with staffs and possibly with a bow; and half human–half animal figures that are typical in Siberian shamanism with regards to human-bird metamorphosis. Furthermore, some petroglyphs in Central Asia dated to these

(a)

(b)

Figure 6.6 Petroglyphs (possibly 4000 years old) representing tailed humans with staffs; upper scene (A) from the Arpauzen Valley in Kazakhstan (traced by the author), the lower one (B) from the Kalbak-Tash in Russian Altai (after Kubarev 2002, courtesy of V. Kubarev).

ancient times appear to reflect ecstatic trance phenomena which, we suppose, were experienced by shamans (Rozwadowski 2001, 2002, 2004:73–80).

Conclusions and Implications

The religious phenomenon of shamanism in Central Asia and Siberia can be better understood using a historical approach. Shamanism is a very important component of the spiritual lives of contemporary nomads. In the last 2000 years these were mainly Turkic-Mongolian peoples. Rock art imagery indicates that not all historically attested shamanic attributes were in use in prehistoric times. In particular, the drum seems to have appeared in rock art only recently, perhaps only from the historical-ethnographical present. Other shamanic elements seem to be well confirmed in prehistoric rock art, starting from around the second to third millennium BC. Moreover, the symbolic association of the main historical shamanic attributes—staffs and drums—with horses or camels strongly suggests their genetic connection with the pastoral-cultural complex, that is, the pastoral/nomadic peoples. In addition, Bronze Age shamanistic rock art is particularly abundant and distributed across the steppes from Central Asia to southern Siberia; we can argue that shamanism in this area was an important cultural component of the steppe cultures since at least the second millennium BC (cf. Hultkrantz 1978).

The theoretical implications of this study first concern the archaeology of shamanism. Shamanism is commonly thought to be foremost a hunter-gatherer religious phenomenon. In the Central Asian and southern Siberian case this supposition does not necessarily hold, with shamanism found among and potentially originating in pastoralist, metal-using cultures.

The prehistoric shamanistic rock art of Central Asia and southern Siberia also provides us with the stimulus to advance more far reaching conclusions with regards to a specific variant of Siberian shamanism, known as "white shamanism" (Vajda 1983). As the archaeology of the region suggests, the eastern Eurasian steppe, since the turn of the Neolithic and Bronze Age, was the territory through which the early pastoralist Indo-European people spread (Mallory 1991). Several studies of white shamanism have noted that this ritual complex bears a resemblance to the Indo-European priesthood. This is suggested by external/visual similarities to Indo-European priesthood traditions, including a ritual emphasis on whiteness, a white horse, and a cult of the highest sky god, and by linguistics, with some terms connected with white shamanism possibly of Indo-European etymology (Dugarov 1991). It is possible then that white shamanism is a consequence of the transformation that occurred in traditional Asian cultures under the influence of Indo-Europeans migrating through and disseminating ideas and rituals across the Asian steppes.

Overall, this emphasizes the importance of contextualizing shamanism in terms of the prehistoric and historical cultural dynamics of Central Asia and Siberia. As demonstrated throughout this paper, a closer examination of Central Asia and southern Siberia has contributed valuable insights into questions about not only the prehistory of Asian shamanism, but also the archaeology of religion in general.

References Cited

Basilov, V. N.
1989   Bowed Musical Instruments. In *Nomads of Eurasia*, edited by V. Basilov, pp. 152–159. Natural History Museum of Los Angeles County in association with University of Washington Press, Seattle.

Boyle, J. A.
1972   Turkish and Mongolian Shamanism in the Middle Ages. *Folklore* 83:177–193.

Chadwick, N. K., and V. Zhirmunsky
1969   *Oral Epics of Central Asia*. Cambridge University Press, Cambridge.

Devlet, E.
2001   Rock Art and the Material Culture of Siberian and Central Asian Shamanism. In *The Archaeology of Shamanism*, edited by N. Price, pp. 43–55. Routledge, London.

Devlet, M. A.
1998   *Petroglify na dne Sayanskogo Morya*. Pamyatniki Istoricheskoy Mysli, Moskva.

Dugarov, D. S.
1991   *Istoricheskie Korni Belogo Shamanstva*. Nauka, Moskva.

Dyakonova, V. P.
1981   Predmety k Lechebnoy Funktsii Shamanov Tuvy i Altaya. *Sbornik Muzeya Antropologii i Etnografii* 37:138–152.

Heissig, W.
1980   *The Religions of Mongolia*. Routledge and Kegan Paul, London and Henley.

Hultkrantz, A.
1978   Ecological and Phenomenological Aspects of Shamanism. In *Shamanism in Siberia*, edited by V. Diózegi and M. Hoppál, pp. 27–58. Akadémiai Kiadó, Budapest.

Kadyrbaev, M. K. and A. N. Maryashev
1977   *Naskalnye Izobrazheniya Khrebta Karatau*. Nauka, Alma-Ata.

Kośko, M. M.
2002   *Szamanizm: Teatr Jednego Aktora*. Wydawnictwo Muzeum Narodowego w Poznaniu, Poznaniu.

Kubarev, V. D.
1988   *Drevnie Rospisi Karakola*. Nauka, Novosibirsk.
2002   Traces of Shamanic Motives in the Petroglyphs and Burial Paintings of the Gorno-Altai. *In Spirits and Stones: Shamanism and Rock Art in Central Asia and Siberia*, edited by A. Rozwadowski, with M. M. Kośko, pp. 33–48. Instytut Wschodni (Institute of Eastern Studies, Adam Mickiewicz University), Poznań.

Leontev, N. V, V. F. Kapelenko and Y. N. Esin
2006   *Izvayaniya i stely Okunevskoy kultury*. Abakan: Khakasskoe Knizhnoe Izdatelstvo.

Lipskiy, A. N.
1961   Novye Dannye po Afanasevskoy Kulture. In *Voprosy Istorii Sibirii i Dalnogo Vostoka*, edited by V. I. Shinkov, pp. 269–278. Izdatelstvo Novosibirskogo Otdela AN SSSR, Novosibirsk.

Mallory, J. P.
1991   *In Search of the Indo-Europeans*. Thames and Hudson, London.

Matochkin, E. P.
1998   Shamanisticheskie Kompozitsii Grota Kuylyu. In *Sibir v Panorame Tysyacheletiy*, vol. 1, edited by V. I. Molodin, pp. 367–378. Izdatelstvo Instituta Arkheologii i Etnografii, Novosibirsk.

Okladnikova, E. A.
1988   Graffiti Kara-Oyuka, Vostochny Altai. In *Materialnaya i Dukhovaya Kultura Narodov Sibiri. Sbornik Muzeya Antropologii i Etnografii 42*, pp. 140–168. Nauka, Leningrad.

Pavlinskaya, L. R.
1994   The Shaman Costume: Image and Myth. In *Ancient Traditions: Shamanism in Central Asia and the Americas*, edited by G. Seaman and J. S. Day, pp. 257–264. University Press of Colorado, Boulder.

Potapov, L. P.
1947   Obryad Ozhivleniya Shamanskogo Bubna u Tyurkoyazychnykh Plemen Altaya. In *Trudy Instituta Etnografii Imeni N.N. Miklukho-Maklaya*, vol. 1, edited by S. R. Tolstov, pp. 159–182. Moskva-Leningrad. Izdatelstvo Akademii Nauk SSSR.

1969   *Etnicheskiy Sostav i Proiskhozhdenie Altaytsev.* Nauka, Leningrad.

1978   K Voprosu o Drevetyurskoy Osnove i Datirovke Altayskogo Shamanstva. In *Etnografiya Narodov Altaya i Zapadnoy Sibiri*, pp. 3–36. Nauka, Novosibirsk.

Prokofeva, E. D.
1961   Shamanskie Bubny. In *Istoriko-Etnograficheskiy Atlas Sibiri*, edited by M. G. Levin and L. P. Potapov, pp. 435–492. Izdatelstvo Akademii Nauk SSSR, Moskva-Leningrad.

Rozwadowski, A.
2001   Sun Gods or Shamans? Interpreting the 'Solar-Headed' Petroglyphs of Central Asia. In *The Archaeology of Shamanism*, edited by N. Price, pp. 5–86. Routledge, London, New York.

2002   Disappearing in the Cliffs: Shamanistic Aspects of Indo-Iranian Mythology As a Context for Interpreting Central Asian Petroglyphs. In *Spirits and Stones: Shamanism and Rock Art in Central Asia and Siberia*, edited by A. Rozwadowski, with M. M. Kośko, pp. 33–48. Instytut Wschodni (Institute of Eastern Studies, Adam Mickiewicz University), Poznań.

2003   Indoirańczycy—Sztuka i Mitologia. *Petroglify Azji Środkowej*. Wydawnictwo Naukowe UAM, Poznań.

2004   *Symbols Through Time: Interpreting the Rock Art of Central Asia*. Institute of Eastern Studies, Adam Mickiewicz University, Poznań.

Sagalaev, A. M.
1984   *Mifologiya i Verovaniya Altaytsev.* Tsentralno-Azyatskie Vliyaniya. Nauka, Novosibirsk.

Samashev, Z.
2002   Shamanic Motifs in the Petroglyphs of Eastern Kazakhstan. In *Spirits and Stones: Shamanism and Rock Art in Central Asia and Siberia*, edited by A. Rozwadowski, with M. M. Kośko, pp. 33–48. Instytut Wschodni (Institute of Eastern Studies, Adam Mickiewicz University), Poznań.

Shirokogoroff, S. M.
1935   *Psychomental Complex of the Tungus.* Kegan Paul, Trench, Trubner, London.

Sidorov, E. S.
1997   *Yakutskie Leksicheskie Skhozhdeniya.* Yakustkiy Gosudarstvenniy Universitet, Yakutsk.

Vajda, M.
1983   Problems of Central Asian and Siberian Shamanism. *Numen* 30 (2):215–239.

Żerańska-Kominek, S., with A. Lebeuf
1997   *The Tale of Crazy Harman.* Dialog, Warsaw.

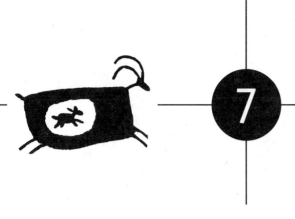

TEXT VERSUS IMAGE: THE IMPLICATIONS OF PHYSICAL EVIDENCE FOR BUDDHIST HISTORY

Robert DeCaroli

Introduction

The use of religious documents as a source of historical information is a practice that can be found in some form wherever religious institutions were associated with the production of written materials. The danger, naturally, lies in the need to interpret the ways in which this type of textual evidence relates to historical events. Such documents were rarely, if ever, written as historical records, at least in the way that history is now generally understood. Still, religious literature is at times the only extant documentation pertaining to the ways communities interpreted and understood the events and ideas that affected their lives.

The opposing tendencies, either to strip down religious documents in pursuit of the barest technical facts or the inverse desire to see fragments of historical evidence as a means to bolster religious claims, have made dealing with this type of evidence particularly complex. The dilemma frequently lies in trying to draw the line between fact and faith. Such distinctions often decline into matters of personal choice and open scholars to criticism from a variety of, often contentious, ideological camps.

It would be naïve to assume that the material culture and physical evidence related to religious histories were immune to many of these same issues. Archaeology and art history deal with forms of evidence that have a solid physicality, which would seem to invite less speculation or disputation than wading through the details of a religious tract. However, artifacts are by no means exempt from intense ideological pressures and polemically charged interpretations. The ongoing and, at times, violent contestations over the history and significance of the Babri Masjid at Ayodhya demonstrate this point all too clearly (Pandey 1995; Van Der Veer 1988).

Both texts and objects are laden with contested historical and religious implications. Therefore, the choice to include or exclude specific materials as historically relevant is often a contested and negotiated process. By privileging one type of document over another we necessarily shape and limit our understanding of the past. While all scholars must exercise judgment in selecting evidence, the inclusion or exclusion of specific forms of evidence largely determines the histories that can or cannot be told. This simple limitation in the process of creating history has had some notable repercussions. The present study will focus on one such example from the academic discourse surrounding Indian Buddhism.

In the study of Buddhism, concerns over the historicity of religious narratives were partially responsible for an early tendency to avoid the use of literary narratives as a means to understand religious change. Overwhelmingly, the scholarship on Buddhism has relied on the Buddhist doctrinal and philosophic literature (largely pulled from the Abhidharma and portions of the Sutra literature) as a preferred method for understanding the religion and its development. Others have noted a similar tendency in the early European scholarship on Buddhism to favor textual sources over the physical evidence provided by archaeological discoveries (Schopen 1991).

Even though the use of artifacts and religious narratives in the recovery of history may at times be fraught with challenges, these forms of evidence provide us access to important information about religious development that would otherwise be lost. While the more canonical textual tradition is unquestionably a central component in understanding Buddhist history, it represents the work of a select intellectual and spiritual elite. To focus exclusively on this aspect of an institution's history is to miss much of its importance and relevance to society. The use of physical evidence and narrative literature can provide access to the contributions made by overlooked portions of the population and allow us to potentially recover some of the vital contributions that Indian popular practices[1] made in shaping the world religion that Buddhism has become.

The Case of Buddhism in India

Frequently there is a divide between the texts that are commonly used to define Buddhist practice (at least in the West) and what the art informs us about the Buddhist monastic world. To a large degree the seeming disjuncture between doctrinal Buddhism and early Buddhist art is a by-product of the way Buddhism has traditionally been studied in the West. Many of the most commonly held assumptions about what is appropriately

Buddhist can be traced back through the history of Buddhist studies, which is intertwined with the history of political relationships between India and the West.

For example, even though the academic scholarship has long recognized the existence of the demigods and spirit-deities[2] which dominate the decoration on early Buddhist monasteries, these figures have commonly been dismissed as unwelcome intrusions whose presence indicates a weakening of Buddhist ideals in the face of overbearing public tastes (Coomaraswamy 1931:33; Hunter 1785:291). In short, these images are usually understood as being little more than reluctant monastic concessions to popular pressure. True Buddhism was seen as being revealed, almost exclusively, by the philosophic textual tradition, which makes relatively infrequent mention of these supernatural beings (de Jong 1975:21). The presence of spirit-deities in the artwork therefore was often seen as indicative of a decline in "true" Buddhism (Cole 1874:13–15; Fergusson 1873:57). The motivations behind these tendencies in the academic literature are complex, long-standing, and closely linked to colonial era histories that sought to describe the history of South Asia as characterized by constant decline from a once-glorious past. Yet, this teleology of decline required that colonial era scholars first posit a golden age. This idealized period was linked to both the Vedas and the earliest forms of Buddhism, which were valorized in order to track a supposed subsequent societal decline[3] (Fergusson 1867:34). Such histories were constructed in the service of the colonial project and, at least in part, functioned to help justify imperialist and missionary agendas.

While the biases inherited from these early histories have had an impact on many areas of study, one repercussion from them, in particular, is central to the project of this chapter. Specifically, one of the consequences of telling Indian history in terms of decline is that Buddhism could in no way be portrayed as dependent on or derivative of the popular religious practices which pervaded a great deal of life in ancient India. All evidence of contact between Buddhism and popular spirit religions of the time, which were seen as even more degraded than Hinduism in the eyes of nineteenth and early twentieth century European academics, had to be explained in terms of conflict or as capitulation to the demands of the unlettered public. Any suggestion of an intentional coexistence between the two traditions would have undermined the accepted teleology of Indian history, which was structured into discrete stages. Specifically, Indian history was said to have begun with Brahmanism (Vedism), the purest religion. Over this time this gave way to Buddhism, which eventually declined into serpent-loving Mahāyāna systems that paved the way for modern Hinduism (Fergusson 1867:34). Within this schema it was impermissible for Buddhism, which was characterized as an early and "rational" religion, to be seen as coexisting or interacting with these "low" spirit religions in any favorable or symbiotic manner (Fergusson 1873:57, 62). To this end the Buddhist doctrinal and philosophic texts, written by a rarefied and erudite intellectual community, were seen as the appropriate means by which to gain a full understanding of Buddhist history. Yet, the primacy of this type of textual evidence was achieved at the expense of the frequently more problematic and informative physical evidence.

Unfortunately even long after the colonial era histories have been rejected, many of the ideas that were originally based on these assumptions still stand. A reexamination of the history of early Buddhism and a reconsideration of the role of Indian popular religion in its formation is therefore warranted. As part of this process, both the physical evidence and the Buddhist narrative literature become central to providing a, potentially, more balanced understanding of early Buddhist practice.

Buddhism, Popular Practice, and the Dead

For example, even a brief examination of the archaeological reports dealing with the earliest Buddhist monastic centers reveals that an impressive number of these sites were built either very near or directly over locations used for funerary practices. Notably, a trend has been identified in the archaeological record demonstrating that many of the early monasteries were built directly adjacent to ancient megalithic burial sites (Schopen 1996). And, while it is true that the form of secondary burial found at many megalithic sites differs from the cremations and charnel grounds often described in the early literature, it is nevertheless significant to note that sites associated with the dead were frequently found in close proximity to monastic centers. This is particularly true in the regions of Andhra and Swat, both of which were on the edges of what had been the Mauryan Empire (323–185 BCE) and, by extension, royally supported Buddhism.

Although the association of monastic complexes with areas linked to popular religion, spirit-deities, and the dead can be seen all over South Asia, this early preponderance of archaeological evidence from the areas on the edges of Magadhan imperial influence suggests that these practices may have played a role in the conversion of new populations. However, it is equally possible that these Buddhist building practices were common across the subcontinent and this trend in the physical evidence may simply be due to differences in regional funerary traditions. After all, it is far easier to identify the massive rocks associated with ancient megalithic burial sites than it is to spot the fragments of ash and bone that might indicate a long-forgotten charnel ground. Even though the specifics of this process may have to remain elusive for now, the physical evidence points firmly to an early association between Buddhism and places related to death and the dead.

In Andhra, megalithic gravesites have been identified under or near the Buddhist remains at Goli, Chandavaram, Panigiri, and Vaddamanu (Deshpande 1978; Ramachandran 1929; Schopen 1996; Sastry 1978; Venkataramanayya 1971–72). Likewise, the well-known sites of Amarāvatī and Nāgārjunakoṇḍa both show evidence of having been constructed in close proximity to megalithic burial sites. The main *stūpa* at Amarāvatī is not only situated directly over the remains of a megalithic grave but the monastery complex is also located in the center of a large area scattered with megalithic remains (Rea 1912). A similar situation can be found at Nāgārjunakoṇḍa where one of the main *stūpas* was located directly over the remains of an ancient grave. It even appears that some of the stones originally employed by the builders of the megalithic structure were reused in the construction of the *stūpa* itself (Subrahmanyam et al. 1975:165–166, 212). Remains of ancient graves have also been identified under the site of Butkara as well as under the Buddhist layer at Mohenjodaro in the far Northwest (Antonini 1963; Banerji 1984).

This litany of sites in no way represents the full extent of the possible archaeological connections between Buddhist sites and the ancient dead. We are unfortunately limited to rather fragmentary evidence due to the fact that the early archaeologists, with few exceptions, were wholly uninterested in excavating the megalithic finds under the more impressive looking Buddhist monuments. For this reason the archaeological reports are spotty at best and only very recently have archaeologists seriously turned their attentions to this earliest layer of construction. Nevertheless, sufficient evidence exists to suggest an association between the construction of Buddhist monasteries and ancient (often megalithic) funerary grounds.

Interestingly, the Buddhist narrative literature is replete with tales involving the conversion, at the hands of the Buddha or his followers, of various ghosts and demigods who dwell in these types of haunted locations. The process usually begins with an unflappable monk or nun transgressing into the domain of a spirit-deity. Then, after a confrontation in which the holy person proves immune to the fearsome or beguiling powers mustered by the angered demigod, the supernatural being acknowledges the superiority of the Buddhist teaching and agrees to be converted. Often this type of encounter is predicated at the request of the community who seeks help in curtailing the excessive habits of the local spirit. For this reason these tales often end with the populace recognizing the power of the Buddhist teachings over that of their local gods and the establishment of a new religious hierarchy with Buddhism at the apex. More often than not this new order is marked by the construction of a monastery over the site where the confrontation occurred (namely, the domain of the spirit-deity).

The following tale is an excellent example of a typical encounter between a monk and spirit-deity. In this particular case the offender is a *nāga* or serpent-deity. This story is from the *Mahāvaṃsa* and even though this is part of the Sri Lankan Buddhist tradition, its conciseness and similarity to longer Indian tales make it worth quoting in its entirety.

> At that time, in Kashmir and Gandhāra, the nāga-king of great miraculous power, Aravāḷa, was causing the rain called 'hail' to pour down upon ripe crops and, being cruel, was having everything washed into the sea. The thera [elder monk] Majjhantika went there quickly by air and performed such acts as walking on the surface of the water of the Aravāḷa-lake. The nāgas saw this and, being enraged, informed the king about it. The nāga-king, too, being enraged, did various terrifying acts: great winds blew; a cloud rained and thundered; here and there, thunder-bolts crashed and lightning flashed; trees and peaks of mountains were hurled down. Nāgas in grisly form caused terror in all directions and he himself spat smoke and fire and uttered abuses in many ways. The thera, through miraculous power, subdued all that terror. Demonstrating his supreme power, he told the nāga-king, "Even if the whole world including devas would come and terrify me, there is none here who would succeed in causing fear and trepidation. Great nāga, even if you were to raise and hurl on me the whole world together with the oceans and mountains, you would not be able to generate fear and trepidation in me. On the other hand, O nāga-king, that would be your own destruction." To him who became humbled hearing these words, the thera preached the Dhamma. Then the nāga-king was established in refuges and precepts. Likewise, eighty-four thousand nāgas and many gandhabbas, yakkhas and Kumbhandakas of the Himālayas. The yakkha named Paṇḍka, too along with yakkhiṇī Harīta and five hundred sons attained the First Fruit. Being admonished as follows, they acted accordingly: "Henceforth do not allow your anger to arise as before. Do not destroy crops, as living beings are desirous of happiness. Develop loving kindness towards beings, thinking 'May human beings live in happiness.'" Then the nāga-king made the thera sit on a gem set throne and stood nearby fanning him. Then the people, residing in Kashmir and Gandhāra, who came to offer homage to the nāga-king, acknowledged the thera as possessing miraculous power, worshipped the thera himself and sat on a side. He expounded to them the Dhamma, Āsivisūpama (Simile of the Serpent). The conversion of eighty thousand persons took place and a hundred thousand persons obtained ordination from the thera. Henceforth even now Kashmir and Gandhāra have shown with yellow robes and been devoted to the three treasures. (*Mahāvaṃsa* 1989:12. 9–12)

This remarkable story provides an ideal example of the complete process, starting with the conversion of a troublesome spirit-deity and ending with the conversion of an entire region to the Buddhist fold. Admittedly, the story is exceedingly fanciful by modern standards with its accounts of flying monks and fire-breathing *nāgas* but the process is repeated in the literature time and again and is almost certainly indicative of a methodology for conversion employed by the Buddhist community. In this case the *nāga* resides in a lake rather than in a funerary ground, but many other tales tell of spirit-deities who dwell in such morbid locales.

For instance, in the *Jayaddisa Jātaka* an ogre's (*rakkhasa*) existence involves residing in a cemetery and eating human flesh (Cowell 1895) and in the *Kathāsaritsāgara* an ascetic and a gambler worship the *yakṣa* Vidyutprabhā who dwells in the banyan tree in the corner of a cemetery (Somadeva 1924).

But no matter the location, the process almost invariably begins with unwavering monks or nuns confronting troublesome or dangerous spirit-deities on their home territory and ends with the populace recognizing the power of the Buddhist teachings over that of their previous local gods. This process not only provided evidence of the worldly and emotional detachment of the Buddhist community but it also provided what must have been perceived as an important social service to the community by creating a mechanism through which potentially troublesome spirit-deities could be kept in check. Repeatedly in the stories, the monastic community positioned itself as an unassailable, impassive buffer between the people and these capricious supernatural beings of desire and whim. By extension, donations to the monastery preserved the institution, which through its teachings and example contained the passions of the spirit-deities and rendered the community a more secure place.

The placement of monasteries over funerary sites and the prominent portrayal of spirit-deities in monastic artwork suggest that these narratives of conversion were understood as far more than just good tales. These encounters between monks and spirits not only provided evidence of the spiritual prowess of the Buddhist community but also provided what must have been perceived as an important social service to the community by creating a mechanism through which potentially troublesome spirit-deities could be kept in check.

Although the narratives alone do not provide sufficient evidence with which to recognize the historical nature of this process, the artistic and archaeological evidence leave little doubt that the Buddhist community intentionally sought out and absorbed spirit-deities into its fold. When taken together, the textual evidence provides an explanation of the activities documented in the material record. Furthermore, by employing evidence from a variety of sources we can begin to understand not only what was done, but also how the Buddhist community understood those actions. Although the texts make it apparent that they believed this process of supernatural conversion to be fraught with danger, it was understood as being worth the risks because it ultimately served to benefit the monastic order, the public and the spirit deities themselves.

This process demanded that the monks and nuns confront their own fear of spirit-deities in order to build monasteries over locations known to be inhabited by the supernatural or in dealing with those beings who were believed to share residency within the monastic complex. Furthermore, the pervasive use of sculptural representation of spirit-deities within and around monasteries signified the Buddhist success in controlling these capricious beings to the public and marked the monastic community as a group that was both worthy of support and capable of generating impressive amounts of merit.

There is even evidence suggesting that the Buddhist monastic community was at times responsible for performing rites that maintained a favorable relationship between the local gods and society. For instance, Faxian, a fourth-century Chinese Buddhist pilgrim to India, writes that the *nāga* at the monastery near Sāmkaśyā "is the patron of this body of priests. He causes fertilising and seasonable showers of rain to fall within their country, and preserves it from plagues and calamities, and so causes the priesthood to dwell in security." (Fa-hien 1965:xli–xlii). However, in return for this kindness the monks were required to provide the *nāga* with a shrine and throne at which daily offerings were presented. And, beyond these daily rituals, once a year they were expected to "place in the midst of his [the *nāga's*] lair a copper vessel full of cream; and then, from the highest to the lowest, they walk past him in procession as if to pay him greeting all round" (Cohen 1998:374–378; Fa-hien 1965:xli–xlii).

Conclusions

These realizations lead us to confront old assumptions about the nature of early Buddhist belief and practice. Buddhism even in its earliest forms was not simply an otherworldly ideology of transcendence, as is at times suggested by the philosophic literature. Parallel to the soteriological concerns was a deep investment in mortuary practices and a persistent concern with strategies for coping with regional spirits and the local dead. Rather than seeing the presence of spirit-deities as signs of flawed practices or as markers of decay, it is clear that visual and textual references to spirit-deities are the hallmarks of a healthy and strong tradition. Instead of signaling periods of decline, the prominent display of spirit-deities often indicates times of active expansion and growth during which the Buddhist teachings and the monastic community were influential enough to claim authority over potential rivals. The incorporation of popular deities into Buddhist contexts becomes simultaneously significant as a methodology for outward expansion, a means of signaling the Buddhist monastic community's purity, and as an act of monastic courage and compassion. The archaeological evidence allows us to realize that far from being marginal concessions to the public, spirit-deities played a central role in the development, growth, and success of Buddhism.

Notes

1. The "popular practices" that I am referring to include the myriad religious practices in India which center on the propitiation and veneration of various local and minor deities. These spirit religions vary greatly according to region and date but they may generally be referred to as non-Brahmanical, non-soteriological forms of religious expression that center on the appeasement of a deity or deities who possess explicitly limited powers.
2. I have employed the hybrid term "spirit-deity" because this category of minor deities (such as *yakṣas*, *nāgas*, *devatās*, *gandharvas*, etc.) hold a liminal position between the realms of ghosts (*preta*, *bhūta*) and gods (*deva*) and frequently seems to share the nature of both. I do realize that combining several categories of supernatural beings under one collective title also poses certain problems. However, given the fluidity and frequency with which the primary sources use these categories interchangeably and the uniformity in the Buddhist response to all these types of beings it is helpful to use this term within the confines of the present discussion.
3. This "decline" was often linked to nineteenth-century ideas of racial determinism. Specifically, this theory sought to explain the gradual decline in Indian civilization by linking it to a watering down of the racial purity of the hypothesized Aryan "invaders." For this reason it was not uncommon for eighteenth and early nineteenth century European scholars to refer to the Buddha as being Aryan (Mitter 1977).

References Cited

Antonini, C. S.
1963   Preliminary Notes on the Excavation of the Necropolises found in Western Pakistan. *East and West* 14(1–2):13–26.
Banerji, R. D.
1984   *Mohenjodaro, A Forgotten Report*. Prithivi Prakashan, Varanasi.
Cohen, Richard
1998   Nāga, Yakṣiṇi, Buddha: Local Deities and Local Buddhism at Ajanta. *History of Religions* 37(4):360–400.
Cole, Henry H.
1874   *Catalogue of the Objects of Indian Art*. Eyre and Spottiswoode, London.
Coomaraswamy, Ananda K.
1931   *Yakṣas*. In two parts. Smithsonian Miscellaneous Collections, Washington, DC.
Cowell, E. B. (editor)
1994   *The Jātaka or Stories of the Buddha's Former Births*. Edited by E. B. Cowell. 6 vols. Motilal Banarsidass, New Delhi. Originally published in 1895.
de Jong, J. W.
1975   The Study of Buddhism Problems and Perspectives, In *Studies in Indo-Asian Art and Culture*. Edited by P. Ratnam. 4ᵗʰ International Academy of Indian Culture, New Delhi, pp. 15–28.
Deshpande, M. N.
1978   *Indian Archaeology 1972–73—A Review*. Indian Ministry of Scientific Research and Cultural Affairs, New Delhi.
Fa-Hien
1965   *A Record of Buddhistic Kingdoms: Being an Account by the Chinese Monk Fa-Hien of his Travels in India and Ceylon (A.D. 300–414) in Search of the Buddhist Books of Discipline*. Translated by J. Legge. Original printing 1886. Dover Press, New York.

Fergusson, James
1867   On the Study of Indian Architecture. J. Murray, London.
1873   Tree and Serpent Worship or Illustrations of Mythology and Art in India in the 1st and 4ᵗʰ Centuries Before Christ from the Sculptures of the Buddhist Topes at Sanchi and Amaravati. Indological Bookhouse, Delhi.
Hunter, William
1785   An Account of Some Artificial Caves in the Neighbourhood of Bombay. Archaeologia 7:286–294.
Guruge, A. W. P. (editor)
1989   Mahāvaṃsa: The Great Chronicle of Sri Lanka, edited and translated by A. W. P. Guruge. Associated Newspapers of Ceylon, Colombo.
Mitter, Partha
1977   Much Maligned Monsters: A History of European Reactions to Indian Art. Clarendon, Oxford.
Pandey, Gyanendra
1995   The Appeal of Hindu History, In Representing Hinduism, edited by Vasudha Dalmia and Heinrich von Stietencron, pp. 369–388. Sage Publications, London.
Ramachandran, T. N.
1929   Buddhist Sculpture from a Stūpa near Goli Village, Guntur District. Madras, New Series. Part 1. Bulletin of the Madras Government Museum.
Rea, A.
1912   Excavations at Amarāvatī. In Annual Reports of the Archaeological Survey of India 1908–1909, pp. 88–91. Government Press, Calcutta.
Sastri, T. V. G., M. Kasturi Bai, and M. Veerender
1992   Vaddamanu Excavations. Birla Archaeological and Cultural Institute, Hyderabad.
Sastry, V. V. Krishna
1978   Annual Report of the Department of Archaeology and Museums, Government of Andhra Pradesh 1976–77. Government of Andhra Pradesh, Hyderabad.
Schopen, Gregory
1991   Archaeology and Protestant Presuppositions in the Study of Indian Buddhism. History of Religions 31(1):1–23.
1996   Immigrant Monks and the Proto-historical Dead: The Buddhist Occupation of Early Burial Sites in India. In Festschrift Dieter Schlingloff, edited by F. Wilhelm, pp. 215–238. Reinbek, Munich.
Somadeva
1924–28 Kathāsaritsāgara: Ocean of Streams of Story. Translated by C. H. Tawney, edited by N. M Penzer. C. J. Sawyer, London.
Sreenivasachar, P.
1963   The Archaeological Bulletin 2. Andhra Pradesh Archaeological Series, Hyderabad.
Subrahmanyam, R.
1975   Nagarjunakonda (1954–60). The Memoirs of the Archaeological Survey of India 75. Archaeological Survey of India, New Delhi.
Van Der Veer, Peter
1988   Gods on Earth: Religious Experience and Identity in Ayodhya. Oxford University Press, New York.
Venkataramanayya, N.
1971–72 Pre-Historic Remains in Andhra Pradesh. Journal of the Andhra Historical Research Society 32:37–58.

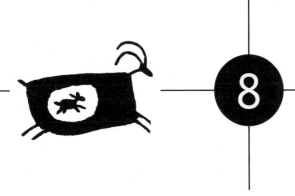

DELEGITIMIZING RELIGION: THE ARCHAEOLOGY OF RELIGION AS ... ARCHAEOLOGY

Lars Fogelin

"If material techniques are easy to infer to, subsistence-economics fairly easy, communal organization harder, and spiritual life hardest of all, you have there a climax of four degrees in reasoning."

—Hawkes 1954:162

I doubt that I am the first archaeologist to be drawn to the archaeology of religion simply because Christopher Hawkes (1954) and Lewis Binford (1965) said it shouldn't be done—that religion was an inappropriate venue for archaeological inquiry. I study the archaeology of religion for the same reason I made gunpowder when I was 12—because I was told not to. Looking back, my interest in religion was little more than postmodern machismo. Fortunately, unlike my juvenile experiments with explosives, I finished my initial forays into the archaeology of religion with my eyebrows intact. I also came away doubting the value of Hawkes's ladder of inference, not because the ladder unwittingly supported the most vulgar forms of materialism, nor because it assumed an artificial separation between the symbolic and material basis of society. All that came later. Rather, I was stunned at how easy an archaeology of religion actually is.

To be fair, Hawkes never meant the ladder of inference to be used in the manner it has been employed. First, it was intended to apply only to contexts where no historical or ethnohistorical sources existed, not as a blanket statement for archaeology as a whole. Second, by its formulation, it inherently rejected environmental or infrastructural determinism. If subsistence and economic patterns determined specific forms of sociopolitical institutions and religious beliefs, the upper rungs of the ladder would not need to be inferred at all. In contrast, Hawkes argued that "there is nothing in North American ecology, by itself, to compel either Iroquois institutions, say, or the Constitution of the United States" (1954:163). Hawkes's position was that, as aspects of human society become less embedded within ecological and subsistence concerns, their form becomes progressively less constrained, less predictable, and ultimately less easily inferred. While I believe that Hawkes's argument is wrong, ecological determinism has nothing to do with it. His arguments, however, still seem to underlie much of the archaeological literature on religion—in some cases even by those who purport to be advocates for its investigation. It is for this reason that I feel it is useful to examine Hawkes's argument, to parse out precisely where he went wrong.

The Archaeology of Religion is Conceptually Simple

While specific religious beliefs may be ecologically unconstrained, or at least mostly so, they are constrained by other religious beliefs, cosmological understandings, and cultural practices. As stated by Geertz, but reflecting common anthropological understanding,

> religion is a system of symbols which acts to establish powerful, pervasive, and long lasting moods and motivations in men by formulating conceptions of a general order of existence and clothing these conceptions with such an aura of factuality that the moods and motivations seem uniquely realistic. (1973:90)

The critical element here is that religions are *systems of symbols*. Not arbitrary symbols. Not unrelated symbols. Religious beliefs are, to varying degrees, constrained by other beliefs (see also Robb 1998:330–331 for other ways that symbolic elements are constrained). Beliefs concerning divine kingship are often tied to conceptions of the afterlife, which can in turn be reflected in cosmological understandings, for example. It is here that Hawkes made his mistake. Religious beliefs are not unconstrained, free-floating units. Hawkes failed to recognize that knowledge of part of a religious system could reasonably be used to infer other, unobserved, parts of the religion. It should be noted that by using the term "system" I am not advocating systems theory or cultural materialism any more than Geertz was. Like Geertz, I am arguing that particular religious beliefs are embedded within a web of meanings and signification (Geertz 1973). The term "system" refers to those webs—no more, no less.

Given all of this, it would seem reasonable for the archaeologists studying religion to start with the aspects of a past religion that are the easiest to identify—the most obvious, those manifested most clearly in the material world—and to work from there to the next easiest, repeatedly. With a bit of luck, we might eventually stumble upon a "key symbol," one that serves to orient and constrain large portions of the total religious system (Ortner 1973). From a small toe-hold, a great deal could potentially be learned. Even Hawkes recognizes that these toe-holds are often easy to come by:

> To infer to the religious institutions and spiritual life may seem, superficially, perhaps, to be easier, and for the first few steps it may sometimes be so. Grave goods indicate a belief that the dead need material supplies or equipment, as though they were still alive. But how much further can one go than that? (1954:162)

Unlike Hawkes, I would claim that identifying a belief in the afterlife in an archaeological setting is an important first step toward understanding a past religion. With a belief in the afterlife established, an archaeologist can start to examine other elements of a mortuary assemblage in an effort to establish how this afterlife was conceived, and how these beliefs might have been employed in the living community. For example, are mortuary symbols associated with patterns of rulership? Is political authority legitimized by reference to deities commonly depicted in mortuary assemblages? The initial statement that a past society had a belief in the afterlife is both obvious and unsurprising. Its generality fails, by itself, to greatly inform upon interpretation. I ask, however, how much more informative are statements such as "In the eleventh century, Chaco Canyon was slightly wetter than it is today"? By itself, this statement says little about past societies. It only gains significance when the implications of this statement are tracked through other social concerns.

This brings me to my major point. The archaeology of religion, conceptually and methodologically, is as easy or as difficult as any other branch of archaeological research and should proceed in pretty much the same way. Yes, some aspects of past religions are difficult or even impossible to study. However, is this so different from zooarchaeology? As we all know, the difficulty of distinguishing between sheep and goats using faunal remains has resulted in that peculiar archaeological animal, the "sheep/goat" (see Redding 1985 for a review of this problem). It is also clear that knowledge of the percentage of sheep compared to goats has important implications on broader issues of subsistence, and ultimately of social organization. However, zooarchaeology has not been invalidated because of this problem. Quite reasonably, zooarchaeologists have focused their efforts on the avenues that are more productive. They have started with things that are easier and built outward from there. By focusing on the aspects of religion that are most unknowable, or immaterial, critics of the archaeology of religion have applied unreasonable standards for its acceptance. Underlying this is the mistake of seeing religion as simply conceptual or ideological. Religion is not only something people think about, but something people do.

This tendency to view religion as abstract or primarily metaphysical even creeps into the writings of some proponents of the archaeology of religion. In a recent discussion, Timothy Insoll repeatedly emphasized the "numinous" aspects of religion, defined as "the irreducible essence of holiness which can be discussed but not defined" (2004:19; see also Otto 1950). It should be noted that Insoll also argues that religion is all-pervasive, informing, and influencing even those actions that archaeologists have typically considered "secular." However, throughout the work there is an air of pessimism concerning the archaeology of religion. If the numinous is treated as unknowable in any and every context, archaeology doesn't have a prayer of getting at it:

> "Thick description" is to be desired and striven for as much as possible but the true answer is that we need to recognize the existence of numinous and irreducible elements as well. In so doing this is essentially providing the necessary recognition that elements of the archaeology of religions are metaphysical by definition. Unfortunately, with much of the archaeology of religions we will never get at its essence no matter how long we boil the pot, because it is in the mind, it defies rationality, and ... it will remain elusive. (Insoll 2004:150)

Perhaps Insoll is right. Perhaps the core of religion is "irreducible," "defies rationality," and will "remain elusive" for archaeologists. Perhaps not. I wonder what value archaeologists gain from focusing attention on the difficult cases—the elements of religion that are least knowable, or the elements with no material indicators. Why are we so fixated upon religious sheep/goats?

In the last 30 years, anthropological studies of religion have focused progressively greater attention on religious practice rather than traditional metaphysical concerns (see Bell 1992, 1997; Bloch 1989; Bourdieu 1977; Comaroff 1985; Ortner 1989). To summarize, practice theorists emphasize the ways in which religion is manifested in people's daily lives. Religions are not simply disembodied metaphysical concepts; they are embedded within human actions. People do religion as much as they think about religion. Religion is embedded in the performance of a funeral, the construction of a shrine, or the references to a god made by a president up for election. These actions inform the metaphysical understandings of religion as much as metaphysics inform people's actions. As stated by Catherine Bell:

> Practice theory claims to take seriously the ways in which human activity, as formal as a religious ritual or as casual as a midday stroll, are creative strategies by which human beings continually reproduce and reshape their social and cultural environments. (1997:76)

In terms of the archaeology of religion, the more recent emphasis on practice is critical. If religion is something that people do, they will, at times, leave material traces of their actions. We, as archaeologists, can examine these traces just as we do in any other domain of archaeological investigation. Does this mean that we can easily determine the metaphysical thought process behind the action? Of course not. This will require careful research and reasoning. Ideology is always difficult to determine or reconstruct, whether it be political, economic, or religious. However, I can see no conceptual reason why investigations of religious ideology should be any more difficult than studying the division of labor among hunters and gatherers.

At the bottom of the ladder of inference, Hawkes (1954:161) argues that "to infer from the archaeological phenomena to the techniques producing them I take to be relatively easy. The modes of research required are themselves no doubt difficult, and in detail often tedious." If religion is something that people do, there is no reason that the initial steps of research should be more conceptually difficult than any other subject, nor the research methods any less difficult or tedious. In the archaeology of religion we should begin with specific material indicators of religious practice, just as an archaeologist focusing on subsistence must identify specific material indicators of the human exploitation of the environment (Hays 1993 makes a similar claim). Rather than discuss this in the abstract, I will illustrate it with a specific case study.

Legitimization

Many archaeological studies of religion, particularly state religion, rely on the concept of legitimization. Derived from Marxist sources, legitimization refers to the ways in which religion serves to reinforce the authority of the elite. Religious legitimization is employed to explain why poor and oppressed members of society do not act in their own economic self-interest by overthrowing the elite. As often as not, legitimization is described in terms that resemble the tide—rolling in at the advent of a state or dynasty only to withdraw at its collapse; the indicators of its passing exhibit as little material evidence as its arrival. Marxist claims that religion acts to legitimize authority, to promote false consciousness, and to reinforce hegemony are assumed *prima facia*, with little attempt to establish where or in what specific way material remains served to promote or retard elite rule.

In modern contexts we know that this simple understanding of legitimization is false. In numerous cases—liberation theology in South America, for example, or the civil rights movement in the United States—religion was employed to legitimize resistance. When examining other cases— roadside shrines memorializing traffic fatalities, for instance—it does not seem that legitimization of elite authority plays any significant role at all. So what sorts of material evidence could serve to identify how, or if, legitimization was employed in the past? What potential material indicators could be used to study legitimization in archaeological contexts?

Jerry Moore (1996:2) has argued that "public buildings are physical testimonies of the use of power." Ceremonial architecture does not simply reflect authority; it is instrumental in creating authority. Thus, ceremonial architecture can be examined with the goal of identifying attempts at legitimization. Moore employs several specific material criteria to evaluate how, and if, ceremonial structures served to legitimize elite authority in coastal Peru (ibid., 139–141). Here I will only mention two. First, in order for legitimization to occur, a religious structure should be located in a position associated with the people who are being legitimized—adjacent to a palace or in the capital city, for example. Moore refers to this as centrality. The second factor is visibility. A religious structure should be visible to the people from whom acquiescence to authority is desired. This does not mean that they must be able to enter the religious structure. Elite authority can be reinforced through preferential access to sacred places—but only if everyone knows it and can see it. Even in cases where the elite perform rituals in secret, it must be a public secret. It might even be the case, paradoxically, that as rituals of legitimization become more exclusive, more secret, religious structures would require larger, more prominent facades.

Legitimization in Buddhist Monasteries

To illustrate both how easily an archaeology of religion can be conducted and how legitimization can be examined through material evidence, I turn to a brief discussion of early Buddhism. An examination of how Buddhist monks architecturally presented their primary ritual symbols shows that they initially attempted to assert authority over the Buddhist laity in the period between the second century BC and the first century AD. By the second to fourth centuries AD, however, Buddhist monks were no longer attempting to legitimize their social position through the manipulation of religious symbols, or at least not to the same degree (see also Fogelin 2003, 2006).

The Buddha is believed to have lived in the mid first millennium BC. Within a few centuries of his death, numerous Buddhist monasteries were constructed throughout the Indian subcontinent. In the earliest phase of Buddhism in South Asia, between the fifth century BC and the second century AD, the primary focus of Buddhist rituals within monasteries were *stupas*—stylized representations of the earthen mound in which the Buddha's cremated remains were interred (Figure 8.1). Starting in roughly the second century AD, however, a new ritual focus emerged within Buddhism—images of the Buddha himself (Figure 8.2).

Figure 8.1 A view of the *stupa* in the main *chaitya* at Bhaja.

Figure 8.2 A Buddha image located within a *vihara* at Aurangabad.

For the purposes of this example I focus on the remains of Buddhist monastic establishments carved into the cliffs of western India between the first century BC and the eighth century AD (Figure 8.3). While numerous other contemporary Buddhist monasteries have been identified, the rock-cut monasteries are far better preserved and studied (Dehejia 1972;

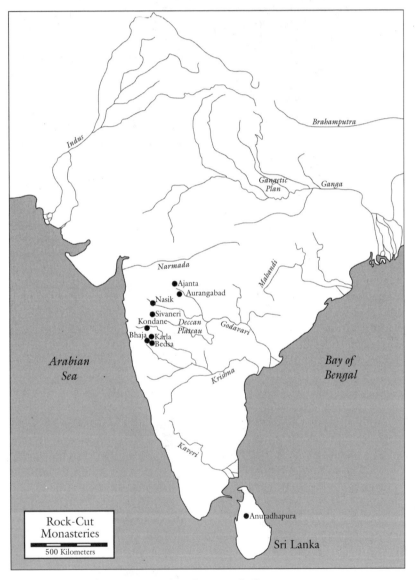

Figure 8.3　Rock-cut monasteries of western India.

Figure 8.4 A typical *vihara* and *chaitya* of the early period.

Fergusson and Burgess 1988 [1880]; Nagaraju 1981). Excellent maps and elevations have been made of these monasteries, providing the basic background necessary for analysis. In the earliest period, rock-cut monasteries consisted of two general types of structures: monastic dormitories, called *viharas*, and larger worship halls called *chaityas* (but see Coningham 2001 for a critique of these terms). *Viharas* were typically small structures, with monastic cells arrayed around a central room. *Chaityas*, on the other hand, were large ritual spaces in which a *stupa* was placed at one end of an apsidal hall (Figure 8.4). *Chaityas* served as the primary ritual space of the monasteries (see Schopen 1997 for a more in-depth discussion of the '*stupa* cult'). Further, using the criteria of visibility and centrality, it appears that these spaces were intended to legitimize monastic authority in the eyes of the Buddhist laity.

The placement of *chaityas* within Buddhist monasteries associated the primary symbol of the Buddha, the *stupa*, with the monks—spatially asserting monastic control over the rituals performed in front of the *stupa*. The design and layout of the *chaitya* halls made them highly visible, even at a great distance. In contrast to the often haphazard placement and low profile of *viharas*, the *chaityas* had large, elaborately carved facades that were visible at great distances (Figure 8.5). Thus, *chaityas*, and the *stupas* contained within them, served to legitimize monastic authority through spatial association with monasteries, together with the visual prominence that proclaimed their importance to the Buddhist laity.

This pattern changed in western India with the emergence of Buddha images, beginning perhaps as early as the second century AD. With this change, rock-cut *chaityas* of the earlier form were no longer constructed in western India. Instead, Buddha images were placed within *viharas*, in monastic cells referred to as "perfumed chambers" (Figure 8.6).

Figure 8.5   The exterior of the main *chaitya* at Bhaja.

The symbolism here was fairly straightforward. The image of the Buddha was installed within a monastic cell, symbolically asserting that the Buddha was a resident of the monastery. In terms of legitimizing monastic authority, this change in the location of the primary ritual focus had profound implications. While the images were still spatially associated with the monks, perhaps even more so than before, the visibility of the images was dramatically reduced. With the abandonment of *chaityas*, the facades of the *viharas* were not elaborated to any great degree (Figure 8.7). The visibility of the monasteries, therefore, was substantially less than it had been in the previous period. Unlike the *stupas* of the earlier period, Buddha images were now sequestered within the *viharas*, with no outside indicator of their presence. It would seem that by this later period Buddhist monks were no longer attempting to assert authority over the laity, or at least they did so to a much lesser degree.

Conclusion

I hope that this brief example has illustrated two points. First, the archaeological use of the concept of legitimization should be materially problematized more than it has been in the past. Not all religious phenomena, even in state societies, served to legitimize elite authority. Even in cases where evidence of legitimization does exist, an examination of the specific techniques used to legitimize authority—and whose authority is

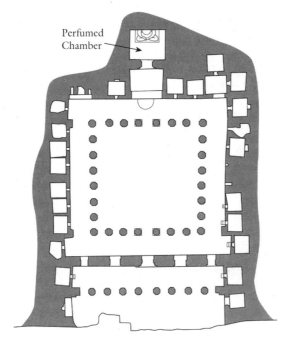

Figure 8.6 The ground plan of *Vihara* IV at Ajanta.

Figure 8.7 The exterior of the *viharas* at Aurangabad.

being legitimized—can be archaeologically useful. The second point is that the archaeology of religion can, and should, follow the same general form as any other branch of archaeological research. It should start with material predictions derived from understandings of particular contexts and general anthropological theory (Hays 1993). These predictions can then be compared to the material evidence and inferences can be made concerning broader social issues. Within the discipline of archaeology, religion has been treated as some special domain, a particularly impenetrable black-box. If nothing else, my intention in this paper is to simply question this treatment. In my experience the archaeology of religion is simply archaeology—as good, bad, or ugly as any other archaeological approach.

References Cited

Bell, Catherine
1992   Ritual Theory, Ritual Practice. Oxford University Press, New York.
1997   Ritual: Perspectives and Dimensions. Oxford University Press, Oxford.
Binford, Lewis R.
1965   Archaeological systematics and the study of culture process. American Antiquity 31(2):203–210.
Bloch, Maurice
1989   Ritual, History, and Power: Selected Papers in Anthropology. Athlon Press, London.
Bourdieu, Pierre
1977   An Outline of a Theory of Practice. Translated by R. Nice. Cambridge University Press, Cambridge.
Comaroff, Jean
1985   Body of Power, Spirit of Resistance: The Culture and History of a South American People. University of Chicago Press, Chicago.
Coningham, Robin
2001   The Archaeology of Buddhism. In Archaeology and World Religion, edited by T. Insoll, pp. 61–95. Routledge, London.
Dehejia, V.
1972   Early Buddhist Rock Temples. Cornell University Press, Ithaca, New York.
Fergusson, J., and J. Burgess
1988   [1880] The Cave Temples of India. Munshiram Manoharlal, New Delhi.
Fogelin, Lars
2003   Ritual and Presentation in Early Buddhist Religious Architecture. Asian Perspectives 42(1):129–154.
2006   Archaeology of Early Buddhism in South India. AltaMira Press, Lanham, Maryland.
Geertz, Clifford
1973   The Interpretation of Cultures. Basic Books, New York.
Hawkes, C.
1954   Archaeological Theory and Method: Some Suggestions from the Old World. American Anthropologist 56(2):155–168.
Hays, Kelley A.
1993   When Is a Symbol Archaeologically Meaningful? Meaning, Function, and Prehistoric Visual Arts. In Archaeological Theory: Who Sets the Agenda, edited by N. Yoffee and A. Sherratt, pp. 81–92. Cambridge University Press, Cambridge.

Insoll, Timothy
2004 *Archaeology, Ritual, Religion.* Routledge, London.
Moore, Jerry D.
1996 *Architecture and Power in the Ancient Andes.* Cambridge University Press, Cambridge.
Nagaraju, S.
1981 *Buddhist Architecture of Western India.* Agam Kala Prakashan, Delhi.
Ortner, Sherry B.
1973 On Key Symbols. *American Anthropologist* 75:1338–1346.
1989 *High Religion: A Cultural and Political History of Sherpa Buddhism.* Princeton University Press, Princeton.
Otto, Rudolf
1950 *The Idea of the Holy.* Oxford University Press, Oxford.
Redding, R. W.
1985 Role of Faunal Remains in the Explanation of the Development of Complex Societies in South-West Iran: Potential Problems and the Future. *Paleorient* 11(2):121–124.
Robb, J. E.
1998 The Archaeology of Symbols. *Annual Reviews in Anthropology* 27:329–346.
Schopen, G.
1997 *Bones, Stones, and Buddhist Monks: Collected Papers on the Archaeology, Epigraphy, and Texts of Monastic Buddhism in India.* Studies in the Buddhist Traditions. University of Hawai'i Press, Honolulu.

BODYLORE AND THE ARCHAEOLOGY OF EMBEDDED RELIGION: DRAMATIC LICENSE IN THE FUNERALS OF THE VIKINGS

Neil S. Price

In the early 1960s, the folklorist and historian of religions Hilda Ellis Davidson put forward a definition of human spiritual aspirations that has seldom been bettered. "A mythology," she wrote, "is the comment of ... one particular age or civilisation on the mysteries of human existence and the human mind, their model for social behaviour, and their attempt to define in stories ... their perception of the inner realities" (Ellis Davidson 1964:9). Whether we follow her in calling it mythology, or choose other terms such as religion or belief, this surely provides one of the keys to what the discipline of archaeology should ultimately address, for it is in such "inner realities" that we see the worldview and mentality of past peoples. In this sense it includes not just their deliberate constructions of reality but perhaps also their subconscious reflections and concerns. Religion and its analogues thus lie at the heart of any meaningful exploration of prehistoric cognition, and of the ancient mind.

However, the obvious problem here is the archaeological inference of the intangible from the material. Put simply, how do we conduct an archaeology of religion? This paper addresses one of the primary difficulties of this task, namely, the way in which we think about ancient religion, which in turn conditions how we look for its material traces. I argue that in any attempt to negotiate the archaeology of prehistoric beliefs, it is first necessary to acknowledge that the manifest spirituality of past societies often bore very little resemblance to our own modern understanding of this concept. Perhaps this is self-evident, but at times it seems far from it when one surveys the current archaeological literature in this field, which feels strangely out of step with anthropological thinking in this respect. In this short text I therefore want to explore a slightly different approach to religion, and to raise some of its archaeological implications.

My research focuses on the Scandinavian world between the eighth and eleventh centuries AD—the Viking Age—looking at the Nordic population and their neighbors, the Sámi (also known, though not to themselves, as the Lapps). It is from these peoples' mental universe that I draw my examples here.

Knowledge, Belief, and the Illusion of Orthodoxy

To most of the populace in the modern, developed West, "religion" conjures up something essentially orthodox, a creed, with more-or-less rigid rules of behavior that usually embody concepts of obedience and worship. These tenets are often set out in holy books, with holy men and women to interpret them for us, with all this implies in terms of social differentiation and power relationships. To a greater or lesser degree, all the world faiths of our time fall into this category: the framework of formalized religion holds true for Christians, Muslims, Jews, Hindus, Buddhists, and many others, and extends to the different doctrines and sects operating within these larger structures. As archaeologists, in far too many instances we tend to project this highly specific understanding of religion back into the prehistoric past.

There are several areas of obvious contention here, and it is not my intention to enter the arena of broader definition patrolled by students of comparative religion (in a northern archaeological context, compare Ahlbäck 1993 and Stausberg et al. 2002). While historians of religion rightly debate the terminologies of "ritual," "sacrifice," "priesthoods," and the very notion of the sacred—in discussions that archaeologists occasionally attempt to follow in material terms—we are forced to acknowledge that the excavated evidence is only very rarely susceptible to such nuances of analysis (for some Scandinavian examples, see the range of papers in Engdahl and Kaliff 1996; Larsson and Wyszomirska 1989; Steinsland 1986).

The modern formalization of ancient religions is clear and beyond doubt, as indicated not least by the appropriately titled chapter in every major synthesis of individual societies. The imposed familiarity of early spiritual practice is more subtle, and is manifested in ways that are not always obvious. One of the clearest media of interpretation in this respect is the reconstruction drawing, a difficult undertaking as it gives such definite shape to what is in reality rather conjectural. How often has one seen a reconstruction purporting to show a prehistoric ceremony of some kind, in which we merely see the elementary structures of modern world faiths replicated in period costume? If we choose Christian imagery for an example, this is a vision of the past in which "priests" address a "congregation," conducting a "service" in what really might as well be a "church" (Figure 9.1). By formulating our ideas on ancient religion through unconscious reference to that which it was not—Christianity and similar world faiths—we are missing something essential.

In a great many early societies—for example all of non-Classical Europe before the coming of Christianity—no one would have understood this concept of formal religion. For much of prehistory all over the globe many scholars now find it more appropriate to speak of a "belief system," a way of looking at the world. What we would now isolate as religion was then simply another dimension of daily life, inextricably bound up with every other aspect of existence. We need to think of cultures that had,

Figure 9.1 Priests and congregations: the Anglican Church projected onto prehistory? Reconstruction of a Bronze Age funeral ceremony at the Bush Barrow, near Stonehenge, southern England. Illustration by Peter Dunn (after Parker Pearson 1993).

among other things, a looser sense than we do of the boundaries between our world and the next, as well as those between the world of humans and the world of animals.

Even so, there are still problems with this more flexible definition. Not least we must question the role that belief—as we understand it in the post-Enlightenment sense of the rational—played in ancient spirituality. Prehistoric humans probably did not believe that the sun moved on a chariot, or that the Northern Lights were the souls of the dead; instead they knew these things, or at least trusted in them (see Smith 1977, 1979 and Good 1994 for further discussion on this theme). If we are to discard belief in favor of knowledge, then we must also to some extent abandon its structure: it may be that the notion of a system of any kind is misleading. An informed review of global ethnographic and anthropological research makes it hard to avoid the conclusion that ancient spirituality only rarely took the form of a consistent orthodoxy. More striking still, it may never have been systematically understood even by those who practised it.

Much of this is linked to the understanding of the past in prehistoric societies, the past in the past (cf. Bradley 2002), reflected in the "religious" link between past and present. In cultures where something of the ancient language has been preserved, we even see this made explicit. The Vikings, for example, had a concept of what they called *fornsed*, literally "the customs of the past"—a combination of tradition, worthy heritage, and spirituality that also embodied the much broader notion of "how one lived," expressed in a relationship between proper conduct in the present and the ancestral world of what has gone before. Similarly, the term that the Sámi people used to encompass their belief system, *noaid-evuohta*, simply means "things that have to do with the noaidi," the latter being an approximate equivalent to the artificial construct of "shaman" and the figure that channeled the crucial link to the ancestral dead (Price 2002). Again, we see the lack of orthodoxy, the loose flexibility of these concepts.

The points made above can also be demonstrated when we look at the gods. Here we can again take those of the Vikings—Odin, Thor, Freyja, and the others—but the example is widely applicable. It is quite clear that the "worship" required by the Norse pantheon was not adoration, or gratitude, or even unreserved approval, and was thus utterly unlike the Christian relationship to the divine. The Viking gods demanded only a recognition that they existed as an integral and immutable part of human nature and society, and of the natural world, and that as such they possessed an inherent rightness—perhaps even a rather terrible kind of beauty. If you wanted to avoid disaster, it was necessary to come to terms with these deities, and the terms would be theirs, not yours. A refusal to acknowledge the powers in this way could have dire consequences, and it would also involve a contradiction, as such an act would be a denial of the undeniable (cf. Vellacott 1973:30–31). For the Vikings, the question of "believing in" the gods was probably irrelevant, like asking if one "believed" in the sea (for further discussion and references to Norse mythology, see DuBois 1999 and Price 2002, Chapter 2).

All this becomes especially apparent when we consider religious transitions, from one culturally constituted understanding of the world to another, fundamentally different in form. If we continue with a Viking Age Scandinavian example, at its simplest this process can be expressed in the change from "paganism" to Christianity, but in reality this extends to encompass a broad range of elements including political structures and the centralization of state power, judicial constructs, social and gender relations, literacy, and many other factors. Common to all these is cognition, mentality, the particular mind-set and worldview of the pre-Christian North.

Bodylore and Religion as Embodied Learning

This view of traditional spiritual knowledge, and its loose formulation within general boundaries, is particularly suited to the archaeology of indigenous religions, for example in North America. However, we need to ask what kinds of material traces this kind of fluid and socially situated practice could leave. To do this we need a new way of looking at the practical activities associated with a flexible, personal understanding of spirituality. The first step is to move away from the idea of ritual, and focus instead on behavior.

The concept I want to introduce here was first developed in 1989 by the folklorist Katherine Young, who subsequently expanded upon it in an edited collection (1993). Young coined the term bodylore to encapsulate the role played by the human body in the production and maintenance of sacred knowledge. Especially important here is the idea of ritual practice as, to a variable degree, actually dependent upon the bodily capacities of the performer(s) involved. We can explore this further through example.

One of those working with bodylore has been the Finnish historian of religions Juha Pentikäinen, in his studies of Siberian shamanism (1998:53). He found that the communities he visited were highly individual in their ritual performances, with an emphasis not on orthodox meaning but on the physical and mental skills of particular shamans. In light of this he used the terminology of bodylore to express the concept of what amounted to a kind of personal theology, in which a clear structure of ritual was absent. Instead the dancing, sacrifice, chanting, and other ceremonies represent sequences of practiced movement and thought, instilled through repetition and unique to each individual shaman. In this sense bodylore appears as something that actually resides in the body itself, similar to what athletes call muscle memory. Most importantly, such rituals are generated and perpetuated in a form that is separated from their perceived meanings, which may have been lost or even unformulated to begin with. This is the same kind of traditional knowledge mentioned above, but expressed differently by different people. This knowledge may have had consistent points of reference from one community to another—a culturally situated meaning—but it may also have been utterly divorced from any desire to understand or analyze it.

Bodylore clearly has many links to the broader exploration of somatics, building on social and anthropological theories of the body (e.g., Csordas 1994; Shilling 2000, 2003) and on feminist studies of gender (e.g., Butler 1993). Turner (1996:24–27) has put forward three key approaches:

- the body as social practice, constantly sustained by regulated activity
- the body as a system of signs, a carrier of social meaning
- the body as a semiotic expression of power.

A fourth reading also emerged over the same period, in which the body is understood in terms of phenomenology and lived experience, in the sense of embodiment (see especially the feminist perspectives of Hekman 1990 and Gatens 1996).

Among archaeologists, especially given the prevalence of phenomenological work in the wake of post-processualism, the study of the somatic past has been surprisingly undervalued. As Meskell has pointed out (1999:42; cf. Meskell 1996, 1998), the studies that have been undertaken tend to concentrate on aesthetics, sexuality, and power, favoring the inscriptive body over its experiential meanings. Archaeological studies of "embodied lives" are certainly possible, however, and have been tackled with impressive results—examples here include explorations of New Kingdom Egypt and the Maya (Meskell 1999; Meskell and Joyce 2003) and the San in southern Africa (Blundell 2004).

Representing as it does a kind of embodied learning, bodylore accords well with this kind of somatic research. In the context of ritual, bodylore is expressed as an ingrained behavior in which conventional religious concepts of "worship" and "cult" are replaced by contextualized gesture and action. Importantly for us as archaeologists, this action is articulated and expressed through material culture: objects, spaces, and landscapes (for further examples from "shamanic" contexts, see Jordan 2003; Jordan this volume; Walter 2001). And, of course, it is here that archaeology gives us a window on religion as praxis, as activity and the traces that it leaves. Perhaps because of its very specific application to the sphere of folklore and religion, as distinct from the general realm of somatic studies and embodied culture, bodylore has hitherto received little or no attention from archaeologists.

Given this, it is reasonable to ask where, and how, should we look? One answer would be in a closer analysis of ritual scenery, the "stages" on which spiritual acts took place and the spaces within which these embodied performances of bodylore played out. For the purposes of this paper, we can take a single, extended example: the extraordinary ship burials of the Viking Age.

The Ship Burials of the Vikings

Figure 9.2 shows the excavation plan of a late-seventh-century boat grave, about a century earlier than the Viking Age, during which such burials continued in many regions of Scandinavia (for reports of the most significant finds see Arne 1934 on Tuna in Alsike; Arwidsson 1942, 1954, and 1977 on Valsgärde; Stolpe and Arne 1912 on Vendel; Sørensen 2001 on Ladby; Müller-Wille 1976 on Hedeby and Groix; Crumlin-Pedersen 2002 on Skuldelev; Petersson 1958 and 1964 on Klinta; for more general discussion of the ship burials see Müller-Wille 1970 [the standard work], Sjøvold 1979; Lamm and Nordström 1983).

In burials like this, vessels ranging from small fishing skiffs to 30-meter longships were dragged up from the water and laid to rest in a trench specially cut for the purpose. The bodies of one or more dead men and women were placed on board, laid out in various ways—lying amidships or resting in bed, sitting in chairs or propped up on cushions, sometimes covered by shaggy bearskins. They were surrounded by weapons and personal belongings, jewelry, tools, household equipment, and fine textiles. The makings of a feast were often laid out—decorated drinking horns and expensive imported glasses, and the mead and wine to fill them; alongside them were offerings of food, herbs, and spices. Sometimes the full range of home furnishings was carried on board: beds, looms for weaving, smiths' tools and agricultural equipment, sledges, ice skates, even entire wagons. Tents and other gear for the outdoor life are also found.

The dead were often accompanied by sacrificed animals or parts of them, everything from domesticated livestock such as cattle, sheep, pigs, and goats, to riding horses and high-status beasts such as hunting dogs and falcons. Even more exotic creatures are sometimes found in the ships: owls, peacocks, eagles and cranes, to name but a few. Sometimes the bodies of other people are discovered, apparently killed during the funeral.

On occasion the ship has been lifted onto a great pyre of wood and set on fire. We find it as a heap of ash with the outline of the vessel preserved as rows of iron rivets, filled with burnt and twisted traces of what had lain inside. Sometimes the dead are found buried in a chamber, on

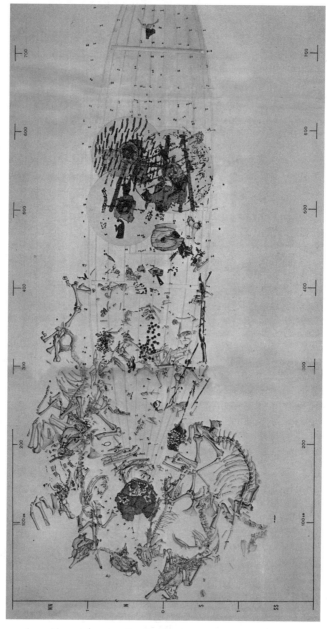

Figure 9.2 Excavation plan of boat burial 7 from Väslgärde in Uppland province, Sweden, dated c. 675 AD. Field drawing and watercolor original by Allan Fridell, reworked by Roger Blidmo (after Arwidsson 1977).

top of which the ship is balanced (occasionally upside down). In almost every case, regardless of the nature of the rituals involved, the graves were covered with a mound of earth, and a barrow was erected over the buried vessel or the remains of its cremation. Sometimes a post might have been set up on top, or the ship's mast allowed to project vertically out of the mound.

Some of the ships are in a superb state of preservation, protected by the anaerobic clay of their burial mounds. Particularly spectacular examples are the ninth-century ships from Gokstad (Nicolaysen 1882) and Oseberg (Brøgger et al. 1917a, 1917b, 1927, and 1928 Christensen et al. 1992) in the Vestfold district of the Oslofjord in Norway. The latter vessel especially—the richest grave of any kind known from Viking Age Scandinavia— preserved an unparalleled variety of organic materials (Figure 9.3).

These ships have been interpreted in many ways: as an impressive possession of the dead person, as a reflection of the status of his or her heirs (expressed in the form of conspicuous disposable wealth), or as something to do with the process of death itself. Perhaps a ship was needed to convey the deceased to the next world, or maybe it was needed where they were going (see Crumlin-Pedersen and Thye 1995 for a range of views and further reading).

Norse mythology certainly contains a great deal of maritime imagery, including the funerary ship of Baldr, the Bright God, pushed onto his pyre by a giantess, who rides to the ceremony on a wolf bridled with vipers. We also have Skidbladnir, the collapsible ship of Freyr (one of the

Figure 9.3 The Oseberg ship burial, Vestfold, Norway, during its excavation in 1904. The extraordinary preservation of the timbers is clearly visible. Dendrochronology suggests a date for the vessel of c. 820 AD.

gods of sexuality), which could be folded up and put into one's pocket. Lastly there is surely the most terrible vessel of any religion, Naglfar (literally "Nail Ship"), made from the fingernails of the dead and moored on the sea-bed. Crewed by all those who have ever drowned, and with the Trickster figure Loki at its helm, on the last day Naglfar will break loose and rise to the surface. Its cargo will be the armies of destruction, journeying to the Ragnarök, the battle at which the universe will end in fire. (These examples all come from the Eddic poem Völuspá and the Gylfaginning section of Snorri's Edda—see Neckel and Kuhn 1983 and Snorri 1988 for the respective Old Norse texts; recent translations may be found in Larrington 1996 and Faulkes 1987.)

Others have seen the burial ships as metaphors, representing the hall buildings characteristic of high-status chieftains, and thus forming a kind of residence for the dead (Herschend 1997). In this interpretation it is important that the dead stay in the mound, protecting or serving their community with spiritual power—the very opposite to the idea of death as a journey. We certainly know that some of the ship burials were left partly open for a short time, with portions of the vessel visible. The most dramatic example here is the Oseberg ship (Figure 9.4; Gansum 2004), while the line of boat burials at Valsgärde may have been housed under open-ended sheds, their occupants and contents accessible to visitors.

Figure 9.4 A reconstruction of the Oseberg ship burial as originally constructed, with the ship left partially uncovered and accessible. Drawing by Morten Myklebust (after Gansum 2004).

Let us now turn to an alternative source of data on the ship graves, which can help us to shed light on the events surrounding their creation. It is in relation to this that the concept of bodylore and embodied religion becomes relevant.

The Diplomat's Report

In the year AD 921, a man called Ahmad ibn Fadlan ibn al-Abbas ibn Rashid ibn Hammad faqh—usually known to modern scholars simply as Ibn Fadlan—set out from Baghdad on a mission of some importance. Trained as a *faqih*, an expert in religious law, Ibn Fadlan seems to have been the secretary of an embassy sent out by the Caliph, with the objective of sealing diplomatic and religious ties with the Bulghars of the middle Volga. After a few months spent in increasingly hostile territory, the man in charge of the expedition's missionary functions seems to have lost his nerve and left the caravan, and thereafter Ibn Fadlan took over his role too. During the two-year journey he encountered a great many different cultures, and he wrote about what he had seen in a document known as the *Risala* (literally "Report"). On the 12th of May 922, Ibn Fadlan arrived on the Volga, a river known to him as the *Atul* or *Atil*. He and his men stayed for some weeks, attending the local dignitaries. Due in part to the Caliphate's sponsorship brought by his mission, the lively trading post that he found there would soon develop into the town of Bulghar, the capital of the tribe of the same name. The site now lies somewhere under the modern city of Kazan' in the Russian Federation, and it was here that Ibn Fadlan first met the people that he called al-Rus' and al-Rusiya, traveling merchants who had come to trade at the market. These were the Vikings.

Ibn Fadlan's text is well known to Viking scholars, but may be less familiar to others working in different branches of archaeology. It has survived in several versions within a number of other manuscripts, mainly geographies of the twelfth, thirteenth, and sixteenth centuries, but the most complete text comes from an eleventh-century work discovered as recently as 1923. There are a great number of modern editions and translations into most European languages (see Dahhan 1959 for the most comprehensive rendering of the Arabic, and Montgomery 2000 for the best English translation and commentary on the sections dealing with the Rus'—Chapters 80–93 of the *Risala*). It may be noted in passing that the Arab use of Rus' as a descriptive term has many connotations, covering not only specific ethnic groups but also "northern foreigners" in general. In Ibn Fadlan's account there is no doubt that it refers to Scandinavians.

In addition to general descriptions of the Rus' appearance, clothing, and personal habits, Ibn Fadlan's main claim to fame today rests on his detailed observation of the rituals following the death of a Rus' chieftain, culminating in his cremation in a ship. This is our only eyewitness account of such an event. The ceremonies include a great many things recognizable with almost unsettling exactitude from excavations: the expensive dress of the dead, the weapons, and other costly possessions laid on board, the animal offerings, and the presence of a human sacrifice, in this case a young slave-girl. What the archaeology does not give us is the rest, the extraordinary unfolding narrative that is enacted in and around the vessel for more than a week prior to its burning.

In summary, the main activities are as follows:

- Some ten days are deliberately allowed to elapse between the chieftain's death and the cremation of the ship, a time during which he is buried in a temporary grave (with temporary grave-goods, including food, drink, and a musical instrument; there is a strong suggestion that all this is intended for his entertainment pending the final funeral).
- The same period sees continuous festivities in the Rus' camp, involving music, sex, and drinking so heavy as to be hazardous to life (the text is explicit that in the past men have died at such feasts); almost the entire band is perpetually drunk.
- The ten-day period also sees the manufacture of special burial clothes for the dead chieftain, on which no less than a third of his wealth is spent; another third goes to the brewing of appropriate quantities of alcohol, while only the remaining third is inherited by his heirs.
- The proceedings are presided over by a middle-aged woman, heavy set and angry, whose title (as Ibn Fadlan understood it through his interpreter) means the "Angel of Death."
- Around the ship, which has been propped up on shore using timbers carved like men, people go back and forth making music and chanting; Ibn Fadlan unfortunately does not understand what they say.
- Early on, the dead man's slaves are gathered together, and asked which of them will volunteer to be killed; a girl steps forward, perhaps around 14 or 15 years old.
- The slave-girl is thereafter referred to as the dead man's "bride," dressed in fine clothes and jewelry, and assigned servants of her own (they are the daughters of the "Angel").
- She spends the ten days prior to the burial drinking and feasting, and during this time has sex with many of the men in the camp (particularly the relatives of the deceased).
- On the tenth day the ship is hauled onto the pyre.
- A wooden tent or cabin is set up on the deck, with a bed of Byzantine gold brocade inside.
- The dead man is exhumed, dressed in his mortuary clothes, and brought to the ship, where he is propped up with cushions in a sitting position on the bed.
- In several successive visits, his possessions are brought on board and a variety of food, drink, and herbs is laid out around him.
- While this is going on, the slave-girl goes from tent to tent around the ship, having sex with each man, who shouts loudly that he has thereby done what his duty demands.
- A dog is then led to the ship and neatly cut in two before the halves are slung on board.

- The man's weapons are then placed in the cabin.
- Horses and cattle are then sacrificed, not cleanly slaughtered but instead hacked to pieces with swords; the horses are exercised first, so their bodies glisten with sweat.
- Some chickens are sacrificed by tearing their heads off, the pieces being first thrown precisely to either side of the ship, and finally onto its deck.
- Before entering the ship, the slave-girl is lifted up to look over a door set up in the open air, and describes three successive visions of the next world and its inhabitants.
- Her jewelry is then taken from her.
- The slave-girl then ascends to the deck of the ship, by walking on the raised palms of the men with whom she has earlier had sex.
- She sings her leave-taking, and is apparently drugged with some kind of special drink.
- Once on board, she becomes confused and is reluctant to enter the cabin.
- When she is forced inside, the slave begins to scream, but her cries are drowned out by men waiting on the deck, beating staves on the shields that they have apparently brought in expectation of such a turn of events.
- Held down on the bed beside the ten-day old corpse of the chieftain, the slave is then raped by six of the dead man's kinsmen.
- After this, while four of the men hold her arms and legs, the other two strangle her with a twisted veil; at the same time, the "Angel of Death" stabs her repeatedly.
- When the living have left the ship, the pyre is then lit by a naked man walking backwards around the vessel, keeping his face averted and covering his anus with his fingers (all orifices of his body are either pointing away from the ship or protected).
- As the fire consumes the ship and its occupants, fanned by a rising wind, the Rus' talk with approval of how the smoke is being carried high into the sky and that therefore their "Lord" is pleased.
- When the ashes cool, a mound is erected over the remains of the pyre and a birch pole is set up on top, on which is cut (in runes?) the dead man's name and that of his king. After this, the Rus' leave.

To all this we need to add the "audio-visual effects," to use a callous phrase: the screaming of the animals; the entrails fouling the ship's timbers; the expensive textiles covered in gore; the confusion and panic of the slave-girl; the flies in the sticky pools of blood; the mingled scents of recent sex, old death, and violent killing. It is hard to believe that anyone could remain entirely calm in the midst of such acts (Ibn Fadlan certainly does not; indeed, he was gently threatened by one of the bystanders).

Despite the detail, it should be stressed that the account given here is merely a synthesis: Ibn Fadlan's description covers several chapters in his report, and ought to be read in its entirety. Not least, it should be viewed in the context of the rest of the document, relating his encounters with other peoples on his journey.

Unsurprisingly, Ibn Fadlan's account has been widely discussed by Viking specialists, and also by archaeologists working more generally with burial studies (e.g., Arne 1941; Kowalska 1973; Lund Warmind 1995;

Parker Pearson 1999; Ritter 1942; Taylor 2002). We do not know the exact location of the grave, and it has not knowingly been excavated. However, it is abundantly clear that the material result would not have looked dissimilar to the ship burials we have briefly reviewed above.

Ritual Drama and Mortuary Theater

To return to the archaeology, a key point here is that each ship burial is different in the exact detail of its contents and their location in the grave: there are dozens of them, and they are all unique. In other words, the actions, rituals, or ceremonies that went into their creation were also individual, albeit enacted within a broadly consistent tradition of "boat burial." It is worth mentioning that we have not even touched upon the related and common phenomenon of symbolic ships, which also form a major class of Viking Age monument (Figure 9.5). Up to 170 meters long (at Jelling, Denmark, though most were much smaller), clearly outlined in standing stones, and found in both cemeteries and on open ground, what exactly do they mean?

Is it possible that the complicated ship burials (and perhaps also their symbolic stone equivalents) are actually the remains of funerary dramas, perhaps days of activity and motion, culminating in the final closure of the grave? To judge from the wealth of actions and performances recorded by Ibn Fadlan, this is not an unwarranted suggestion.

The idea of mortuary plays has been explored at length for Anglo-Saxon burial grounds in the sixth to eighth centuries, enacted in this case within the agenda of fledgling kingdoms. The main work in this vein has been conducted at Sutton Hoo, and suggests that the rituals behind the elaborate ship burials resembled small stories, literally acted out around a grave (Carver 1992, 1995, cf. 2002). The final locations of objects ("grave-goods") and animals ("sacrifices") represent their final position when their roles were played to completion. In this respect the dead themselves are among the main characters, "acting" in their own funerals. "The Sutton Hoo ship burial, with its curious assemblage of artefacts, is not a truthful reference to real life at all; it is itself a heroic text ... a poem, like Beowulf, in another medium, and has many of the same problems of interpretation" (Carver 1992:181). For the early Anglo-Saxon kingdoms, such performances are seen as taking place in a "theater of death" subtly different from a mere cemetery, the stage for political statements and public messages of ideological allegiance (Carver 1998). The stories of the English burials are ancestral ones, linking the dead kings and their living successors not only with their Nordic heritage but also with a new idea of royal authority in a colonial territory.

So, is what we excavate and reproduce in our neatly ordered plans essentially what is left at the close of a play? If this is the case, the gulf

Figure 9.5 "Ale's Stones," the Viking Age ship setting in its impressive cliff-top location at Kåseberga in Skåne province, Sweden. Photo L. Bergström (after Janson and Lundberg 1987).

between what survives and what it represents may be even greater than we have previously supposed. Perhaps we should picture an entire performance of Hamlet, in all its subtle richness of language and imagery, represented only by the pile of bodies on stage at the end, their clothing and equipment, and the few props that surround them. We can go further and envisage a unique play, a special commission, composed for each funerary occasion.

If Carver's Sutton Hoo kings are making political theater, there may be many other themes. A similar idea has been addressed for a kind of pictorial memorial stone found on the Baltic island of Gotland in the late Iron Age and Viking period (Figure 9.6). Covered in carved images arranged either in horizontal panels or as jumbles of pictures, some of the stones relate recognizable mythological and heroic stories, while the majority of the designs remain obscure. Some of the stones are also set up at intervals along the boundary lines of Viking Age farms, suggesting that the Gotlanders were commemorating the dead in a way that also staked out (and thereby laid permanent claim to) the family land on which they had lived. Most excitingly, it is on these particular stones that the pictorial stories form sequences—in one case from the tale of Sigurd the Dragon-Slayer—with the narrative "continuing" from the lower panel of one stone to the upper panel of the next, in a line from one monument to the next around the property boundary. Anders Andrén (1993) suggests that these may be stories connected to an individual family, and that each successive funeral involves a symbolic enactment of the "next chapter" in the ancestral tale. In this way the dead are not only bound closer to their family, absorbed into the story, but they also serve to reinforce their kin's right to land. The stones' "keyhole" shape also resembles the doors preserved in later wooden churches, and it has been argued that the memorials may have symbolized (or even been thought to actually represent) doorways to the other world beyond.

Another feature of the Gotland stones is that most of them have a large ship in the lower part of the scene, sometimes taking up more than half its surface. Actual ship burials are not known from Gotland, and in general the island's Viking Age material culture takes a slightly different form to that of the mainland. Andrén has therefore suggested that the picture stones may be an equivalent to boat graves but expressed in a different form, in which the stories are illustrated rather than literally acted out. The majority of uninterpreted scenes on the stones merely serve to emphasize the sheer range of stories involved.

The wider role of drama in the enactment and communication of early Scandinavian religious ideas has been extensively examined by Terry Gunnell (1995), who has argued that several of the surviving mythological poems were originally performed as plays. There are indications of

Figure 9.6 A damaged Viking Age picture stone from Gotland, found at Lärbro Stora Hammars I. The stone is 3.9 m high, of the type depicting multiple narrative panels with a ship in the lower field (after Lindqvist 1942).

several "parts" in the dramas (as in the poem Lokasenna, in which Loki and the gods exchange ritualized insults), and in some cases even the "stage directions" appear to be preserved.

In following the suggestions put forward by Carver, Andrén, and Gunnell, in combination with the nuanced reality of the boat graves, we arrive at a startling conclusion. Given the huge variety in the repertoire of ship burials and the images on the Gotland stones, it seems possible that all the funerary narratives were tailored or composed as required. Were the Vikings in effect augmenting their own mythology with each new burial, adding to the cycle of tales?

And why should this not have extended beyond the ship burials into more ordinary mortuary behavior? Figure 9.7 shows a map of population distribution in southern Scandinavia during the Viking Age, represented as hundreds of individual areas of settlement. This image was compiled by Johan Callmer in an extensive survey of excavated data undertaken in the 1980s, and it is important to stress that the variation we see results from the spatial plotting of differences in burial ritual (Callmer 1991, 1992). While there are clear patterns in funerary customs all over Scandinavia,

Figure 9.7   Settlement distribution in southern Scandinavia, c. 800 AD, based on differentiation in the detail of funerary custom. Circled areas show affinities of burial ritual (after Callmer 1992).

the variation in terms of exact practice extends to the level of individual villages and farms, as Callmer has shown so vividly. The implications are suggestive.

The funerary tales of kings and elites may have had formal conventions, but for others we may be looking at a whole world of stories, within the orbit of which individuals and families lived their lives and died. If we put all this together, it is here that bodylore returns, in the sense of improvised, even spontaneous, dramas for the dead—a very different kind of "religion," but one that has left dramatic archaeological traces.

From Religion to Society

We can return to the points with which we began this paper. When we try to theorize ancient religions, and then complain about how hard it is, what we are often doing is seeking something that was never there to begin with. In prehistoric cultures all over the world we will not always find formal religious structures of the kind familiar from Europe and the Orient. There are exceptions, of course, especially in state-based societies, but in general we should be looking for the local patterns of personal belief, of individual relationships with the supernatural powers and the equally unique negotiations that were conducted with them.

We shall find these patterns in the equipment of such negotiators, buried with the dead "shamans" and ritual specialists; we shall find them in the cognitive analysis of everyday material culture and its symbolic associations; and we shall find them in the spatial analysis of the grave fields and the landscape itself, the world in which past peoples understood themselves to move.

Not least, we must remember the social theater of the rituals themselves, what they say about those who took part and those who were present. In the acts witnessed by Ibn Fadlan, how did the onlookers feel, watching the loading of the ship, the slaughter of the animals, the slow build-up to the rape and murder of the slave and its accompaniments? Perhaps the slave was someone they knew and cared for, or perhaps she signified less to them than the dog. To us this whole event seems unthinkably horrible, and yet to at least some of the people of the Viking Age, at an institutionalized and socially sanctioned level, it clearly was not. Why? What does this tell us about them, and in this how far can we trust the judgment of a thousand years of hindsight?

The implications and possible parallels are legion here—to take just one recent instance, we may think of the debate about violence and cannibalism in the American Southwest, and its challenges to preferred views of a peaceful prehistory (see Lekson 1999 for an overview of the arguments, including contributions by LeBlanc, Turner, and Walker; LeBlanc 1999 provides an in-depth study). There are many other topical examples. In this light the explicitly archaeological study of religion becomes imperative, with a unique research agenda that alone can address the total social context that gave meaning to such embedded beliefs. Another crucial point here is archaeology's relationship with other disciplines, especially what is often called history of religions, comparative theology, or religious science. It is very important that we as archaeologists have faith in our own research agendas—we are not trying to pursue the history of religions by other means. Archaeology in fact has the potential to give us something very different, something nuanced and varied that goes far beyond the relatively limited world of purely textual scholarship. Both material culture and the written word are equally eloquent testimonies to the mental landscape of the past, but whether approaching objects or approaching text, our work here is entirely archaeological in its inspiration and its agenda.

This notion of embedded and embodied religion, interlaced with every other element of life, also works both ways. If an ancient religion essentially provides a particular understanding of the nature of reality, then its effects stretch far beyond the artificial compartment of faith. We can conclude this paper with the thought that in rejecting a notion of formalized religion, and in recognizing individual attitudes to the spiritual, we may find our best chance at understanding not only prehistoric beliefs but also the rest of society whose every aspect they informed.

References Cited

Ahlbäck, Tore (editor)
1993   The Problem of Ritual. Donner Institute, Åbo.
Andrén, Anders
1993   Doors to Other Worlds: Scandinavian Death Rituals in Gotlandic Perspective. Journal of European Archaeology 1:33–56.
Arne, Ture J.
1934   Das Bootgräberfeld von Tuna in Alsike, Uppland. KVHAA, Stockholm.
1941   Ibn-Fadlans resa till Bulgar: en nyupptäckt handskrift. Fornvännen 36:193–212.
Arwidsson, Greta
1942   Valsgärde 6. Almqvist & Wiksell, Uppsala.
1954   Valsgärde 8. Almqvist & Wiksell, Uppsala.
1977   Valsgärde 7. Almqvist & Wiksell, Uppsala.
Blundell, Geoffrey
2004   Nqabayo's Nomansland: San Rock Art and the Somatic Past. Uppsala University Press, Uppsala.
Bradley, Richard
2002   The Past in Prehistoric Societies. Routledge, London, New York.
Brøgger, A. W., Hjalmar Falk, and Håkon Shetelig (editors)
1917a   Osebergfundet. I. Universitetets Oldsaksamling, Kristiania.
1917b   Osebergfundet. III. Universitetets Oldsaksamling, Kristiania.

Brøgger, A. W., and Håkon Shetelig (editors)
1927   *Osebergfundet. V.* Universitetets Oldsaksamling, Oslo.
1928   *Osebergfundet. II.* Universitetets Oldsaksamling, Oslo.
Butler, Judith
1993   *Bodies that Matter: On the Discursive Limits of "Sex."* Routledge, London, New York.
Callmer, Johan
1991   Territory and Dominion in Late Iron Age Southern Scandinavia. In *Regions and Reflections. In Honour of Märta Strömberg*, edited by Kristina Jennbert, Lars Larsson, Rolf Petré, and Bozena Wyszomirska-Werbart, pp. 257–273. University of Lund, Lund.
1992   Interaction Between Ethnical Groups in the Baltic Region in the Late Iron Age. In *Contacts Across the Baltic Sea*, edited by Birgitta Hårdh and Bozena Wyszomirska-Werbart, pp. 9–107. University of Lund, Lund.
Carver, Martin
1992   Ideology and Allegiance in East Anglia. In *Sutton Hoo: Fifty Years After*, edited by Robert Farrell and Carol Neuman de Vegvar, pp. 173–182. American Early Medieval Studies, Oxford.
1995   Boat Burial in Britain: Ancient Custom or Political Symbol? In *The Ship As Symbol in Prehistoric and Medieval Scandinavia*, edited by Ole Crumlin-Pedersen and Birgitta Munch Thye, pp. 111–124. National Museum, København.
1998   *Sutton Hoo: Burial Ground of Kings?* British Museum Press, London.
2002   Reflections on the Meaning of Anglo-Saxon Barrows. In *Burial in Early Medieval England and Wales*, edited by Sam Lucy and Andrew Reynolds, pp. 132–143. Society for Medieval Archaeology, London.
Christensen, Arne Emil, Anne Stine Ingstad, and Bjørn Myhre (editors)
1992   *Osebergdronningens grav.* Schibsted, Oslo.
Crumlin-Pedersen, Ole
2002   *The Skuldelev Ships.* Roskilde Museum, Roskilde.
Crumlin-Pedersen, Ole, and Birgitta Munch Thye (editors)
1995   *The Ship As Symbol in Prehistoric and Medieval Scandinavia.* National Museum, København.
Csordas, Thomas J. (editor)
1994   *Embodiment and Experience: The Existential Ground of Culture and Self.* Cambridge University Press, Cambridge.
Dahhan, Sm
1959   *Rislat Ibn Fadln.* Matbu'at al-Majma al-Ilmi al-Arabi bi-Dimashq, Damascus.
DuBois, Thomas A.
1999   *Nordic Religions in the Viking Age.* University of Pennsylvania Press, Philadelphia.
Ellis Davidson, Hilda R.
1964   *Gods and Myths of Northern Europe.* Pelican, Harmondsworth.
Engdahl, Kerstin, and Anders Kaliff (editors)
1996   *Religion från stenålder till medeltid.* Rikantikvarieämbetet, Stockholm.
Faulkes, Anthony (translator)
1987   *Snorri Sturluson. Edda.* Dent, London.
Gansum, Terje
2004   *Hauger som konstruksjoner—arkeologiske forventninger gjennom 200 år.* Göteborg University, Göteborg.
Gatens, Moira
1996   *The Imaginary Body.* Routledge, London, New York.
Good, Byron J.
1994   *Medicine, Rationality and Experience: An Anthropological Perspective.* Cambridge University Press, Cambridge.

Gunnell, Terry
1995   *The Origins of Drama in Scandinavia*. Brewer, Woodbridge.
Hekman, Susan
1990   *Gender and Knowledge: Elements of a Postmodern Feminism*. Polity Press, Cambridge.
Herschend, Frands
1997   *Livet i hallen: tre fallstudier i yngre järnålderns aristokrati*. Uppsala University Press, Uppsala.
Janson, Sverker, and Erik B. Lundberg (editors)
1987   *Med arkeologen Sverige runt*. Forum, Stockholm.
Jordan, Peter
2003   *Material Culture and Sacred Landscape: The Anthropology of the Siberian Khanty*. AltaMira Press, Walnut Creek.
Kowalska, Maria
1973   Ibn Fadlan's Account of his Journey to the State of the Bulghars. *Folia Orientalia* 14:219–230.
Lamm, Jens-Peder, and Hans-Åke Nordström (editors)
1983   *Vendel Period Studies: Transactions of the Boat-Grave Symposium In Stockholm, February 1981*. Statens Historiska Museum, Stockholm.
Larrington, Carolyne (translator)
1996   *The Poetic Edda*. Oxford University Press, Oxford.
Larsson, Lars, and Bozena Wyszomirska (editors)
1989   *Arkeologi och religion*. University of Lund, Lund.
LeBlanc, Steven A.
1999   *Prehistoric Warfare in the American Southwest*. University of Utah Press, Salt Lake City.
Lekson, Stephen H. (editor)
1999   War and Peace in the Southwest. *Discovering Archaeology* (May/June) 1999:38–64.
Lindqvist, Sune
1942   *Gotlands Bildsteine*, vol. 2. Wahlström & Widstrand, Stockholm.
Lund Warmind, Morten
1995   Ibn Fadlan in the Context of His Age. In *The Ship As Symbol in Prehistoric and Medieval Scandinavia*, edited by Ole Crumlin-Pedersen and Birgitta Munch Thye, pp. 130–135. National Museum, København.
Meskell, Lynn
1996   The Somatisation of Archaeology: Discourses, Institutions, Corporeality. *Norwegian Archaeological Review* 29:1–16.
1998   The Irresistible Body and the Seduction of Archaeology. In *Changing Bodies, Changing Meanings: Studies of the Human Body in Antiquity*, edited by Dominic Montserrat, pp. 139–161. Routledge, London, New York.
1999   *Archaeologies of Social Life: Age, Sex, Class et cetera in Ancient Egypt*. Blackwell, Oxford.
Meskell, Lynn, and Rosemary Joyce
2003   *Embodied Lives: Figuring Ancient Maya and Egyptian Experience*. Routledge, London, New York.
Montgomery, James
2000   Ibn Fadln and the Rsiyyah. *Journal of Arabic and Islamic Studies* 3:1–25.
Müller-Wille, Michael
1970   *Bestattung im Boot: Studier zu einer nordeuropäischen Grabsitte*. Offa, Neumünster.
1976   *Das Bootkammergrab von Haithabu*. Berichte über die Ausgrabungen von Haithabu 8. Neumünster.
Neckel, Gustav, and Hans Kuhn (editors)
1983   *Edda: die Lieder des Codex Regius nebst verwandten Denkmälen*, vol. 1 Text. 5th ed. Winters, Heidelberg.

Nicolaysen, Nicolay
1882   *Langskibet fra Gokstad ved Sandefjord.* Kristiania, Hammermeyer.
Parker Pearson, Michael
1993   *Bronze Age Britain.* Batsford/English Heritage, London.
1999   *The Archaeology of Death and Burial.* Sutton, Stroud.
Pentikäinen, Juha
1998   *Shamanism and Culture.* Etnika, Helsinki.
Petersson, K. G.
1958   Ett gravfynd från Klinta, Köpings sn., Öland. *Tor* 4:134–150.
1964   *Det vikingatida Köping på Öland.* Unpublished licenciate thesis. University of Uppsala, Uppsala.
Price, Neil S.
2002   *The Viking Way: Religion and War in Late Iron Age Scandinavia.* Uppsala University Press, Uppsala.
Ritter, Hans
1942   Zum Text von Ibn Fadlns Reisebericht. *Zeitschrift der Deutschen Morgenländischen Gesellschaft* 96:98–126.
Shilling, Chris
2000   The Embodied Foundations of Social Theory. In *The Handbook of Social Theory,* edited by George Ritzer and Barry Smart, pp. 439–457. Sage, London.
2003   *The Body and Social Theory.* 2nd ed. Sage, London.
Sjøvold, Torsten
1979   *The Viking Ships in Oslo.* Oslo University, Oslo.
Smith, Wilfred Cantwell
1977   *Belief and History.* University of Virginia Press, Charlottesville.
1979   *Faith and Belief.* University of Virginia Press, Charlottesville.
Sturluson, Snorri
1988   *Edda: Prologue and Gylfaginning.* Edited by Anthony Faulkes. Viking Society for Northern Research, London.
Sørensen, Ann Christine
2001   *Ladby: a Danish Ship-Grave from the Viking Age.* Roskilde Museum, Roskilde.
Stausberg, Michael, Olof Sundqvist, and Anna Lydia Svalastog (editors)
2002   *Riter och ritteorier: religionshistoriska diskussioner och teoretiska ansatser.* Nya Doxa, Nora.
Steinsland, Gro (editor)
1986   *Words and Objects: Towards a Dialogue Between Archaeology and History of Religion.* Instituttet for sammenlignende kulturforskning, Oslo.
Stolpe, Hjalmar, and Ture J. Arne
1912   *Graffältet vid Vendel.* KVHAA, Stockholm.
Taylor, Timothy
2002   *The Buried Soul: How Humans Invented Death.* Fourth Estate, London.
Turner, Bryan S.
1996   *The Body and Society: Explorations in Social Theory.* 2nd ed. Sage, London.
Vellacott, Philip
1973   Introduction. In *Euripedes. The Bacchae and Other Plays,* translated by Philip Vellacott, pp. 9–38. Penguin, Harmondsworth.
Walter, Damian
2001   The Medium of the Message: Shamanism As Localised Practice in the Nepal Himalayas. In *The Archaeology of Shamanism,* edited by Neil S. Price, pp. 105–119. Routledge, London, New York.
Young, Katherine (editor)
1993   *Bodylore.* University of Tennessee Press, Knoxville.

HISTORICAL-PROCESSUAL ARCHAEOLOGY AND CULTURE MAKING: UNPACKING THE SOUTHERN CULT AND MISSISSIPPIAN RELIGION

Thomas E. Emerson and Timothy R. Pauketat

"We do not believe our religion ... we dance it!"

—Plains Indian informant
(quoted in Brown 1977:123)

A few years ago, Colin Renfrew called for an archaeology of ancient religions, seeking in particular the "causes of religious change" by looking to "early cults" (1994:48–49). While his "cognitive-processual" approach retained the sense that religions were shared "belief systems," Renfrew emphasized the importance of the experiential component of religion—ritual and cult practices—in order to understand how religions change from within. The early Mississippian period of eastern North America provides an excellent case of just this sort of religious circumstance.

Structural and functional approaches have traditionally predominated analyses of the religious phenomena of the so-called Mississippian peoples of the Eastern Woodlands of North America between the eleventh and sixteenth centuries AD. Archaeologists attempting to reconstruct Mississippian-period meanings and religious themes have labeled them the "Southeastern Ceremonial Complex" (SECC) or the "Southern Cult" (Galloway 1989). The goal of such reconstruction ostensibly is to understand how interrelated American Indian religious traditions changed from place to place through time to shape the broad pan-regional contours of social life. Like other approaches to religion, reconstructions of

167

broad-brush meanings and institutions are typically given precedence over measures of actual religious practices, presumably since the latter were structured by and thus reflected the former.

From an early Mississippian vantage point, however, there is ample reason to cease viewing the SECC as a belief system that evolved through its institutions (e.g., temples, priests) to constrain the actions and experiences of its practitioners. Instead, we argue that separation of religious beliefs, meanings, and institutions from the lived experiences of people is ill advised. Indeed, recent theoretical approaches challenge the utility of analyzing religion in structural or functional terms, or as an inviolate and widely shared cognitive system. In a series of related moves toward theories of practice, performance, landscape, and embodiment, archaeologists have assumed more historical and phenomenological views of cultures. Cultures are participatory phenomena that were continuously constructed, produced, and experienced by people (e.g., Hodder and Cessford 2004; Meskell and Joyce 2003; Tilley 1994). *Culture-making* as a process (rather than culture as a structure or system) thus becomes a central focus of research (Pauketat and Loren 2005).

Elsewhere, Pauketat (2000, 2001a, 2001b, 2003) has laid out the principles of such "historical-processual" approaches, arguing that traditions, including religious traditions, were lived by people through their "continuous and historically contingent enactments or embodiments of ... attitudes, agendas, and dispositions" (Pauketat 2000:115). For our present purposes, it is important to note that these enactments and embodiments are not difficult to recover. Instead, they are routinely recovered by archaeologists who mistakenly use the details of practices, performances, landscapes, and embodiments to reconstruct traditions and institutions that, in reality, only exist in the moments of lived experience (Pauketat 2003). Archaeologists recover those details as a matter of course. Indeed, as we shall see, in the archaeology of religion, the devil is in the details.

Reconsidering the time-honored approaches to the so-called Southeastern Ceremonial Complex, we propose that Mississippian religion was an embodied, experiential process. New archaeological finds from the greater Cahokia region question the assumption that broad religious themes can characterize all Mississippian peoples. The details of Cahokian archaeology support our contention that people lived their religion through the practice of it, and in so doing continuously redefined that which we commonly consider to be the religious traditions and institutions of the Eastern Woodlands. We focus on the twelfth-century greater Cahokia region, which is particularly well known due to its research history (see Emerson 1997a, 1997b; Pauketat 1998, 2004), viewing it as a phenomenon with historical priority in the formation of "Mississippianism" (the historical patterns of practice associated with the period). We consider three lines of evidence manifest at three different analytical scales: monumentality, the sociality of gaming, and materiality of pot use. In featuring these evidentiary lines, our archaeology of Mississippian religion stresses how the practical experiences of ordinary farmers constructed on a continuous basis that which we call Mississippian religion.

Unpacking Mississippian Religion

The monuments and art of Mississippian peoples are among the most striking from the Eastern Woodlands. These people lived in major towns typically centered around four-sided plazas and large raised earthen platforms topped by pole-and-thatch temples and elite houses, some of which also served as cemeteries for the honored dead. Rich in multi-referential symbolism, Mississippian artifacts of copper, shell, ceramic, wood, woven fabrics, and stone have attracted the interest of many antiquarians, collectors, and archaeologists. Mississippian lifestyles have also caught the attention of researchers because of the rich textual legacy left by the early conquerors, merchants, missionaries, and travelers who encountered the historic descendants of these people. Insights gained from the admittedly biased accounts of the sixteenth-century Spanish or the seventeenth-century French have been a mainstay in the interpretation of Southeastern peoples' polity, economy, society, and religion. The art and the extensive ethnographic and ethnohistoric records have been both a blessing and a curse to the study of Mississippian religion.

During the early and middle decades of the twentieth century, scholars began to draw together the objects from Mississippian art and the ethnohistoric accounts of Southeastern native belief systems and rituals (especially of the Muskogee). They recognized the similarity of designs, motifs, and composite supernatural beings in late pre-Columbian art from across the southeastern United States. This vision of homogeneity was encouraged by the recovery of burial caches of elaborate and artistically crafted objects from premier mound sites such as Etowah and Moundville, and especially from the 1930s commercial looting of the Spiro Mound complex (Brown 1996; Moore 1905, 1907; Moorehead 1932). Their initial attempt to synthesize this growing body of iconographic objects commenced in an era when archaeologists were organizing native cultures by identifying their unique cultural traits (i.e., the Midwestern Taxonomic System). Antonio Waring and Preston Holder's (1945) now classic analysis of this body of art objects, iconography, and settlement features produced a "trait" list that primarily emphasized the thematic homogeneity of Mississippian art. Further interpretive work built on this approach, ultimately creating a cohesive interpretation that meshed Muskhogean beliefs and rituals with pre-Columbian material culture under the label of the "Southern Cult" or the "Southeastern Ceremonial Complex" (Howard 1968; Waring 1968; Waring and Holder 1945; Willoughby 1932; Witthoft 1949). Some researchers postulated that, in fact, the "Southern Cult" was best understood as the iconography and ritual practices of the Mississippians, which is to say their religion (Howard 1968; Hudson 1976, 1984).

The initial belief in the homogeneity of the Southern Cult was encouraged by the nature of the early work conducted at the sites. Many of the artifacts included in the trait lists were from early pre-scientific excavations with poorly understood archaeological context and supported by only rudimentary local or regional chronologies. Often lacking detailed chronological and/or contextual associations, artifacts were linked primarily by perceived stylistic similarities. Several decades of additional excavations, stylistic studies, and reanalyses of older collections have, however, begun to disassemble the unity of the Southern Cult. Especially important in this process of reinterpretation were detailed studies of Spiro shell engravings and southeastern shell gorgets (Brown 1989; Muller 1966, 1989; Phillips and Brown 1978, 1984). These analyses demonstrated that shell art was not homogeneous and was in fact divisible into distinctive styles that vary geographically and chronologically.

Our understanding of the potential heterogeneity of Southern Cult assemblages was enhanced when Brown's (1996) reanalysis of the Craig Mound burial caches, earlier considered as the archetypical Southeastern Ceremonial Complex (SECC) assemblage, demonstrated that it represented composite groupings of artifacts whose geographical origins were diverse and whose manufacture had occurred over at least a two-century-long period! By the time of the publication of the comprehensive review volume *The Southeastern Ceremonial Complex: Artifacts and Analysis* (Galloway 1989), most of the symposium participants had serious doubts about the reality of the Cult as a unified iconographic and religious entity (e.g., Brose 1989; Brown 1985, 1989; Hall 1989; Muller 1989).

In more recent times, research on Mississippian iconography has shifted to an increased interest in identifying stylistic variation and identifying how it "functioned" within society (e.g., the earlier work of Philips, Brown, and Muller cited above). James Brown has been in the forefront of efforts to categorize SECC artifacts and art in terms of socio-political roles. Working primarily with the extensive Spiro collections, Brown (1975, 1976) proposed that rather than representing an iconography of Mississippian religion, SECC art could be functionally differentiated into three symbolic realms associated with warriors and weaponry, the paraphernalia of falcon dancers, and the trappings of a mortuary cult. Knight (1986) expanded upon this idea in his exploration of ethnohistoric and archaeological evidence in an effort to define pan-Mississippian "cult institutions" that he believed revolved around warfare, platform mounds, and temple statuary.

These strands of thought have, most recently, culminated in the conclusion that the SECC has no overarching integrity (e.g., Knight 2006; Knight et al. 2001). It is, instead, a geographically, chronologically, and functionally variable ideological phenomenon, further complicated by the effects of extensive interregional exchange of centrally produced craft objects overlaid on locally complex iconographies and cultural object assemblages. In this most recent reinvention, the SECC is portrayed as representing cosmological themes that are "primarily [references] to the celestial realm of a layered cosmos" (Knight et al. 2001:129). These authors have restricted the SECC to a body of repoussé copper plates, engraved shell gorgets, and engraved shell cups and similar materials that depict "personages and zoomorphic" figures. They have also chosen to confine their "primary analytical focus to imagery as opposed to artifacts and their functional uses" (Knight et al. 2001:131). This focus is commensurate with the work of the leading scholar in Eastern Woodland cosmology, Robert Hall (e.g., 1977, 1989, 1997). For at least three decades, Hall has championed the thematic unity of Eastern Woodlands native cosmology through time and across national boundaries. Reaching into the rich ethnographic and ethnohistoric records of North America and Mesoamerica, Hall has argued for the continuity of belief systems across these regions as well as their linkage to pre-Columbian and historic iconography and practice.

From Imagery to Belief Systems?

There are three closely related problems with the approach of isolating belief systems through an analysis of imagery. First, religion, politics, economy, and identity may have been near-inseparable domains of the Mississippian experience. In fact, such inseparability is the foundation of current theories of the rise of Cahokia (e.g., Pauketat and Emerson 1999). Whose beliefs were represented by images on certain cultural objects that were used in elite ceremony or public display? This matters, since those images clearly constitute a miniscule fraction of the totality of a population's cultural practices. Moreover, even if this imagery did approximate some person's or group's belief system, and even if the imagery was shown in public, why assume that it was anything more than a projection of a minority belief into the public domain that otherwise might have been pervaded by opposing beliefs, alternate memories, and contradictory meanings? That is, why would we ever assume a uniform sharing of beliefs and practices, even where elites appear to have achieved a hegemony over common people? (Pauketat 2000).

The second problem in attempting to isolate belief systems via imagery is that of multivocality. Perhaps one central idea, theme, or "dominant symbol" was at the heart of some image, icon, or motif (*sensu* Turner 1967). However, as it turns out, such symbols are particularly susceptible to politicization—where the referents may be altered or meanings invented to suit contemporary purposes (e.g., Kertzer 1988, as cited by Pauketat 2001a). Thus, even apparent continuity in symbolic form belies potentially profound change in cultural meanings. Multiple, ambiguous, and even contradictory meanings are conveyed by symbols contingent on the context of use.

This problem of multivocality is closely related to the third problem, which is how to interpret meaning. What is meaningful? Clearly, meaning resides in more than imagery. Space, speech, dress, bodies, and cultural objects (with or without iconography) are all laden with meaning. Separating artifact function from meaning—as archaeologists are prone to do—is therefore additionally suspect, given two corollaries of phenomenological and practice-based theorizing: (1) technologies involve cultural "know-how" and thus necessarily incorporate cultural meanings, and (2) certain material objects and tools may be thought of as "extensions" of the human body, and thus would be intimately wrapped up in cultural categories associated with the body—gender, sexuality, individuality, and identity (e.g., Dobres 2000; Sassaman 1998). In the final analysis, limiting our scope of inquiry to specific imagery or to particular media necessitates a partitive view that holds religious systems or cosmologies apart from other dimensions of the human experience. Unfortunately, such positions ultimately beg the question of how religion changes.

This is not to dismiss the goal of comprehending the meanings of Mississippian religious practices (Emerson 1989:46–47, 1997a, 1997b, 2003a, 2003b; Emerson et al. 2000:511–512)—rather, it is to understand meaning as a more fluid domain that was in practice fraught with tensions and ambiguities and that was constantly under negotiation and reinterpretation. Thus, isolating meaning "in any complete sense (as it would have been understood by their makers) is hardly a feasible undertaking" (Renfrew 1994:53). Instead, we may consider the SECC themes in the same way that Mississippians probably did: as ambiguous, negotiated generalities that were memorialized, inscribed, or marked differently contingent upon the histories of people, events, and localized social movements. Interpreting meanings, that is, hinges on measuring the genealogies of meaning production. Meanings did not exist as homogeneous unchanging structures outside of the moments in which those meanings were lived, experienced, or practiced.

Dimensions of Religious Experience at Cahokia

To begin, we do need to identify the aggregate patterns—"the specific developmental trajectory of regional iconography" (Emerson et al. 2000:511)—through studies of the systematic co-occurrence of motifs on artifacts or the nonrandom associations of objects within secure archaeological contexts (Emerson 1989, 1997a, 1997b; Emerson et al. 2000). We do need studies that identify phenomena such as the SECC. However, iconographic patterns are not isomorphic with the belief systems shared by all people. The latter cannot be derived from the former, and the patterns are just the first step in an archaeology of religious practice.

It is instructive to examine how one localized variant of a Mississippian religion was constructed—spatially, materially, and bodily—around the earliest and largest Mississippian polity in North America, Cahokia (Fowler 1997). Cahokia's rise from a village in the Mississippi River floodplain near St. Louis, locally called the "American Bottom," to a political capital of 10,000 or more inhabitants was marked by an abrupt and region-wide political consolidation at about AD 1050 (Pauketat 2004). A significant aspect of this event was the incorporation of preexisting cosmological beliefs and practices into what appears, in the aggregate, to have been a centrally mediated religion, perhaps featuring a priestly elite with formalized religious practices, ritual paraphernalia, and dedicated spaces (Emerson 1997a, 1997b, 2002).

Our knowledge of the dense, heterarchically complex and hierarchically organized American Bottom populations of the eleventh to fourteenth centuries indicates that the scale of the Cahokian polity was unique among its North American contemporaries (Pauketat 1998, 2004). Its magnitude becomes evident when one considers that Cahokia—containing more than 120 mounds or earthen pyramids (including Monks Mound, the largest in North America) and nearly 2 sq km of habitation area—was only a portion of the sprawling and possibly undifferentiated "central political-administrative complex" of some 200 mounds, plazas, and habitation zones that encompassed the Cahokia, East St. Louis, and St. Louis sites (Pauketat 2004). It probably rivaled other early centers around the world in spatial extent, monument construction, and social and political complexity. And, as in other such primal centers, religion likely was a pivotal factor in its creation and existence. But how?

Constructing the Cosmos

If there was a single overarching pattern to the grounds and features of the central political-administrative complex, it was the pervasive dualism and quadripartitioning of the spatial dimension of social life (Emerson 1989,

1997a, 1997b). In fact, this partitioned spatiality seems apparent in the Cahokia region as early as AD 900 in the grounds and buildings of pre-Mississippian village courtyards (Kelly 1990). There, above-ground public buildings and the central posts of courtyards were counterbalanced by four-sided and semi-subterranean domiciles, all arrayed around an open courtyard that sometimes featured four subterranean storage pits.

After AD 1050, this same patterning is even more obvious, literally built into the planned Mississippian grounds of Cahokia proper or embodied by the associated practices (Figure 10.1). There were, for instance, great rectangular plazas leveled and surrounded by carefully engineered, steep-angled and flat-topped earthen pyramids, built by scooping out earth from nearby borrows. Most pyramids were four-sided rectangles, but in a bit of monumental dualism, some were paired with mounds having circular shapes in plan view. The circle-and-rectangle dualism was played out atop the platforms as well, in the plans of the oversized pole-and-thatch public or elite buildings (e.g., Pauketat 1993). It was also played out via the elaborate mortuary rituals of the unique ridgetop mounds (e.g., Fowler et al. 1999; see Pauketat 2004, 2005).

Figure 10.1 Reconstruction of a Cahokia Grand Plaza with surrounding mounds and chunkey yard in foreground (from a painting by L. K. Townsend, courtesy Cahokia Mounds State Historic Site).

Perhaps the duality and quadripartitioning of the central grounds of these early Mississippians was an ideological projection of someone's perceived relationship between an upper sky realm and a lower earthly realm, as it was several centuries later when observed by European explorers. Perhaps the four-sided platform mounds may have graphically portrayed the cosmos as "earth-islands" in which the world was flat-topped and four-sided (Knight 1989). In other contexts, the mound icon has been symbolically linked to agricultural and fertility themes involving world renewal rituals, effectively tying it to Cahokian representations in other media.

Then again, it is equally important to note that flat-topped, four-sided earthen pyramids have a discontinuous construction history in the Mississippi valley (Pauketat and Alt 2003). Although there *may have been* up to several earthen pyramids under construction at the Pulcher site a few kilometers south of Cahokia (and *perhaps* at Cahokia as well) during the tenth century AD, few people might have seen them, much less participated in these modest constructions. Fewer still may have understood what they meant. After all, these mounds were the first to have been built for centuries, following a regional hiatus in mound construction between about AD 400 and 900. Earthen pyramids akin to the later Mississippian kind were built during the fifth through tenth centuries AD, but only several hundred kilometers to the south in Arkansas, Mississippi, and Louisiana. Thus, the dramatic surge in construction around Cahokia after AD 1050 (never mind the likely immigration of diverse people from other places into the greater Cahokia region) represents a "historical disjuncture," perhaps indicating that mound construction was an idea "imported" by someone into the region (Pauketat and Alt 2003).

Certainly, as argued elsewhere, the Mississippian mounds and surmounting architecture built after AD 1050 were not one-time constructions, but were works in progress (e.g., see Dalan 1997; Dalan et al. 2003). After AD 1050, many people would have been routinely—probably annually—involved in the reconstruction of both mound and mound-top architecture (Pauketat 2000). Would these people, particularly those of the first generation following AD 1050, have shared the same sense of what the scores of huge platforms meant? Or, were the meanings and memories of the planners of the new mound-and-plaza complexes of greater Cahokia at ca. AD 1050 different from those of the thousands of participants who helped carry the earth? That is, even if we were to concede that the new mounds and plazas of eleventh-century Cahokia represented a four-cornered, two layered cosmos—perhaps even an up-scaled version of an apparent traditional settlement plan—the break with past practice must have been palpable to many of the participants who had not, up to that point, built a mound, experienced a grand plaza, or participated in any events located at Cahokia before this time! After the mid-eleventh century, however, these neophyte Mississippians were helping to inscribe new or significantly altered meanings into the landscape of the Mississippi valley (Pauketat and Alt 2003). Would their own understanding of this new landscape have been the same as the Cahokians overseeing construction? If not, would their subaltern sensibilities have been built into Cahokia too?

Disciplining the Body at Cahokia

Spaces are meaningless without people experiencing them, moving through them, and understanding themselves in relation to the natural and supernatural associations inscribed there (see Tuan 1977). As Pauketat (2004:78) explains elsewhere, the new spaces of Cahokia were probably "intended to generate certain physical sensations if not emotional responses. … [T]hey constrained or freed-up the movement of human bodies within them." The movement of those bodies, in turn, would have engendered "an appreciation of the proportions and relationships between the pyramids and the plaza" and between the "upright posts, thatch-roof buildings, and gathered peoples" who "would have been part of the experience of movement and changing perspectives" (Pauketat 2004:78). The sensibilities and dispositions of anyone attending a plaza ritual would have been defined in relation to the experience. Presumably, this would include the religious ideals and meanings implied or unambiguously associated with Cahokian ritual.

Likewise, as noted above, the participants in such rites would have brought their varied understandings and religious practices to bear on the central event, so that they too, in some small way, were intimately involved in a grand negotiation of religious meanings via the construction and experience of Cahokian space. This negotiation appears to have involved great religious festivals, featuring gargantuan feasts attended by thousands of people and accompanied by the inhalation of large amounts of nicotine, the parading of weaponry, display objects, and the bones of ancestors, and the manufacture and use of a variety of "magico-ritual" objects, paints, and bodily ornaments (Emerson 1989; Pauketat et al. 2002; Pauketat and Koldehoff 2002). Closely related to these ceremonies may have been the periodic mortuary rituals, where life and death appear to have been celebrated through a very public if not theatrical retelling of legendary histories and mythical memories (Emerson and Pauketat 2002; Pauketat 2005).

Also a prominent component of such gatherings would have been the playing of a traditional sport, similar to the game known as "chunkey" in historic times (Culin 1992). The chunkey game involved opposing teams alternately rolling a finely polished disk-shaped stone across a level playing field (courtyard or plaza) and hurling gaming sticks after it to score points. It is intriguing that the game, which may have been invented in the greater Cahokia region centuries earlier, had been played at that time by most pre-Mississippian villages. Like the analog "hoop-and-pole" game of various historic American Indians, it may have been a favorite game of children, who grew up with some sense of what the game meant: historically, the rolling stone was likened to the movement of the sun across the sky's arched ceiling; the sticks and stone may have been gendered male and female, so that the game recapitulated stories of cosmological creation, where a masculine sky deity or the rays of the sun penetrated the feminine forces of earth and darkness.

At AD 1050, the playing of chunkey appears to have been centralized to a degree, so that most residents of the Mississippi floodplain around Cahokia lacked the gaming stones, while Cahokians and their high-status kin maintained (and probably manufactured) the stones, which were sometimes buried with the elite dead in their ridgetop mounds (DeBoer 1993; Pauketat 2004). Besides their association with elite mortuaries, the stones are sometimes engraved with cosmograms (simple crosses or cross-hatchings) or a diamond-and-dot motif, on occasion interpreted (based on comparative analogies) as the eye of the sky-world thunderer (Figure 10.2). Whatever the varied meanings of the motif, the cosmological meanings of the chunkey game, in this way, seem to have been unambiguously projected into the game itself.

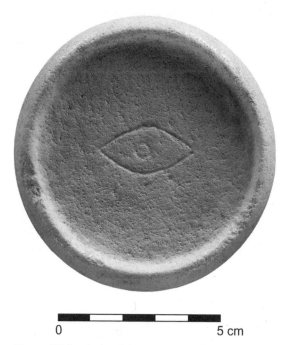

0   5 cm

Figure 10.2 A chunkey game groundstone discoidal with eye motif (photo by Mera Hertel, used with permission of ITARP, University of Illinois).

It is this projection, in fact, that holds greatest importance for our present analysis. Playing chunkey at Cahokia—where the largest, most high-stakes games may have occurred—would have entailed a certain sort of "disciplining" of the bodies of the people involved (following Foucault 1979; e.g., Hodder and Cessford 2004). Moving through the plaza on one of two teams would have engendered a coordination of action on a scale that far exceeded the earlier games of children in courtyards. It may have united a disparate series of familial and village-based groups into uniform, and perhaps dual, corporate identities.

Playing chunkey also would have positioned the game's action—and the bodies of the players in general—in the cosmological dramas of old, in turn set in the spaces of greater Cahokia's mounds and plazas. Ancient legends of hero twins who played a game against the forces of the underworld may have found new currency in Cahokia's up-scaled chunkey matches (see Pauketat 2004, 2005). The identities of teams—Cahokians versus others—may have emerged, overlaid on the earlier less polarized ones. Those identities now may have entailed the invention of new traditions or the imagining of new memories to bring new immigrants, visiting families, or disparate families and village identities into alignment with the ancestors of Cahokians.

In short, in playing the game in the grand spaces of Cahokia and its outliers, people would have participated in an ancient drama rich with cosmological imagery. The game recapitulated the creation of the cosmos and placed into new perspective the opposing dualisms: life and death, day and night, sky and earth, and male and female. The disciplining of bodies in this way aligned certain emotions and physiological functions of the body with the new realities of Cahokian society and the Cahokian *axis mundi*. Given the scale of the early Cahokian festivals—where thousands of people gathered to work on monuments, smoke tobacco, feast, sing, and dance—the disciplining of bodies via the chunkey game would have had profound historical implications.

Similarly, we must acknowledge that the players would have brought their own rules, memories, and religious meanings to bear on the sporting events of the day. In this way, the movement of the hundreds to thousands of bodies—at once or in sequence, building up a genealogy of winners and losers—through the plaza spaces virtually created or re-created the cosmos.

The Phenomenology of Pots

At these same events, Cahokians probably distributed medicinal potions and foods ceremonially to ritual participants (Emerson 1989). Indeed, we have previously argued that "Ramey Incised" jars—deep, blackened, burnished, sharp-shouldered earthenware containers with restricted orifices—were twelfth-century objects produced by a few potters at Cahokia and its outliers for use in communal rituals (Pauketat and Emerson 1991). These were not "elite" wares, strictly speaking, since they appear to have been relatively unrestricted in their usage (save their decreasing availability with distance from Cahokia). However, they did bear standardized decorative motifs in symmetrical design fields.

Ramey iconography was both focused and homogeneous (Emerson 1989, 1997a, 1997b; Pauketat and Emerson 1991). Fully 65 percent of the motifs can be related to the imagery of the sky world, while the remaining 35 percent appear to connote the earth/fertility motifs of mounds and underworld deities (Emerson 1997a, 1997b). Viewed from above, as one would if presenting, accepting, or using the vessel, the motifs were arrayed about the exterior of the in-turned jar rim as symmetrical pairs, giving the design field both a dualistic and quadrilateral pattern. When firing the jar, the potter often seems to have allowed the vessel's slip to oxidize to a reddish color around the jar lip, while the rest of the pot's body was smudged black. Thus, color symbolism and the imagery of the decorative motifs bespeak a vessel laden with meaning.

In the case of the Ramey Incised jar, however, what the pot "meant" was inextricably linked to "how" it meant it. First, the biography of the pot—who made it, what clay was used, who presented it as a gift, what it contained, who received it, and who used it (and in front of whom)—would have been among the most meaningful associations of each vessel. Thereafter, however, the bodily movements involved in accessing the contents of the pot were also meaningful (Pauketat and Emerson 1991; see Figure 10.3). Consider that the pot, made of earth and containing solids or liquids possibly associated with the earth or underworld, was accessed by passing through the decorated red-and-black orifice. The user, in removing the contents through this meaning-laden, two-dimensional field, was in effect enacting the cosmological relationship between self (and any onlookers), the earthly realm, and the supernatural forces of the cosmos (the sky-world motifs set in their symmetrical field). In a sense, then, the Ramey Incised pot embodied the cosmos. In holding a Ramey pot, devotees possessed the entire cosmos in their hands.

Discussion

As noted, the history and the grand scale of Cahokia give it historical priority in our reconsideration of Mississippian religion. It was large and influential at a time when there was nothing quite like it elsewhere

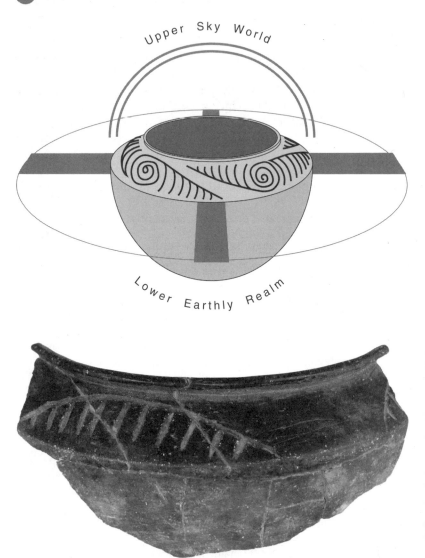

Figure 10.3 A schematic depiction of the Ramey vessel as cosmos (modified from Pauketat 2004) and an archaeological specimen of a Ramey vessel (photo by Linda Alexander, used with permission of ITARP, University of Illinois).

in the American mid-continent. The events of AD 1050 were not in fact restricted to greater Cahokia. A host of people in the late eleventh and twelfth centuries adopted, emulated, or avoided the Cahokian brand of Mississippianism—or "Cahokianism." It may thus be said that Cahokia had a "cultural ripple" effect across the varied peoples of the Eastern Woodlands (Pauketat and Emerson 1997). However, our approach to understanding this ripple effect is not to use the trappings of Cahokia to define a Mississippian belief system or a set of Southern Cult institutions that presumably would have been exported to the four corners of the Mississippian world. The historical process of the spread of religion instead is more complex than such a simple structural view of religion permits. Would not all American Indians, after all, have experienced religious phenomena in the same manner as did the early Cahokians? That is, they too would have participated in and actively reconstituted their religion through practices such as earth-moving, gaming, and using pots to cook, serve, and distribute comestibles. This being so, what would the archaeology of the religious experience of Mississippianization look like elsewhere? Probably like the various "localizations" identified by Emerson (1991).

Artifacts produced during the late eleventh and twelfth centuries by the predominantly Siouan-speaking peoples of the upper Midwest (and to a lesser extent the non-Siouan-speaking peoples of the interior Midsouth) included a few (sometimes hoarded) cultural objects from Cahokia, many more hybridized Cahokia-like objects made locally, and localized iconographic repertoires that served to parallel, emulate, or attempt to counter Cahokianism (see Emerson and Lewis 1991; Pauketat 2004; Stoltman 1991). For instance, after centuries of effigy-mound construction, the terminal Woodland peoples of Wisconsin, Iowa, and Minnesota seem to have abandoned the practice at or shortly after the mid-eleventh century AD, simultaneous with the intrusion of Cahokianism in the north (Stoltman and Christiansen 2000).

At that time, ostensibly Mississippian platform mounds appeared at several key northern sites, from the Collins site in east-central Illinois to Silvernale in southeastern Minnesota. These mounds were apparently modest adaptations of Cahokian monuments, and may have been surmounted not by elite housing but by modest religious temples holding the bones of ancestors. At around the same time, Cahokia chunkey stones and Ramey Incised pots appeared in small numbers among the northern Midwestern people, along with a few other calling cards of Cahokians (see summary in Pauketat 2004). Among these were the elaborate sculpted redstone images of Cahokia, produced around the American Bottom in the early twelfth century and widely dispersed across the upper Midwest and Midsouth (Emerson et al. 2002, 2003). These include depictions of gendered religious scenes and the supernatural forces of life and death (Figure 10.4).

What would have been the effect of such materializations of Cahokian ideas in the hands of a shaman in Wisconsin or an heir to chiefly office in Oklahoma? Can we assume that the thick polysemic imagery of such objects was readily interpreted by the recipient of such a gift in some far-off land?

Figure 10.4 A Cahokia female deity carved from the local red flint clay (photo by Linda Alexander, used with permission of ITARP, University of Illinois).

Perhaps the receipt of such a "piece of Cahokia" accompanied an elaborate adoption ritual or trade event (see Pauketat 2005). In the Mississippian past, such political-religious ceremonies might have created "fictions of kinship between the powerful leader of a large polity [Cahokia] and his political clients in outlying areas" (Hall 1991:33, citing Gibbon 1974). Such Cahokia-centric adoption rituals appear to explain the pan-midcontinental distribution of "Long-Nosed God" ear ornaments. These small, shield-shaped heads with long noses evoked the story of hero twins and the creation of the cosmos while serving patently political ends (see Hall 1989, 1991, 1997).

In any event, the adoption of Cahokianism was probably not accompanied by the creation of a uniform religious tradition or a series of Mississippian institutions even if that was the intent of Cahokians or their northern converts. In considering the materiality of Cahokianism and its likely historical effects across the Mississippi valley, Pauketat has recently concluded that:

> foreign visitors to Cahokia went home and, to the degree that they aspired to replicate what they had seen, overlaid to varying degrees the new Cahokian principles and cultural practices on to their local "traditional"

ones. They would have become, hence, the proselytizers for or missionaries of some new anomalous Cahokianism visibly emanating from the American Bottom. (2004:114)

But they did not succeed in transferring a belief system to far-off regions where historical circumstances were unlike those of the American Bottom.

Conclusions

Was the spread of any world religion over the centuries any different? Does the Pope in Rome make edicts because all Catholics already share the same understanding of Catholicism? Do Iranian ayatollahs or Iraqi clerics represent the views of all followers of Islam? Does a Hollywood actor who professes fervent beliefs in Buddhism embody those beliefs in the same way as Buddhist monks in Nepal? The answer to all of these questions is clearly no, because the religious meanings created through the localized practices of a seemingly widespread belief system are not the same. World religions take on local flavors and are syncretized with "traditional" beliefs, re-imagined and re-invented through practice (*sensu* Appadurai 1996).

Similarly, the Southern Cult of the Mississippians of the eleventh through sixteenth centuries was not one belief system, or even several regionally based belief systems. Belief systems are themselves projections, or political ideologies, either of the people whose interests were served by the notion of a shared common religion (e.g., Cahokians), or of present-day analysts who recognize patterns but lack the details of landscape construction, bodily movements, and object biographies that are necessary to come to grips with the historical processes that generated those patterns.

An archaeology of religion, as envisioned by Renfrew (1994) and others, remains to be pieced together. The case of Cahokia and the Southern Cult provides a beginning that permits us to imagine religion not as a system but as an experience. Such a re-imagining of an archaeology of the Southern Cult is not possible without looking beyond the imagery of elites. Such an archaeology of religion in general may not be possible without simultaneous archaeological control over local, regional, and pan-regional patterns of religious practice and representation. Both are impossible without theories that address the phenomenological principles currently expressed through theories of practice, performance, and landscape where human experiences are embodied, and the bodies of humans are intimately connected with the physical world of things and landscapes.

Religions are performed, projected, and negotiated. The Cahokians did not "believe" their religion, and the institutions did not define religion for people, per se. The sky realm and the powers of the earth were experienced, not merely idealized. Cahokians, like other American Indians, danced their religion. They constructed it, played it, held it in their hands, and gave it away.

References Cited

Appadurai, Arjun
1996   *Modernity at Large: Cultural Dimensions of Globalization.* University of Minnesota Press, Minneapolis.
Brose, David S.
1989   From the Southeastern Ceremonial Complex to the Southern Cult: "You Can't Tell the Players without a Program." In *The Southeastern Ceremonial Complex: Artifacts and Analysis*, edited by P. Galloway, pp. 27–37. University of Nebraska Press, Lincoln.
Brown, James A.
1975   Spiro Art and its Mortuary Context. In *Death and the Afterlife in Pre-Columbian America*, edited by E. P. Benson, pp. 1–32. Dumbarton Oaks Research Library and Collections, Washington, DC.
1976   The Southern Cult Reconsidered. *Midcontinental Journal of Archaeology* 1:115–135.
1985   The Mississippian Period. In *Ancient Art of the American Woodland Indians*, pp. 93–145. Harry N. Abrams, New York.
1989   On Style Divisions of the Southeastern Ceremonial Complex: A Revisionist Perspective. In *The Southeastern Ceremonial Complex: Artifacts and Analysis*, edited by Patricia Galloway, pp. 183–204. University of Nebraska Press, Lincoln.
1996   *The Spiro Ceremonial Center: The Archaeology of Arkansas Valley Caddoan Culture in Eastern Oklahoma.* Museum of Anthropology Memoir No. 29. 2 vols. University of Michigan, Ann Arbor.
Brown, Joseph E.
1977   *The Spiritual Legacy of the American Indian.* Crossroad Publishing, New York.
Culin, Stewart
1992   *Games of the North American Indians.* Originally published in 1907. University of Nebraska Press, Lincoln.
Dalan, Rinita A.
1997   The Construction of Mississippian Cahokia. In *Cahokia: Ideology And Domination in the Mississippian World*, edited by T. Pauketat and T. Emerson, pp. 89–102. University of Nebraska Press, Lincoln.
Dalan, Rinita A., George R. Holley, William I. Woods, Harold W. Watters, Jr., and John A. Koepke
2003   *Envisioning Cahokia: A Landscape Perspective.* Northern Illinois University Press, DeKalb.
DeBoer, Warren R.
1993   Like a Rolling Stone: The Chunkey Game and Political Organization in Eastern North America. *Southeastern Archaeology* 12:83–92.
Dobres, Marcia-Anne
2000   *Technology and Social Agency.* Blackwell, Oxford.
Emerson, Thomas E.
1989   Water, Serpents, and the Underworld: An Exploration into Cahokian Symbolism. In *The Southern Ceremonial Complex: Artifacts and Analysis*, edited by P. Galloway, pp. 45–92. University of Nebraska Press, Lincoln.
1991   Some Perspectives on Cahokia and the Northern Mississippian Expansion. In *Cahokia and the Hinterlands: Middle Mississippian Cultures of the Midwest*,

edited by T. Emerson and R. B. Lewis, pp. 221–236. University of Illinois Press, Urbana.

1997a *Cahokia and the Archaeology of Power*. University of Alabama Press, Tuscaloosa.

1997b Cahokia Elite Ideology and the Mississippian Cosmos. In *Cahokia: Ideology and Domination in the Mississippian World*, edited by T. Pauketat and T. Emerson, pp. 190–228. University of Nebraska Press, Lincoln.

2002 Chiefly Power, Priestly Temples, and Shamanistic Practices at Pre-Columbian Cahokia. Paper presented in The Rise of Priestly Societies symposium at the Annual Meeting of the American Anthropological Association, New Orleans.

2003a Materializing Cahokia Shamans. *Southeastern Archaeology* 22(2):135–154.

2003b Crossing Boundaries Between Worlds: Changing Beliefs and Mortuary Practices at Cahokia. In *A Deep-Time Perspective: Studies in Symbols, Meaning, and the Archaeological Record: Papers in Honor of Robert L. Hall*, edited by J. Richards and M. Fowler. The Wisconsin Archeologist 84(1–2):73–80.

Emerson, Thomas E., and R. Barry Lewis (editors)

1991 *Cahokia and the Hinterlands: Middle Mississippian Cultures of the Midwest*. University of Illinois Press, Urbana.

Emerson, Thomas E., Brad Koldehof, and Timothy Pauketat

2000 Serpents, Female Deities, and Fertility Symbolism in the Early Cahokian Countryside. In *Mounds, Modoc, and Mesoamerica: Papers in Honor of Melvin L. Fowler*, edited by Steven R. Ahler, pp. 511–522. Illinois State Museum, Scientific Papers, vol. 28. Springfield.

Emerson, Thomas E., Randall E. Hughes, Mary Hynes, and Sarah U. Wisseman

2002 Implications of Sourcing the Cahokia-Style Flint Clay Figures in the American Bottom and the Upper Mississippi River Valley. *Midcontinental Journal of Archaeology* 27(2):309–338.

2003 The Sourcing and Interpretation of Cahokia-Style Figures in the Trans-Mississippi South and Southeast. *American Antiquity* 68(2):287–314.

Emerson, Thomas E., and Timothy R. Pauketat

2002 Embodying Power and Resistance at Cahokia. In *The Dynamics of Power*, edited by M. O'Donovan, pp. 105–125. Center for Archaeological Investigations, Occasional Paper No. 30. Southern Illinois University, Carbondale.

Foucault, Michel

1979 *Discipline and Punish: The Birth of the Prison*. Vintage Books, New York.

Fowler, Melvin L.

1997 *The Cahokia Atlas: A Historical Atlas of Cahokia Archaeology, Revised*. Studies in Archaeology No. 2. Illinois Transportation Archaeology Research Program, University of Illinois, Urbana-Champaign.

Fowler, Melvin L., Jerome Rose, Barbara Vander Leest, and Steven A. Ahler

1999 *The Mound 72 Area: Dedicated and Sacred Space in Early Cahokia*. Illinois State Museum, Reports of Investigations No. 54. Springfield.

Galloway, Patricia (editor)

1989 *The Southeastern Ceremonial Complex: Artifacts and Analysis*. University of Nebraska Press, Lincoln.

Gibbon, Guy E.

1974 A Model of Mississippian Development and its Implications for the Red Wing Area. In *Aspects of Upper Great Lakes Anthropology*, edited by E. Johnson, pp. 129–137. Minnesota Prehistoric Archaeology Series 11. Minneapolis.

Hall, Robert L.

1977 An Anthropocentric Perspective for Eastern United States Prehistory. *American Antiquity* 42:499–518.

1989 The Cultural Background of Mississippian Symbolism. In *The Southeastern Ceremonial Complex: Artifacts and Analysis*, edited by P. Galloway, pp. 239–278. University of Nebraska Press, Lincoln.

1991   Cahokia Identity and Interaction models of Cahokia Mississippian. In *Cahokia and the Hinterlands: Middle Mississippian Cultures of the Midwest*, edited by T. E. Emerson and R. B. Lewis, pp. 3–34. University of Illinois Press, Urbana.

1997   *The Archaeology of the Soul: North American Indian Belief and Ritual.* University of Illinois Press, Urbana.

Hodder, Ian, and Craig Cessford

2004   Daily Practice and Social Memory at Catalhöyük. *American Antiquity* 69(1):17–40.

Howard, James H.

1968   The Southern Ceremonial Complex and its Interpretations. *Missouri Archaeological Society*, Memoir 6, Columbia.

Hudson, Charles

1976   *The Southeastern Indians.* University of Tennessee Press, Knoxville.

1984   *Elements of Southeastern Indian Religion.* E. J. Brill, Leiden.

Kelly, John E.

1990   The Emergence of Mississippian Culture in the American Bottom Region. In *The Mississippian Emergence*, edited by B. Smith, pp. 113–152. Smithsonian Institution Press, Washington, DC.

Kertzer, David I.

1988   *Ritual, Politics and Power.* Yale University Press, New Haven, Connecticut.

Knight, Vernon J., Jr.

1986   The Institutional Organization of Mississippian Religion. *American Antiquity* 51(4):675–687.

1989   Symbolism of Mississippian Mounds. In *Powhatan's Mantle, Indians in the Colonial Southeast*, edited by P. H. Wood, G. A. Waselkov, and M. T. Hatley, pp. 279–291. University of Nebraska, Lincoln.

2006   Farewell to the Southeastern Ceremonial Complex. *Southeastern Archaeology* 25(1):1–5.

Knight, Vernon J., Jr., James A. Brown, and George E. Lankford

2001   On the Subject Matter of Southeastern Ceremonial Complex Art. *Southeastern Archaeology* 20(2):129–141.

Meskell, Lynn M., and Rosemary A. Joyce

2003   *Embodied Lives: Figuring Ancient Maya and Egyptian Experience.* Routledge, London.

Moore, Clarence B.

1905   Certain Aboriginal Remains from the Black Warrior River. *Journal of the Academy of Natural Sciences of Philadelphia* 13:5–170.

1907   Moundville Revisited. *Journal of the Academy of Natural Sciences of Philadelphia* 13:336–405.

Moorehead, Warren K.

1932   *Etowah Papers: Exploration of the Etowah Site in Georgia.* Yale University Press, New Haven, Connecticut.

Muller, Jon

1966   Archaeological Analysis of Art Styles. *Tennessee Archaeologist* 22(1):25–39.

1989   The Southern Cult. In *The Southeastern Ceremonial Complex: Artifacts and Analysis*, edited by P. Galloway, pp. 11–26. University of Nebraska Press, Lincoln.

Pauketat, Timothy R.

1993   *Temples for Cahokia Lords: Preston Holder's 1955–1956 Excavations of Kunnemann Mound.* Museum of Anthropology, University of Michigan, Memoir No. 26. Ann Arbor.

1998   Refiguring the Archaeology of Greater Cahokia. *Journal of Archaeological Research* 6:45–89.

2000   The Tragedy of the Commoners. In *Agency in Archaeology*, edited by Marcia-Anne Dobres and John Robb, pp. 113–129. Routledge, London.

2001a   A New Tradition in Archaeology. In *The Archaeology of Traditions: Agency and History Before and After Columbus*, edited by T. R. Pauketat, pp. 1–16. University Press of Florida, Gainesville.

2001b   Practice and History in Archaeology: An Emerging Paradigm. *Anthropological Theory* 1:73–98.

2003   Materiality and the Immaterial in Historical-Processual Archaeology. In *Essential Tensions in Archaeological Method and Theory*, edited by T. L. VanPool and C. S. VanPool, pp. 41–53. University of Utah Press, Salt Lake City.

2004   *Ancient Cahokia and the Mississippians*. Cambridge University Press, Cambridge.

2005   The Forgotten History of the Mississippians. In *North American Archaeology*, edited by T. R. Pauketat and D. D. Loren, pp. 187–212. Blackwell Press, Oxford.

Pauketat, Timothy R., and Susan M. Alt

2003   Mounds, Memory, and Contested Mississippian History. In *Archaeologies of Memory*, edited by R. Van Dyke and S. Alcock, pp. 151–179. Blackwell Press, Oxford.

Pauketat, Timothy R., and Thomas E. Emerson

1991   The Ideology of Authority and the Power of the Pot. *American Anthropologist* 93:919–941.

1997   Introduction: Domination and Ideology in the Mississippian World. In *Cahokia: Ideology and Domination in the Mississippian World*, edited by T. Pauketat and T. Emerson, pp. 1–29. University of Nebraska Press, Lincoln.

1999   The Representation of Hegemony as Community at Cahokia. In *Material Symbols: Culture and Economy in Prehistory*, edited by J. Robb, pp. 302–317. Occasional Paper No. 26. Southern Illinois University, Carbondale.

Pauketat, Timothy R., Lucretia S. Kelly, Gayle J. Fritz, Neal H. Lopinot, Scott Elias, and Eve Hargrave

2002   The Residues of Feasting and Public Ritual at Early Cahokia. *American Antiquity* 67(2):257–279.

Pauketat, Timothy R., and Brad Koldehoff

2002   Cahokian Ritual and the Ramey Field: New Insights from Old Collections. *Southeastern Archaeology* 21:79–91.

Pauketat, Timothy R., and Diana D. Loren

2005   Alternative Histories and North American Archaeology. In *North American Archaeology*, edited by T. R. Pauketat and D. D. Loren, pp. 1–29. Blackwell Press, Oxford.

Phillips, Philip, and James A. Brown

1978   *Pre-Columbian Shell Engravings from the Craig Mound at Spiro, Oklahoma*, Part 1. (Paperback edition). Peabody Museum Press, Cambridge.

1984   *Pre-Columbian Shell Engravings from the Craig Mound at Spiro, Oklahoma*, Part 2. (Paperback edition). Peabody Museum Press, Cambridge.

Renfrew, Colin

1994   The Archaeology of Religion. In *The Ancient Mind: Elements of Cognitive Archaeology*, edited by C. Renfrew and E. Zubrow, pp. 47–54. Cambridge University Press, Cambridge.

Sassaman, Kenneth E.

1998   Crafting Cultural Identity in Hunter-Gatherer Economies. In *Craft and Social Identity*, edited by C. Costin and R. Wright, pp. 93–107. Archeological Papers of the American Anthropological Association No. 8. Washington, DC.

Stoltman, James B. (editor)

1991   *New Perspectives on Cahokia: Views from the Periphery*. Prehistory Press, Madison.

Stoltman, James B., and George W. Christiansen

2000   The Late Woodland Stage in the Driftless Area of the Upper Mississippi Valley. In *Late Woodland Societies: Tradition and Transformation Across the Midcontinent*, edited by T. E. Emerson, D. L. McElrath, and A. C. Fortier, pp. 497–524. University of Nebraska Press, Lincoln.

Tilley, Christopher
1994   *A Phenomenology of Landscape: Places, Paths and Monuments.* Berg, Oxford.
Tuan, Yi-Fu
1977   *Space and Place: The Perspective of Experience.* University of Minnesota Press, Minneapolis.
Turner, Victor
1967   *The Forest of Symbols.* Cornell University Press, Ithaca.
Waring, Antonio J.
1968   The Southern Cult and Muskogean Ceremonial. In *The Waring Papers*, edited by S. Williams, pp. 30–69. Papers of the Peabody Museum of Archaeology and Ethnology 58. Harvard University, Peabody Museum, Cambridge.
Waring, Antonio J., and Preston Holder
1945   A Prehistoric Ceremonial Complex in the Southeastern United States. *American Anthropologist* 47(1):1–34.
Willoughby, Charles C.
1932   Notes on the History and Symbolism of the Muskhogeans and the People of Etowah. In *Etowah Papers: Explorations of the Etowah Site in Georgia*, edited by Warren K. Moorehead, pp. 7–105. Yale University Press, New Haven.
Witthoft, John
1949   *Green Corn Ceremonialism in the Eastern Woodlands.* University of Michigan Museum of Anthropology Occasional Publication No. 13. Ann Arbor.

DISCONTINUITY BETWEEN POLITICAL POWER AND RELIGIOUS STATUS: MOUNTAINS, POOLS, AND DRY ONES AMONG VENDA-SPEAKING CHIEFDOMS OF SOUTHERN AFRICA

Johannes H. N. Loubser

Like most traditionalists worldwide, traditional Venda-speaking people of southern Africa make a distinction, albeit not a rigid one, between mundane linear time and sacred cyclical time (cf. Eliade 1959). Whereas their recognition of linear time is crucial for the successful completion of everyday tasks, such as metal smelting or preparing food, their notions about cyclical time come to the forefront when recounting oral traditions or during ritual performances, public or private (though this does not negate the fact that technical tasks are accompanied by ritualized behaviors or that ritual ceremonies often involve matters of technological nature). Recognition of linear time allows traditionalists to acknowledge the existence of a more distant past (Figure 11.1a).

According to Singo Venda traditionalists, this distant past is replete with supernatural events, starting when a pool within a mountain cave gave birth to their first king, Nwali (Aschwanden 1982; Hodza and Fortune 1979; Wentzel 1983). The legendary Singo king Dimbanyika, son of Nwali, migrated south from Zimbabwe and crossed the Limpopo River to conquer Venda-speaking chiefdoms in the Soutpansberg Mountains. By beating a magical drum, known as Ngoma-Lungundu, the early warrior king of the Singo generated a sound that killed those autochthonous Venda people who dared resist this invasion (Mudau 1940). The drum of the Singo royalty retained its magical properties as long as it was kept suspended above the ground. Singo hegemony over a vast area south of the Limpopo River crumbled when this drum accidentally touched the ground during infighting between king Thoho-ya-Ndou and his brothers. This catastrophic event in early Venda history is believed to have angered the ancestor spirits, including Nwali, so much that they withdrew from their everyday involvement in the affairs of the Singo royalty. The dropping of the drum, Thoho-ya-Ndou's defeat in battle by the hands of his brothers, and his disappearance into Lake Fundudzi mark the termination of the supernatural period in Venda history.

Traditionalists among the Singo Venda believe that ever since the termination of the early period they can only access the supernatural through ritual and libations (Mudau 1940). Even though Singo traditionalists believe in a definite break from the supernatural past, they see the supernatural as keeping up with the present; the sacred normally intersects with the profane during annual ritual occasions (Blacking 1969). In terms of this underlying logic of cyclical sacred time, the final supernatural event in time would reflect the first (Figure 11.1a); many traditionalists among the Singo Venda believe in a millenarian fashion that Nwali would emerge from his mountain birthplace to reestablish the Singo Empire when the world comes to an end (Gottschling 1905; Stayt 1931).

Like traditionalists elsewhere, traditional Venda people maintain that the distant past cannot be understood in terms of everyday processes that are known to operate in linear time. There are two main reasons for this belief. First, traditionalists see processes operating in the supernatural world, or in cyclical time, as ultimately responsible for historical events in this world of linear time (Figure 11.1a). Second, traditionalist oral histories represent the catastrophic collapse of early history as creating a barrier between early supernatural history and more recent mundane history. This catastrophist view of the past differs from the Enlightenment uniformitarian view, which holds that the same processes observed in recent linear time also apply to the remote past.

Materialist processual archaeologists use uniformitarian principles when they reconstruct prehistoric behavior in terms of ethnographic parallels (Figure 11.1b). However, materialist processual archaeologists tend to ignore the religious beliefs of indigenous traditionalists. Several reasons seem to explain their rejection of religious notions (see critiques in Whitley 1998). First, processual archaeologists see religious views as epiphenomenal and consequently as having indirect to no value for understanding past material processes, such as metallurgy or ceramic production. Second, for many processual archaeologists linear time and change in material cultures equal change in religion, especially considering the assumed dependence of religion on a material base. Third, many

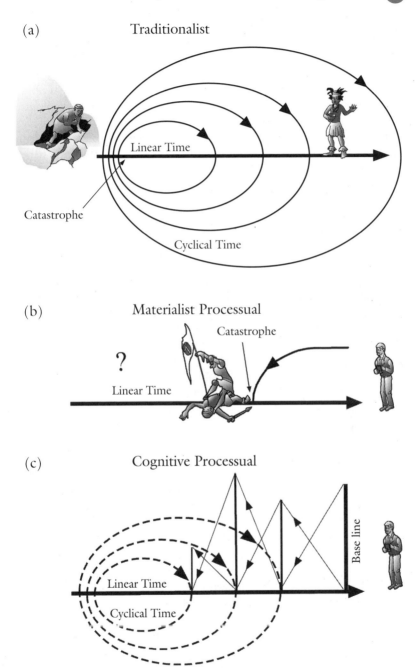

Figure 11.1 Different views of religion and time: (a) traditionalist, (b) materialist processual, and (c) cognitive processual.

processualists cite colonial conquest as a catastrophic event that created a barrier between history and prehistory. One result of this position is the processualist tendency to dismiss indigenous traditionalist accounts of the past as mere post hoc explanations.

Realizing that the traditionalist belief in cyclical time and ritual observance favors religious conservatism, cognitive processual archaeologists tend to emphasize the continuity of religious notions (Figure 11.1c). Within this paradigm the passing of time or change in material culture do not necessarily imply change in religion (e.g., Bloch 1977). Whereas cognitive archaeologists might accept a link between a material political-economic base and religion, the historical record suggests that religion has a relative autonomy and therefore does not necessarily change with shifts in the associated political economy. But the relative autonomy of religion does not mean that archaeologists can automatically project religious notions in the past or that they can uncritically assume that past religious notions are mirror images of the present; only by means of empirical investigation can cognitive processual archaeologists trace the continuity or discontinuity of religious views back into the remote past. Starting at a base line constructed from observed and documented ethnographic and historic sources, the cognitive archaeologist can look at the archaeological record for material points of similarity and difference. By "triangulating" back into the past in this fashion the archaeologist can construct secondary base lines, some of which might be similar to the starting line, while others might be radically different. I propose that this brand of cognitive processualism can map the relationship between political power and religious status among the Venda-speaking peoples back into prehistory.

Origin Stories and Burial Modes

Venda autonomy was terminated by the beginning of the twentieth century with the military subjugation of the last independent Singo ruler, chief Mpephu. Missionaries have had various degrees of success in converting traditionalist Venda to Christianity (Beuster 1879; Grundler 1899; Ralushai 1977). It might be erroneously assumed that conversions introduced a complete break from traditional religion conceptions. Moreover, population shifts and underdevelopment brought about by conquest, crop failures, epidemics, and migrant labor may be interpreted as introducing new religious notions among the Venda. For example, some scholars maintain that the Singo Venda peoples' account of their early history was influenced by other traditions and religions, ranging from Malawi origin stories (Wilson 1969) to the biblical account of Exodus (Wessmann 1908). According to these views the European subjugation of the Venda people brought about a change of catastrophic events that drove a wedge between the ethnographic present and the preconquest past. One outflow of such perspectives is that archaeologists can never hope to understand the proto- or prehistoric religion of the Venda. However, widespread similarities in core religious concepts among the Venda and neighboring groups, particularly the Shona of Zimbabwe and the Northern Sotho, suggest considerable antiquity. This is supported by similarities in religious customs as documented in accounts that predate mission work, conquest, and migrant labor (e.g., Beuster 1879; Da Silva Rego and Baxter 1962; Liesegang 1977).

Venda clans, or *mitupo* (singular *mutupo*), distinguish between themselves primarily by referring to their place of origin and by the way in which they bury their chiefs (Ralushai 1977). In this paper the following three *mitupo* are used as examples (simply because their practices and archaeology are best documented): the ruling Singo *mutupo* that inhabits the south-central, central, and southeastern Soutpansberg; the Mianzwi Mbedzi *mutupo* that inhabits the eastern Soutpansberg; and the Dzivhani Ngona neighbors of the Mianzwi Mbedzi (Figure 11.2).

The prominent Singo *mutupo*, whose members variously claim to come from Matangoni Mountain (Mudau 1940) or from Mbelengwa Mountain (Mudau 1940) in Zimbabwe, bury their chiefs within a mountain, or

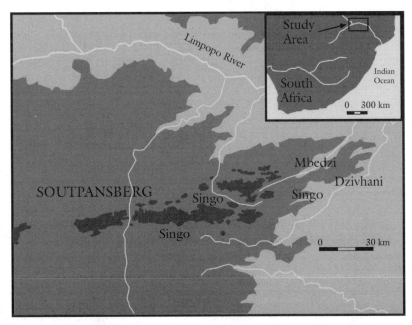

Figure 11.2 Map of the Soutpansberg region showing the location of the *mitupo* mentioned in the text.

thavha. Prior to the 1900s this burial location was within a mountain cave. After their conquest by the Boers, the Singo placed their deceased chiefs in a hut that is located on comparatively high ground behind the chief's stone-walled royal compound. Whether they bury their chiefs in a cave or in a hut, the Singo divide royal burial into distinct stages. An important component of all royal burials is to dehydrate the bodies of the deceased chiefs on a specially constructed platform and then collect the bones for final placement in the high-lying cave or hut (Ralushai 1977). It is said that a new chief has to swallow a river pebble that dropped from his dehydrated predecessor's stomach. According to tradition, this pebble initially came from a crocodile's stomach. The transmission of the pebble in this fashion symbolizes continuity of chieftainship.

The Mianzwi Mbedzi rainmaking *mutupo*, most of whose members claim to come from Manaledzi Pool in the central Mutale River valley, also bury their rulers in this pool. The Mbedzi first place the body of their deceased ruler in a shallow grave. After a while they exhume the bones and throw these directly into Manaledzi Pool. Other prominent *mitupo* with roughly equal status as the Mbedzi, such as the Tavhatsindi and Famadi, first cremate their deceased rulers before scattering the ashes into specific river pools, or *thivha*. In light of their origin stories and burial practices, it is perhaps not surprising that these people claim that they do not have a mountain; they claim that their mountain is a river pool (Ralushai 1977).

Venda people generally, and the Singo in particular, fear and try to avoid the Dzivhani Ngona *mutupo* from the Mutale River area. Dzivhani Ngona people do not like to talk about their place of origin and have no set burial mode for their leaders. Deceased Dzivhani rulers are typically placed in a hut or sacred grove outside their settlement. These locales are feared and avoided, especially by non-Ngona *mitupo*. Like other so-called Ngona groups in the Soutpansberg, these people have the lowest status among the Venda, but are nevertheless feared as powerful sorcerers (Ralushai 1977). Such Ngona groups are also known as "dry ones," or *zwiomo*.

The Dual Powers of Venda Chiefs as Expressed in Royal Settlements, Artifacts, and Oral Traditions

As a divine ruler who enjoys the supernatural sanction of the ancestor spirits, the death of a Singo chief is considered disruptive to the natural order. For this reason a chief's departure is kept secret from his followers (Mudau 1940). Hidden behind the stone walls that enclose the royal compound from the commoners' gaze farther downslope, the royal family and their functionaries try their utmost to conduct burial rites and succession disputes in private. Only once the departure of a deceased chief becomes known to the general populace and a successor is chosen, do the royalty block the entrance to the high-lying royal residence and make a new one within the stone wall barrier.

A Singo Venda chief has dual powers; one is political and the other ritual. A chief not only has ultimate control over political decision making, but he also officiates at annual renewal rituals (e.g., Kuper 1982). Political intrigue and decision making primarily occur on the comparatively private "mountain," or *thavha*, which is the high-lying area characterized by a labyrinthine network of stone walls (Figure 11.3). A public annual ancestral dedication ceremony, or renewal ritual, known as *tshikona*, occurs in the assembly area within a walled enclosure that is below and in front of the chief's "mountain." The assembly area, or *khoro*, is also known as a "pool," or *thivha*. It is here that premarital initiates are reborn during the *domba* (python) dance, very like the apical ancestors during creation (Blacking 1969).

In Venda and Shona cosmology a mountain is seen as male, hard, isolated, and consumptive (e.g., Lan 1985; Van Warmelo and Phophi 1948). The same people view a pool as female, soft, populated, and generative. The juxtaposition of the political/male sphere and the ritual/female sphere within the royal settlement, or *musanda*, is thus a spatial

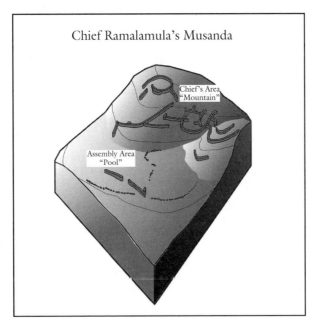

Figure 11.3 The distinction between "mountain" and "pool" in Chief Ramalamula's *musanda*.

expression of a chief's dual powers. These dual powers are also alluded to in stories about outside threats to the safety of the chief and his *musanda*. Medicated sticks or bullfrogs buried below the entrance to the assembly area are intended to deter malicious outsiders from entering the *musanda* (e.g., Davison 1984; Du Plessis 1945). These medicines are supposed to turn the assembly area into a pool that magically hides the chief's mountain within. However, if the intruder proves to be too strong for the medicines, the chief's mountain might disappear permanently inside the pool. This account is a metaphorical allusion to the fact that the chief can use his ritual potency to trick his enemies and so retain his political power. However, if the enemy proves too strong, the chief loses his "mountain," or political power, but retains his "pool," or ritual status.

The duality between politics/mountain and rituals/pool evident in royal settlements was also expressed at the much smaller physical scale of a royal artifact. This artifact is a carved wooden divination bowl (*ndilo*) that was stored within the chief's royal "mountain" quarters (Nettleton 1984). Use of such bowls apparently ceased in the early twentieth century. These bowls were used in public only when a big calamity threatened the well being of the entire chiefdom, such as during severe droughts or after a death caused by lightning. Venda informants say that when the chief's specially appointed diviner (*mungoma*) filled the bowl with water, then it represented a pool hiding the royal *musanda*; the submerged knob in the center of the bowl signified the chief's compound, or "mountain." Bas-relief motifs carved on the bottom of the bowl represented areas within the capital town (Figure 11.4a), such as the cattle byre. Relief motifs on the outside rim represented the different Venda clans. It is said that most people within the chiefdom, royals and commoners, were present in the public assembly when the bowl was used to divine the cause of misfortune. Zigzag and concentric rings carved on the underside of the bowl represented ancestor spirits who lived in the underworld below the assembly area, or "pool."

Just as when outsiders threaten the *musanda*, a divination bowl filled with water marks a crisis occasion when the chief's ritual, or "pool" role predominated over his political, or "mountain" role. The self-similarity between the royal settlement and the royal bowl demonstrates the ubiquity of the symbolic opposition between mountain-related politics and pool-related rituals. Soapstone bowl fragments with zebra and cattle motifs carved around the exterior of bowls from the 700-year-old hill ruins of Great Zimbabwe (Summers 1971) are reminiscent of the divination bowls of Venda royals (Figure 11.4b). The discovery of these fragments within prehistoric royal quarters suggests that divination and associated beliefs have considerable antiquity. It is interesting that ceramic similarities and Venda oral histories strongly suggest a link between the Singo chiefs and vestiges of the Zimbabwe empire of Shona-speakers.

(a)

(b)

Figure 11.4 (a) Carved wooden *ndilo* divination bowl from the Soutpansberg, (b) carved soapstone bowl fragment from Great Zimbabwe.

The dual powers of powerful Venda chiefs, or kings, are also expressed in oral traditions of the early supernatural period recalled by Singo traditionalists. Like powerful Shona chiefs, the powerful Singo king Dimbanyika subjugated the indigenous Soutpansberg communities by stepping like a giant from one mountain top to the next (Blacking 1969). When the ambitious Dimbanyika "overstepped" at Tshiendeulu Mountain (Figure 11.5a) and incurred the wrath of his sons, it is said that he disappeared in the mountain (some say that his resentful sons trapped him in the cave). Whether the mountain spontaneously fell on the king or whether ambitious princes set a trap (Dzivhani 1940; Motenda 1940), this story is reminiscent of euphemistic references among the Shona and Venda to the death of a chief as "the mountain has fallen." Some Venda insist that Dimbanyika still lives within a cave in the mountain, and like his father Nwali, would one day emerge to reestablish Singo hegemony. Certain caves that formed in weathered sandy and clayey sedimentary layers within the quartzite formations of the Soutpansberg contain streams and pools. Such mountains with pools are indeed apt natural models of chiefly political power that contains ritual potency.

Dimbanyika's son, commonly remembered as Thoho-ya-Ndou, expanded Singo rule throughout the Soutpansberg and beyond. His jealous brothers opposed his rule and with the assistance of local Venda chiefs they created a unified front that proved too powerful for Thoho-ya-Ndou. In a legendary battle near Lake Fundudzi (Figure 11.5b), they defeated Thoho-ya-Ndou and he reputedly disappeared into the lake. His watery death is a variation of Shona and Venda stories of chiefs, or "mountains," who are overcome by pools and so lose their dominant political position but retain their ritual potency. It is interesting to note that Lake Fundudzi was actually formed when a mountain next to the Mutale River valley collapsed along an unstable fault-line and so blocked the flow of the river. This small lake, or large river pool, is an apt landscape metaphor for political decline and retention

(a)

(b)

Figure 11.5 (a) Tshiendeulu Mountain, reputed burial place of Singo kings in the early eighteenth century, (b) Lake Fundudzi in the upper Mutale River valley.

of ritual status. Like at specific river pools elsewhere in the Soutpansberg, the mountain inside Lake Fundudzi is said to rise above water level during annual *tshikona* ceremonies (e.g., Stayt 1931). Descendants who visit these pools not only claim to see the old capital town of their former chiefs on the rising mountain, but also hear the sounds of drums, flutes, and sheep. Overall, at these annual ceremonies on the edge of river pools or within abandoned assembly areas, participants appear to commemorate and reactivate the former glory of their ancestors.

Although Thoho-ya-Ndou's departure marked the end of an extensive Singo trade-based polity centered on Dzata in the Nzhelele Valley, this did not end Singo political expansion in the Soutpansberg, bearing in mind that Thoho-ya-Ndou's brothers established their own dynasties in different portions of the region. Based on royal genealogies recalled in oral histories, the collapse of the Singo Empire occurred around AD 1750 (Loubser 1990). Descendants of the Tshivhase Singo dynasty in the eastern Soutpansberg eventually conquered the Mianzwi Mbedzi under the Luvhimbi dynasty of rainmakers in the nineteenth century (Ralushai 1978). Prior to the Singo conquest, the Luvhimbi chiefs were prominent players in long-distance trade with the Indian Ocean. After the Singo conquest the main sister of the last Luvhimbi chief took over as leader of the Mianzwi Mbedzi. This sister became an influential rainmaker for the Tshivhase Singo chiefs and also a ritual functionary at Singo premarital *domba* ceremonies. It is said that when they were conquered by the Singo, the Mbedzi *musanda* turned into a pool (Blacking 1969). Ever since the death of the last male Luvhimbi chief, his sister and her descendants, known collectively by the dynastic name of Tshisinavhute, were buried in Manaledzi Pool, not far from their *musanda* in the Mutale River valley.

During my archaeological fieldwork in 1986, the then current headwoman Tshisinavhute revealed to me that her male ancestors were buried in a sacred grove on Tswingoni Mountain (Figure 11.6) and not within Manaledzi Pool as mentioned in documented oral histories. I also learned that Tshisinavhute, who was married to a Tshivhase Singo chief, had political ambitions and wished to be buried in the mountain grove of her Luvhimbi male ancestors instead of Manaledzi Pool of her female predecessors.

On the opposite, southern side of Tswingoni Mountain, descendants of the Dzivhani Ngona told me that they once lived near Tswingoni and Tshilavhulu Mountains in the Mutale River valley. It is intriguing that the Dzivhani remember Tshilavhulu Mountain as "the pool of water" and as a former burial place of their early chiefs. The ruins of the earliest recalled *musanda* of the early Mbedzi Luvhimbi chief in the Soutpansberg is also located on Tshilavhulu Mountain. Although not mentioned explicitly by informants, this implies that the Mbedzi replaced the Ngona at the Tshilavhulu Mountain settlement. Moreover, certain published Mianzwi

Figure 11.6 Headwoman Tshisinavhute at the Tshitaka-tsha-Makoleni Ruins on the slopes of Tswingoni Mountain.

Mbedzi oral histories claim that they did not originate from the local Manaledzi Pool, but came from the more distant Malungudzi Mountain in Zimbabwe to the north of the Limpopo River (Ralushai 1978).

On closer scrutiny then, Dzivhani and Mbedzi informants acknowledge origins and burial locales that differ from commonly mentioned ones. It is argued here that this ostensible incompatibility in traditions actually reflects changes in political power and ritual status of the Mbedzi and Dzivhani. The archaeological record, furthermore, reflects these changes and gives dates as to when they most likely occurred.

The Archaeological Record

According to the "long chronology" of the most detailed royal Singo genealogies (e.g., Van Warmelo 1932), the Singo rulers had settled in the Nzhelele River valley of the central Soutpansberg by the late seventeenth century (Loubser 1991). Radiocarbon dates from Dzata, the first Singo capital town in the Soutpansberg and center of the Singo trading empire, support the "long chronology." A few Khami type ceramics with diagnostic chevron designs occur at Dzata and its satellite towns in the Soutpansberg (Figure 11.7). These ceramics are similar to seventeenth-century ceramics made by Shona-speaking communities in Zimbabwe.

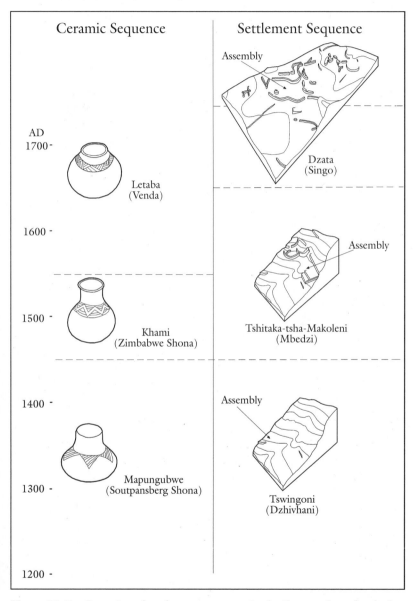

Figure 11.7 Ceramic and settlement sequence in the Soutpansberg for the last 800 years.

The appearance of the Khami ceramics alongside indigenous Letaba-type ceramics at Dzata and contemporary sites in the Soutpansberg accordingly implies an influx of people from the north and therefore supports those Singo accounts that claim origins in Zimbabwe. It is during their reign at Dzata that the Singo buried their powerful kings in Tshiendeulu Mountain. The abnormally big size of Dzata (20 hectares) and the concentration of ivory and other long-distance trade items at the site support oral recollections of it being a prominent capital town. The big assembly area suggests that it was an important ritual center as well. The concentration of walls at the back and higher portion of the settlement represented the "mountain" where the Singo king resided, whereas the clean-swept assembly area lower down the gradual slope represented the "pool" where subjects from across a widespread area attended rituals such as *tshikona* and *domba*.

The Letaba style pots found at Dzata and its satellite towns developed locally in the Soutpansberg area from existing Shona and Sotho ceramic traditions. The earliest Letaba pots come from sites such as Tshitaka-tsha-Makoleni, former capital town of the Luvhimbi Mbedzi dynasty. According to radiocarbon assays of associated charcoal, the earliest Letaba ceramics date to the mid-sixteenth century (Figure 11.7). Since Letaba ceramics are closely associated with sites known to have been occupied by Venda speakers and are still made by Venda-speaking potters today, the development of these ceramics most probably marks the emergence of the Venda language as it is spoken today (Letaba pots combine elements of Soutpansberg Shona motifs and Sotho shapes, the Venda language combines elements of Shona grammar and Sotho vocabulary). The presence of Letaba pots at the Mbedzi capital show that they probably spoke Venda prior to the arrival of the Singo, as indeed mentioned in some oral histories (Motenda 1940; Mudau 1940). But the Zimbabwe style ruins of Tshitaka-tsha-Makoleni also contain Khami type pottery from Zimbabwe, features that support those origin stories that mention the Mbedzi as migrating from north of the Limpopo River (Ralushai 1978). Located on the comparatively steep slope of Tswingoni Mountain, the walls of Tshitaka-tsha-Makoleni contain a "mountain" residence for the chief and his functionaries and an assembly "pool" area that is slightly lower down (Figure 11.7). The mid-sixteenth-century date for the stone-walled capital is probably later than the arrival of the Luvhimbi dynasty from Zimbabwe, since the earliest Luvhimbi chiefs lived at Tshilavulu Mountain prior to their construction of Tshitaka-tsha-Makoleni.

Deposits directly underneath the stone walls and associated Khami and Letaba ceramics at Tshitaka-tsha-Makoleni contain an earlier ceramic style known as Mapungubwe. These Mapungubwe ceramics occur in layers that have been dated to between the late thirteenth and mid-sixteenth centuries.

The layers have far fewer walls than the Mbedzi period occupation but some terraced walls lower down the slope date to the Mapungubwe period occupation of Tswingoni Mountain (Figure 11.7). As at other prominent Mapungubwe period sites in the Soutpansberg and Limpopo River valley, terraced walls separate the assembly area from the royal area on the uphill side (e.g., Huffman 1986).

The Dzivhani Ngona people are the most likely candidates to have lived at Tswingoni Mountain prior to the arrival of the Mbedzi, including on Tshilavulu Mountain not far north of Tswingoni Mountain. If the Dzivhani claim that their former chiefs were buried on Tshilavhulu Mountain is true, then the burials must predate the settlement of the Mbedzi immigrants on the mountain. Judging from the ceramic and radiocarbon record at Tswingoni, Dzivhani occupation must be associated with Mapungbwe ceramics that predate the sixteenth century. Historians and linguists associate Mapungubwe ceramics with very old Shona-speaking inhabitants of the Soutpansberg area, and the so-called Ngona people such as the Dzivhani are descendants of these autochthones (Beach 1980; Ehret 1972). The more prominent Mapungubwe sites in the region have yielded evidence of "mountain" burials, assembly areas, and long-distance trade items from the coastal trade (Loubser 1991). Even though Mapungbwe period walls are comparatively scarce and simple, the mountain/pool dichotomy still seems to be present within Mapungbwe settlements that date back to the middle of the twelfth century. Prior to this date, which marks the beginning of a fully fledged long-distance trading empire centered on Mapungubwe Hill, mountain burials seem to be absent (Gardiner 1963).

Status Misrepresented as Stasis

Variants of the mountain/pool symbolism as outlined above are present among most Bantu-speaking groups in sub-Equatorial Africa, but this dichotomy is perhaps nowhere as pronounced and elaborate as among the Venda and Shona-speaking peoples of far northern South Africa and Zimbabwe. According to the archaeological record this belief system can be traced back for nine centuries in the Soutpansberg. A change in the burial location from mountain to pool can be interpreted as indicative of a change in belief, however. Yet, the ethnographic record unequivocally shows that the two burial modes are part of the same belief system that is acted out on the landscape; mountain burials demonstrate ancestrally sanctioned political power, whereas pool burials accentuate religious potency. Internal logic, oral historical recollections, and archaeological evidence show that this is not a static system but a dynamic process. This process not only accentuates the ruling group's current status and presents it as eternal, but it also masks the previous status of subverted groups.

The pool within the mountain signifies the religious potential of a political ruler; a defeated chief without a mountain retains or even enlarges his/her pool status and normally becomes an important ritual functionary for a new ruler (Figure 11.8a). The mountain within the pool signifies the political potential of the conquered chief; through renewed alliances with

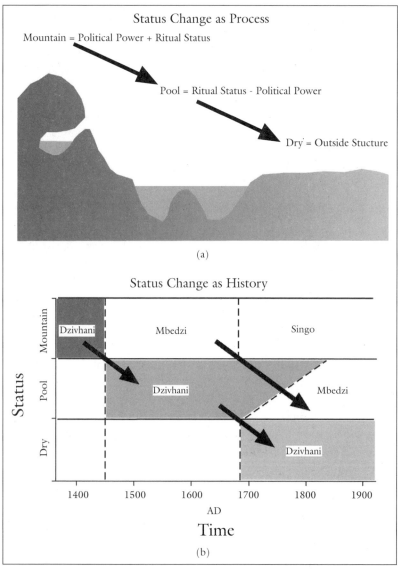

Figure 11.8   (a) Status change as process, (b) status change as history.

the current rulers a ritual functionary can always work his/her way back up the political system to regain mountain status. The case of the Mianzwi Mbedzi female rainmaker dynasty is but one of the better documented examples that illustrate this notion. However, a ruler without a mountain or a pool is outside this system and has no potential for upward mobility. The leaders of the Dzivhani Ngona are one of many such ambivalent figures in the Soutpansberg who live outside the periphery of the Venda political system. Yet, these seemingly powerless and impotent rulers, also known as "dry ones," or *zwiomo*, are feared and avoided by mountain and pool leaders. One reason for this respect for the weak lies in changing political fortunes during historic and prehistoric times.

Archaeological evidence and certain oral testimonies indicate that the ancestors of the Dzivhani Ngona once occupied at least two prominent mountain-slope settlements in the Mutale River valley—Tshilavhulu Mountain and Tswingoni Mountain. Based on the comparatively big size of these Dzivhani settlements and recollections of their chiefs being buried in these mountain locations, the Dzivhani probably were once powerful rulers in the region (Figure 11.8b). Dzivhani rule lasted until the Mbedzi immigrants from Zimbabwe settled in the Mutale valley some 500 years ago. Subjugated by the Mbedzi, the Tshilavhulu Mountain of the Dzivhani changed into a "pool of water." The Mbedzi first ruled from Tshilavhulu and later from Tswingoni Mountain until they in turn were subjugated by the eastern Singo Tshivhase dynasty in the nineteenth century. With their loss of political power and mountain status, the Mbedzi rulers were relegated to pool status. At the same time the Dzivhani lost their pool status to become the "dry ones."

When traditionalists view status grades in terms of cyclical time alone, without consideration of politico-religious process or linear time, status grades appear as divinely ordained juxtaposed units (Figure 11.8a). However, viewed in terms of politico-religious process and punctuated linear time, status grades resemble stratified geological layers with an underlying dynamic (Figure 11.8b). In the latter sense, status grades among the Venda *mitupo* are a function of relative antiquity; those at the bottom of the hierarchy are the oldest. But the oldest are also in a sense the most potent, considering that they have the most intricate link with the land and its spirits. Perhaps in tacit recognition of the Dzivhani Ngona's previous power, the ruling Singo people respect and fear these autochthonous people. Another reason why the Singo and their allies fear the various Ngona groups is that these ousted people no longer fall within commonly recognized politico-religious boundaries. Metaphorical allusions among the Venda emphasize the notion of socially acceptable boundaries; in the court language of Singo royals a chief is called a crocodile that does not leave its pool, whereas Ngona rulers are generally seen as anomalous crocodiles, or sorcerers, wandering about on dry land (Nettleton 1984). Such allusions to mountains, pools, and crocodiles are indeed ancient; they are part of the same religious system that has informed the settlement layouts and burial practices of peoples that have lived on both sides of the Limpopo River for the last 900 years.

Acknowledgments

This paper is based on fieldwork I conducted among the Venda-speaking people of the Soutpansberg between 1984 and 1986. I would like to thank the inhabitants of this area for the hospitality and assistance that they spontaneously provided in so many different ways. The South African Human Sciences Research Council, Henry Bradlow Scholarship, Rusterholz Memorial Scholarship, and University of the Witwatersrand Senior Bursary are thanked for their financial assistance. I appreciate that Joe Joseph, President of New South Associates, Inc., supported my attendance at the Society of American Archaeology in Montreal, Quebec. My gratitude is also due to David Whitley for asking me to contribute to this volume as well as for his pioneering theoretical and organizational contributions towards studying religion in archaeological contexts.

References Cited

Aschwanden, H.
1982   *Symbols of Life*. Mambo Press, Gwelo.
Beach, D. N.
1980   *The Shona and Zimbabwe AD 1000–1850*. Mambo Press, Gwelo.
Beuster, C. L.
1879   Das Volk der Vavenda. *Zeitschrift fur Geschichte Erdkunde* 14:236–240.
Blacking, J.
1969   Songs, Dances, Mimes, and Symbolism of Venda Girls' Initiation Schools: Part 1, Vhusha; Part 2, Milayo; Part 3, Domba; Part 4, The Great Domba Song. *African Studies* 28:28–35, 69–118, 149–199, 215–266.
Bloch, M.
1977   The Disconnection Between Power and Rank As a Process: An Outline of the Development of Kingdoms in Central Madagascar. In *The Evolution of Social Systems*, edited by J. Friedman and M. J. Rowlands, pp. 303–340. Duckworth, London.
Da Silva Rego, A., and T. W. Baxter (editors)
1962   *Documents on the Portuguese in Mozambique and Central Africa, 1497–1840*. Vol. 1, 2, and 3. National Archives of Rhodesia and Nyasaland, Lisbon.
Davison, P.
1984   Lobedu Material Culture. *Annals of the South African Museum*. 94:41–201.
Du Plessis, H.
1945   Die Territoriale Organisasie van die Venda. *African Studies* 4:122–127.

Dzivhani, S. M.
1940   The Chiefs of Venda. In *The Copper Miners of Musina and the Early History of the Soutpansberg*, edited by N. J. Van Warmelo, pp. 33–50. Ethnological Publications No. 8. Government Printer, Pretoria.
Ehret, C.
1972   Outlining Southern African Prehistory: A Re-Evaluation AD 10–1500. *Ufahamu* 3:9–27.
Eliade, M.
1959   *The Sacred and Profane*. ET Harcourt, Brace, and World, New York.
Gardiner, G. A.
1963   *Mapungubwe (Vol. 2)*. Van Schaik, Pretoria.
Gottschling, E.
1905   The Bawenda: A Sketch of their History and Customs. *Journal of the Royal Anthropological Institute* 35:365–386.
Grundler, W.
1899   *Geschichte der Bawenda-Mission in Nord-Transvaal*. Berlin. Buchhandlung der Berliner Evangelischen Missionsgesellschaft.
Hodza, A., and G. Fortune
1979   *Shona Praise Poetry*. Clarendon Press, Oxford.
Huffman, T. N.
1986   Iron Age Settlement Patterns and the Origins of Class Distinction in Southern Africa. *Advances in World Archaeology* 5:291–338.
Kuper, A.
1982   *Wives for Cattle: Bridewealth and Marriage in Southern Africa*. Routledge and Kegan Paul, London.
Lan, D.
1985   *Guns and Rain: Guerrillas and Spirit Mediumship in Zimbabwe*. James Currey, London.
Liesegang, G.
1977   New Light on Venda Traditions: Mahumane's Account of 1730. *History in Africa* 4:163–181.
Loubser, J.
1990   Oral Traditions, Archaeology, and the History of Venda Mitupo. *African Studies* 49:13–42.
1991   The Ethnoarchaeology of Venda-Speakers in Southern Africa. *Navorsinge van die Nasionale Museum, Bloemfontein* 7:145–464.
Motenda, M. M.
1940   History of the Western Venda and of the Lemba. In *The Copper Miners of Musina and the Early History of the Soutpansberg*, edited by N. J. Van Warmelo, pp. 51–70. Ethnological Publications No. 8. Government Printer, Pretoria.
Mudau, E.
1940   Ngoma-Lungundu and the Early Invaders of the Venda. In *The Copper Miners of Musina and the Early History of the Soutpansberg*, edited by N. J. Van Warmelo, pp. 10–32. Ethnological Publications No. 8. Government Printer, Pretoria.
Nettleton, A. C. E.
1984   The Traditional Figurative Woodcarving of the Shona and Venda. Unpublished Ph.D. dissertation, University of the Witwatersrand, Johannesburg.
Ralushai, V. N. M. N.
1977   Conflicting Accounts of Venda History with Particular Reference to the Role of the *Mutupo* in the Social Organization. Unpublished Ph.D. dissertation, Queens University, Belfast.
1978   Further Traditions Concerning Luvhimbi and the Mbedzi. *Rhodesian History* 9:1–12.

Stayt, H.
1931   *The Bavenda.* Oxford University Press, London.
Summers, R.
1971   *Ancient Ruins and Civilisations of Southern Africa.* T. V. Bulpin, Cape Town.
Van Warmelo, N. J.
1932   *Contributions Towards Venda History, Religion, and Tribal Ritual.* Ethnological
Publications No. 3. Government Printer, Pretoria.
Van Warmelo, N. J., and W. W. Phophi
1948   *Venda Law: Part 1, Betrothal.* Ethnological Publications No. 23. Government
Printer, Pretoria.
Wentzel, P. J.
1983   *The Relationship Between Venda and Western Shona 3.* University of South Africa,
Pretoria.
Wessmann, R.
1908   *The Bawenda of the Spelonken.* African World, London.
Whitley, D. S.
1998   *Reader in Archaeological Theory: Post-Processual and Cognitive Approaches.*
Routledge, London.
Wilson, M.
1969   The Sotho, Venda, and Tsonga. In *The Oxford History of South Africa*, edited by
M. Wilson and L. Thompson, pp. 131–182. Clarendon Press, Oxford.

SHRINES OF THE LAND AND PLACES OF POWER: RELIGION AND THE TRANSITION TO FARMING IN WESTERN EUROPE

Chris Scarre

"To the minds of the lower races it seems that all nature is possessed, pervaded, crowded, with spiritual beings."

E. B. Tylor, *Primitive Culture* (1871)

Thus, in language characteristic of the period, did anthropologist Sir Edward Tylor 130 years ago describe the beliefs that he labeled animism, and that have particularly been associated with hunter-gatherer societies in the ethnographic record. Like shamanism, with which it is closely related, animism might all too easily be considered an early or pristine form of human religion. As Hultkrantz has observed, however, shamanism is not itself the religion of any "primitive" society, but rather is a set of practices "to establish means of contact with the supernatural world by the ecstatic experiences of a professional and inspired intermediary, the shaman" (Hultkrantz 1996:4, quoted in Jordan 2001). Animism, likewise, may be considered not a religion but a set of beliefs about the world. Matthias Guenther, for example, states that "hunter-gatherers regard nature as pervasively animated with moral, mystical and mythical significance; there is a 'hovering closeness of the world of myth to the actual world'" (1999:426).

In an important recent study of the Nayaka of southern India, Nurit Bird-David (1999) has sought to locate the basis for animistic beliefs in a set of social relationships. Her primary conclusion is not so much that these communities project their own image of society onto the animate and inanimate world, as that they seek to enter into sharing relationships with salient or relevant features of their world, whether alive (like plants or animals) or inanimate (such as rocks or hills). The Nayaka refer to the spirits in question as *devaru*:

> The devaru objectify sharing relationships between Nayaka and other beings. A hill devaru, say, objectifies Nayaka relationships with the hill; it makes known the relationships between Nayaka and that hill. Nayaka maintain social relationships with other beings not because, as Tylor holds, they a priori consider them persons. *As and when* and *because* they engage in and maintain relationships with other beings, they constitute them as kinds of person: they make them "relatives" by sharing with them and thus make them persons. (Bird-David 1999:S.73)

As Bird-David makes clear, it is not every rock or plant that is a *devaru*, but only those that manifest themselves to humans by certain actions. A stone, for example, that was said to have jumped onto the lap of a woman resting in the forest was considered a *devaru* and was brought home to the village and placed on a mud platform among the houses. But the many other stones lying nearby were not considered alive in this way; they did nothing to manifest themselves or enter into relationship with human actors.

If Bird-David is right, then this kind of animistic belief may be peculiar to the kind of social sharing that is characteristic of most hunter-gatherer societies. The animism involves an anthropomorphization of apparently inanimate things (along with animate plants and animals) but in the specific sense of social interaction. The *devaru* brought back to the village are invited to feasts and are conversed with during certain ceremonies.

The significance of such animistic practices has, I believe, been only tangentially considered in archaeological research. There is indeed a major methodological problem, since the attribution of life to an inanimate object would be difficult to determine unless that object were modified in some way. Hence most archaeological reference to what has been called the "numinous landscape" has confined itself to general observations about the likely importance of specific locales such as springs, trees, and caves. Numerous ethnographic accounts indicate that such features were commonly held to be places of special significance. This significance— this manner of reading the landscape—does however extend far beyond hunter-gatherer societies.

My archaeological examples will be drawn from western Europe. Indeed, my main focus is to understand the changes in belief systems that accompanied or may even have underpinned the transition from hunting and gathering to farming in the Atlantic zone, from Portugal to Scandinavia. The most conspicuous surviving indicators of the new farming communities are without question the various categories of field monument: enclosures marked by ditches and banks; circles and rows of upright timber posts and standing stones; burial mounds containing or covering chambers of timber or stone with multiple inhumations. In some areas of western Europe these monuments are so numerous that they must have been widely apparent throughout the whole of the landscape; they created a pervasive cultural landscape. Yet it is unlikely that they entirely replaced previous understandings based on the sacred character accorded to unmodified features and locales. So one part of my enquiry seeks to establish in what ways the new constructions may have related to existing understandings of a numinous landscape "possessed, pervaded, crowded, with spiritual beings," to quote Tylor again (1871).

A second question concerns the specific materialities of the new constructions. Many are of timber, earth, or chalk, but others again are characterized by the deployment of extravagantly large "megalithic" blocks. This feature has long intrigued antiquarians and archaeologists, but attempts to explain why this particular use of massive and often unshaped blocks was so prevalent have hitherto been unpersuasive. My argument is that the significance of megalithic construction relates closely to the qualities—symbolic as much as physical—of the megalithic slabs themselves, and the sacred character of the outcrops or boulder scatters from which they were taken. They might thus have provided a direct link between the "old" understandings of a numinous or animistic landscape and the "new" understandings of culturally constructed places.

Places of Power and Shrines of the Land

African ethnography provides several examples that illustrate the overlapping yet distinct meanings associated with natural places and cultural monuments. A number of ethnographers working among traditional societies in central and southern Africa have drawn a distinction between "places of power" associated with nature spirits and "shrines of the land" dedicated to ancestral spirits. Elizabeth Colson expresses the distinction as follows:

> Places of power are permanent features of the landscape regarded as inherently sacred or as the loci of spiritual power. If they are associated with particular named spirits rather than generic spirits or unpersonified force, these spirits are usually mythologized as ancient heroes who existed before present political units or communities came into existence or they are conceived of as spiritual forces of non-human origin. (1997:48)

Land shrines, unlike places of power, are built by humans and the spirits commonly associated with them are the spirits of those reputed to have first settled the locality or to have subsequently conquered and ruled it. They require offerings from those who now occupy their places, and adherence to routines established by themselves ... They represent ... the continuity of human life forces, not the power inherent in nature. (1997:52)

Places of power throughout Africa typically take the form of prominent landscape features such as mountains, cliffs, caves, pools, waterfalls, hot springs, and large trees. Such "places" are not restricted to Africa, but are widely encountered in the ethnographic literature of Australia, North America, and northern Europe (e.g., Basso 1996; Drucker 1951; Helskog 1999; Morphy 1991). In some instances, acoustic or other sensory properties may contribute to the sense of place, but such features cannot adequately explain why some cliffs or trees are regarded as sacred while others are not. Places of power are generally isolated from areas of everyday activity, and may in part represent the religious significance of the "wild" for subsistence farmers. In Africa, they are loci of ritual danger and are to be approached cautiously, usually by delegations or pilgrims guided by mediums or priests (Colson 1997:51). In broad cross-cultural perspective they resemble the kinds of landscape location regarded as sacred by hunter-gatherer societies (though by other societies also), and it is possible therefore that we may deduce from them a continuity of landscape understanding and belief. These sacred landscape features are associated with powerful spirits that sometimes act on behalf of local communities: thus the Agole mountain god in northern Ghana sent a swarm of bees to ward off raiders from a neighboring community and thereby protected the local people (Mather 2003:53).

Shrines of the land, by contrast, are human-made, and are associated with particular named individuals or ancestors. These shrines may take the form of a small hut in which offerings can be left. In northern Ghana, however, they consist of large stones set into the ground, sometimes beside natural features but often at the compounds of village founders. Thus they are ancestor-shrines, providing a memorial of common origin for the members of a community (Mather 2003:33).

The distinction between "places of power" and "shrines of the land" may be less clear cut than these accounts suggest (T. Insoll, personal communication 2004), but they do provide a valuable venue for thinking about the distinction between humanly created shrines and natural features of the landscape to which special powers or significances are attributed. The opposition between natural places and humanly created shrines is not absolute but can be broken down. This happens where founding lineages seek to establish a claim to the land by forging a special relationship with the local spirits or deities. Mather describes the shrine of the land god Akasong in the settlement of Zorse in northern Ghana.

This shrine takes the form of a large stone set in the ground at the foot of an enormous baobab tree. The stone was placed in front of the compound established by the founder of the settlement, and this founder was buried next to the land god's shrine.

> The association of the stone and the grave illustrates the melding of land and social groups represented by the land gods. The spirit of the land is fused with the spirit of the founding ancestor, and this provides the ultimate rationalization for establishing and maintaining reciprocal relations with the land ... the land god is, at least in part, infused with the spirit of the apical ancestor of the residents of Zorse. (Mather 2003:33)

Mather goes on to explain this fusion of land gods and ancestors as part of a domestication process:

> The anthropomorphism of land gods is part of an overall strategy of domestication, of integrating land and spiritual forces within human communities. Enshrinement is the initial stage in this strategy. The living can negotiate with an enshrined spirit, whereas an unenshrined spirit is impossible to predict and capricious, tries to create discord, and is largely beyond human influence ... Enshrinement bridges the divide between the "wild" and the "house," giving the living opportunity to influence the spiritual causes of physical events and circumstances. (Ibid., 40–41)

The proposal, then, is that the human-made land shrines overlie and partially incorporate an earlier set of sacred meanings that were not marked by permanent human action. As Mather puts it, "the natural features comprising 'places of power' exist prior to and independent of humans, while the constituent parts of 'shrines of the land' exist as a result of human activity and interaction" (2003:40). Places of power are in essence timeless places, formed by natural forces prior to human occupation; they commemorate the initial covenant between the founders of human settlement and the spirit of the land. Yet, alongside their timelessness, there is a distinct sense of chronological precedence; they were the original sacred places, before human communities began specifically to build shrines or monuments.

It is interesting to note that a similar layering of belief and sacred significance is to be found in the central highlands of Madagascar. Kus and Raharijaona (1998) have recounted how, for the Merina, the boulders that litter the countryside are the result of a mythical battle between Earth and Sky. An alternative or more specific belief associates stones with the Vazimba, the original inhabitants of the land who were replaced by the Merina. Some traditions suggest that these people were hunter-gatherers; other details suggest to Western commentators that they were dryland farmers and herders displaced by wet rice agriculturalists. Vazimba are associated with boulders in streams and boulders that mark the locations of springs. Boulders lying on valley floors are also sometimes associated with Vazimba, but usually involve a wetland connection (such as the presence of a marshland plant), referring to the belief that Vazimba can live underwater. The Merina respect and avoid these boulders, leaving around them an undisturbed area at least 5 meters across (Kus and Raharijaona 1998:54).

In contrast to these natural, unmodified stones associated with Vazimba are the many stone monuments erected by the Merina themselves (Figure 12.1). These include standing stones in the countryside or at village entrances, stones used to line the edges of sunken cattle corrals, or stones used to build the collective tombs for which the Merina are particularly famous.

Thus once again on Madagascar we find a distinction between natural, unmodified landscape features (in this case, boulders) and human constructions in which the symbolism of stone is used in an entirely different way. Furthermore, the ethnographic accounts suggest that here also the sacred places of an initial or natural order have been succeeded or overlain by a secondary order of human-built shrines and monuments. This need not represent a single event, however, nor need it be a manifestation of a universal process. In part it conforms to a more general and continuous process of reincorporation and reworking, in which natural and cultural features are subject to reinterpretation by succeeding generations, whether of hunter-gatherers or farmers. What is significant is that the construction of enduring cultural features such as monuments is associated much more frequently with farmers.

Megalithic Monuments and the Cult of Stones

The many hundreds of megalithic monuments that dot the landscapes of western Europe from Scandinavia to the Mediterranean have naturally invited a wide variety of approaches and explanations since they first attracted the attention and wonderment of antiquarians in the seventeenth and eighteenth centuries. A century ago, debate raged as to whether these monuments might have been built by "a single race in an immense migration or series of migrations" (Peet 1912:152) or were instead testimony to the spread of a megalithic "influence" (Peake and Fleure 1929:5). In 1940, Gordon Childe put forward the notion of a "megalithic religion," its content almost unknown, but lying behind the construction of elaborate tombs in the various regions of western Europe. The distribution of tombs, he argued, predominantly along the coasts and radiating from coastal ports, indicated the channels of the

Figure 12.1 Orthostat marking tomb of village founder, Merina (Madagsacar) (photo by R. Joussaume).

religion's propagation and the area of its domain (Childe 1940:46). The subsequent reaction against such diffusionist notions set aside the cultic associations of these monuments in order to propose that megalithic monuments and related structures might have arisen independently in several different areas of western Europe through processes of parallel social development. A key part of that argument was the chronological association between these monuments and the transition to farming. The monuments were seen as having served as territorial markers and statements of land rights, especially the tombs, in which the collective remains of community ancestors were interred (Renfrew 1976). Subsequent structuralist and marxist interpretations also focused on the social significance of the tombs and the collective burial practices (Shanks and Tilley 1982).

It is only within the last 15 years that renewed attention has been paid to the specific character of the monuments, and in particular the practice of megalithic construction and the manner in which this creates links between the monuments and the surrounding landscape (Bradley 1998, 2000; Scarre 2002; Tilley 1994, 1996). At the same time, there has been a new interest in the archaeology of natural places—the western European prehistoric equivalents of the "places of power" of African ethnography. The major methodological difficulty is to determine the significance of landscape features that by definition may not have been altered by human action. A persuasive case may sometimes be made, however notably, where monuments in the surrounding landscape appear to make reference, by their form, location, or orientation, or through their materials, to prominent features such as ridges or distant mountains (Cummings 2002; Tilley 1994).

These approaches have the significant advantage of regarding the monuments as elements of a sacred geography, one that extended beyond human-built structures to include features of the natural world. It is in this context that a possible equivalence between the African notions of places of power and shrines of the land suggest itself. The megalithic monuments of western Europe, like shrines of the land, may be invoking the agency of founder-ancestors or of spirits or deities with which they had become associated. Mountains, rocks, and springs may conversely have been places of power.

This simple equivalence, however, does not fully address the symbolism of materials, and most especially the symbolism of the oversized stones used in megalithic construction. Here it must be at once admitted that many western European monuments of this period were built of earth and timber, or of dry-stone blocks of more manageable proportions. Megalithic construction was not universal, and megalithic monuments themselves frequently incorporated earth, timber, and dry-stone alongside the megalithic elements. Yet the particularity—or peculiarity—of using massive stone slabs necessarily raises specific questions about the symbolism of stone. Individual elements may weigh 30 or more tons and though most of these slabs were taken from sources in the immediate vicinity of the monuments (Thorpe and Williams-Thorpe 1991), a few cases involved the transport of blocks over much greater distances. The most extreme example is the Stonehenge bluestones, brought 130 miles from South Wales (Green 1997). Such long-distance transport suggests that the source of the stone may in itself have been highly significant. Two further observations strengthen this argument. First, most megalithic monuments consist of unmodified blocks that have not been further shaped or smoothed once they were detached from the parent material. Second, some monuments incorporate stone slabs taken from a number of different sources, that may be distinguished by qualities of color or texture. Studies show that such slabs are incorporated in intentionally patterned ways, employing, for example, principles of alternation and symmetry (Scarre 2004).

This careful and specific way in which the megalithic slabs were handled and arranged is emphasized by their impressive size and their sometimes striking shape, color, and texture. Together, these features suggest that qualities perceived to lie in the individual stone slabs were a powerful reason behind the adoption of megalithic architecture. We may doubt Childe's model of a "megalithic religion" spread by missionaries, but the distribution of megalithic monuments in contiguous areas of western Europe argues that they may indeed be the result of a shared set of understandings and beliefs. That they are interrelated is further supported by their chronology, which indicates that the first megalithic tombs in Iberia and northwest France date to the mid fifth millennium BC, while in Britain, Ireland, and northern Europe the sequence of monument construction began a few centuries later, shortly after 4000 BC.

Throughout most of this large region, the construction of monuments began within a few centuries of the introduction of pottery, cereals, and domestic animals; they coincide with the transition from hunting and gathering to farming and food production. The nature of the transition continues to be the subject of considerable debate, with some arguing for the movement of colonist farmers and others proposing exclusively acculturationist models, in which indigenous communities adopted the various elements of the new lifestyle from farming neighbors who had already made the transition. Recent studies of human genetics have been unable to resolve the issue, indicating only that Near Eastern genetic markers become progressively less significant from eastern to western Europe (Chikhi et al. 2002). At the same time, isotope studies of skeletal remains of early farmers in the Rhineland have suggested that early farming communities in that region may have combined individuals of varied geographical origin, perhaps representing the incorporation of indigenous hunter-gatherers as well as immigrant farmers in the new farming communities (Bentley et al. 2002).

The western and northwestern fringes of Europe, where the megalithic monuments are found, are the areas with the strongest argument for continuity of population across the foraging to farming transition. This is shown, for example, by the evidence for social and mortuary complexity among the final hunter-gatherer communities of Portugal, Brittany, and southern Scandinavia. Thus the origin of the shared understandings that lay behind the selection and use of massive megalithic blocks may perhaps be sought among these hunter-gatherer communities. It was perhaps in their mythology or cosmology that the significance of certain boulders or rock outcrops developed a salient importance, as the dwellings or indeed the materialization of spirits. We may suppose, then, an animistic understanding of the many crags and boulders that characterized the landscapes upon which megalithic monuments subsequently came to be built. The megalithic monuments, in taking stones from places of "natural" power, represent a reworking or reinterpretation of earlier beliefs similar perhaps to the overlay of human-built structures—shrines of the land—onto an ancient pattern of unmodified sacred locales—places of power.

What the individual stones used in megalithic monuments may represent can be explored further through ethnography and folklore. In Madagascar, standing stones are known as *vatolahy* or "man stones" (Parker Pearson and Ramilisonina 1998). They are erected to commemorate well-known individuals or those who have died away from home and whose bodies cannot be returned for burial in the communal tomb. They often appear to be identified with individual ancestors. The identification of standing stones with people is recorded in numerous folk tales, and relates both to the mystery of the megalithic structures—inviting mythological and often moralizing explanations—and to the general shape of the stones: frequently tall and narrow, and easily envisaged as fossilized humans.

One such tradition concerns the Merry Maidens, a circle of standing stones in southwest Britain:

> One Sabbath evening some thoughtless maidens of the neighbouring village, instead of attending vespers, strayed into the fields, and two evil spirits, assuming the guise of pipers, began to play some dance tunes. The young people yielded to the temptation; and, forgetting the holy day, commenced dancing. The excitement increased with the exercise, and soon the music and the dance became extremely wild; when, lo! A flash of lightning from the clear sky, transfixed them all, the tempters and the tempted, and there in stone they stand. (Hunt 1856)

Another attributes the Carnac stone rows of southern Brittany (Figure 12.2) to an early Christian miracle:

> The inhabitants of Carnac ... say that Saint Corneille, whom they call Cornély, was pursued by a pagan army, and fled before them to save himself, until he arrived at the sea edge. There, finding no boat and on the point of being captured, he employed his saintly power and transformed into stones the soldiers who were thinking to seize him. (Mérimée 1836; author's translation)

These folklore traditions may have little to do with the original meaning of the stones, but they highlight the prevalence of anthropomorphism: the attribution of human qualities to animate and inanimate objects, which is a pervasive feature of all religion (Boyer 1996; Guthrie 1993). In the context of European megalithic monuments such anthropomorphism may take a more specific form, focusing on human-like details of particular stones. Thus George Smith, writing in 1752 of another British stone circle, Long Meg and her Daughters, observed rather scathingly that "the vulgar notion that the largest of these stones has breasts, and resembles the remainder of a female statue is caused by the whimsical irregularity of the figure, in which a fervid imagination may discover a resemblance of almost any thing." The process continues in recent years, with some claiming to see human faces in the stones of Stonehenge and Avebury (Meaden 1999).

Figure 12.2 The Carnac alignments of southern Brittany imagined as a petrified Roman army (F. Debret, early nineteenth century).

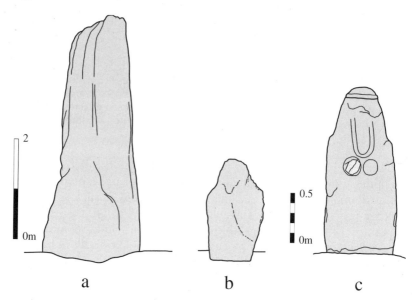

Figure 12.3 Anthropomorphism in Neolithic menhirs: (a) Lann-Saliou, Côtes-d'Armor (unshaped); (b) Ile Gaignog, Finistère (shouldered); (c) Le Câtel, Guernsey (statue-menhir); (a) after Marchat and Le Brozec, (b) after L'Helgouach, (c) after Shee-Twohig.

These instances underline the widespread human tendency to interpret large stones in anthropomorphic terms. The relevance of this observation to prehistoric beliefs is strengthened by the effective elision in northwest France between a small group of megalithic slabs that clearly bear human form and features, to those which have a "shouldered" shape suggesting the human form, and those which finally have no specific human features but may well have stood in a continuity of representation with the others (L'Helgouach 1993; see Figure 12.3). These date to the fifth and fourth millennia BC. Other stones, less human-like in overall form, bear rows of carved pairs of breasts, or enigmatic incised motifs, some of which may represent elements of the human body. Thus the idea that the megalithic slabs contain or embody human-like beings finds some direct support, though it should be noted that such carvings are restricted in geographical distribution and are absent from many areas of western Europe in which megalithic monuments are found.

An Evolution of Religion?

It remains to bring together the different strands of this argument and to consider the process of religious change. In seeking to understand the religious significance that lies behind the construction of megalithic monuments I have highlighted the relationship between the monuments themselves and the landscapes (and more particularly the landscape features) from which their materials were drawn. The careful selection of particular kinds of stone suggests that the specific sources may have been places of special significance. This may be coupled with the limited but suggestive evidence from iconography (carvings on or shaping of those stones) that appears to indicate that at least some of the stones were considered to embody or incorporate human-like powers or qualities. If we are allowed to speculate further, we may suggest that these stones were thought to be animate in some way.

This can be related directly to ethnographic evidence, which from Tylor onwards has indicated the widespread belief in a world "possessed, pervaded, crowded, with spiritual beings." The concept of "places of power" among African societies (and elsewhere) arises directly from such a belief. What I have sought to show here is how this kind of belief, anchored in landscape locales, may have been drawn upon and transformed in a way that makes sense of the predilection for using unshaped megalithic slabs. The process may indeed be analogous to the way in which "shrines of the land" in Africa sometimes draw upon "places of power" or the gods and spirits associated with the land to gain greater legitimacy.

What is suggested here is both a transformation and a sequence, in which unmodified places held sacred by previous generations are supplemented by the creation of human-built shrines by early farming communities. The limited or subtle anthropomorphism that can be observed in these megalithic structures may variously be interpreted as either the clearer manifestation and representation of existing beliefs about these stones or the development of new beliefs.

This scenario, in which a set of religious beliefs and practices widely associated with hunter-gatherers was enhanced by another widely associated with farming communities, raises the issue of religious evolution. Ethnographic and archaeological evidence is consistent with the view that animistic beliefs focusing on sacred places in the landscape remained an important feature after the agricultural transition. A number of studies have interpreted Neolithic imagery in terms of shamanistic practice and this too might be an example of the continuance of beliefs and practices of earlier origin (Bradley 1989; Dronfield 1996; Lewis-Williams and Dowson 1993;). Guenther associates shamanism (along with totemism) "typically (though not exclusively) with hunter-gatherer, and incipiently agricultural societies" (Guenther 1999).

While I have suggested an animistic interpretation, individual stones (especially those few carved and shaped examples) might equally represent ancestors. The commemoration and veneration of individual ancestors is widely associated with farming communities but does not appear to have been a widespread practice among hunter-gatherers. As an explanatory device within British archaeology, ancestors have attracted legitimate criticism in recent years (Whitley 2002), and it is clear that they must be invoked with greater caution than has sometimes hitherto been the case. Ethnographic literature does, however, support the general argument that ancestors become important to farming communities in legitimizing claims to land, in a way not found necessary among hunter-gatherers (Meillassoux 1972). This is not to say that ancestors were not important to hunter-gatherer societies also. The process I am proposing is not one of replacement but of reworking and addition, in which older beliefs and the places associated with them become part of a newer understanding, with a new emphasis on *created places*, among early farming societies.

The greater emphasis on ancestors, and possibly also the representation of deities (if that is what we are seeing in megalithic art) suggest, however, a significant innovation in belief. Does this, then represent a "stage" in the progressive evolution of religion? A number of earlier authors have viewed religious change in such a perspective. We may recall Tylor's words: "To the minds of the lower races it seems that all nature is possessed, pervaded, crowded, with spiritual beings" (1871:271). Tylor considered animism an erroneous understanding of the world held by primitive peoples who believed in a soul or spirit divisible from the physical body—a mistaken belief to be contrasted with scientific knowledge of the world. Bellah subsumed it within his category of "primitive religion," characterized by

> the very high degree to which the mythical world is related to the detailed features of the actual world. Not only is every clan and local group defined in terms of the ancestral progenitors and the mythical events of settlement, but virtually every mountain, rock and tree is explained in terms of the actions of mythical beings. (1964:362–363)

The concept of a unilinear sequence of "stages" of religion was widely held in the late nineteenth century but has fewer adherents today (Insoll 2004:42–46). Bellah interprets his successive stages of religion in terms not of the evolution of religious beliefs in themselves, but of society. This is an interpretation of religious change with which many archaeologists and anthropologists would feel more comfortable. We may recall how Bird-David (1999) interprets the animistic beliefs of the Nayaka of southern India as their attempt to enter into sharing relationships with salient or relevant features of their world, both animate and inanimate. It is essentially an extension of social relationships beyond the human community. Ancestor cults may be interpreted in similar terms, as a reflection of the social relationships within farming communities for whom kinship and descent were all-important.

The proposal then is not for a succession of religious "stages," in which animism and natural places precede ancestor-worship and human-built shrines. Such a succession would be simplistic and flawed. It is clear, for example, that hunter-gatherers do sometimes build shrines (e.g., the Inuit; see Vitebsky 1995), and it would be entirely misleading to consider the construction of monuments as the exclusive preserve of farming communities. In the European case, indeed, it is far from clear that the communities who built megalithic monuments during the fifth, fourth, and third millennia BC fit easily within the category of "farmers," since residential mobility may have remained a key feature of their lifestyle (Scarre 2001; Thomas 1999). It is also no part of my purpose to suggest that such singular forms of religion as animism or shamanism (insofar as they can be defined) should be correlated with particular prehistoric periods. Nor are these religious forms to be considered as mutually exclusive: there is no reason why animism and ancestors should not sit comfortably together. My argument focuses instead on continuity, accumulation, and reinterpretation, as new beliefs were added to old, and old beliefs subtly modified or reworked. It is through such a process of addition and modification that we may best seek to understand the megalithic monuments of western Europe, which draw so evidently on the powers of the land in the choice of materials that they use, and the particular forms that they espouse; yet they mark important processes of change, inscribing new beliefs on the landscape and creating new places of power by their scale and physical presence.

These monuments did not replace older understandings. On the contrary, they bound them together with newer socially embedded beliefs and concerns to create an interpretation of the world that probably shared much with that of previous generations, but was novel in its willingness to alter the landscape by the construction of monuments. The monuments may well have been associated with a growing concern with ancestors and genealogy, and we have noted the anthropomorphic qualities of some of the stones from which they were built. In that respect they may resemble the "shrines of the land" of African ethnography. There is, however, no need to argue for this specific distinction, since fundamentally both natural places and human-built monuments will have constituted "places of power" in their different ways. What is most intriguing is the way in which the monuments drew upon natural places in their use of materials such as stone, earth, and timber. In incorporating and reworking stone slabs and other elements that may already have been held significant by previous generations, these human-built monuments appropriated and reinterpreted the powers of natural places, creating new kinds of Neolithic meaning.

Acknowledgments

I wish first of all to thank David Whitley for inviting me to participate in the session "Faith in the Past: Theorizing the Archaeology of Religion" at the Montreal SAA meeting in April 2004 at which this paper was delivered. The published version has benefited greatly by comments from Tim Insoll, to whom I am particularly grateful for his careful reading of my original text. Attendance at the SAA meeting was made possible through the support of the McDonald Institute for Archaeological Research, Cambridge.

References Cited

Basso, K.
1996   Wisdom Sits in Places: Notes on a Western Apache Landscape. In *Senses of Place*, edited by S. Feld and K. Basso, 53–90. School of American Research Press, Santa Fe.
Bellah, R. N.
1964   Religious Evolution. *American Sociological Review* 29:358–374.
Bentley, R. A., T. D. Price, J. Lüning, D. Gronenborn, J. Wahl, and P. D. Fullagar
2002   Prehistoric Migration in Europe: Strontium Isotope Analysis of Early Neolithic Skeletons. *Current Anthropology* 43:799–804.
Bird-David, N.
1999   "Animism" Revisited: Personhood, Environment, and Relational Epistemology. *Current Anthropology* 40:S69–S91.
Boyer, P.
1996   What Makes Anthropomorphism Natural: Intuitive Ontology and Cultural Representations. *Journal of the Royal Anthropological Institute* 2:83–97.
Bradley, R.
1989   Deaths and Entrances: A Contextual Analysis of Megalithic Art. *Current Anthropology* 30:68–75.
1998   Ruined Buildings, Ruined Stones: Enclosures, Tombs and Natural Places in the Neolithic of South-West England. *World Archaeology* 30:13–22.
2000   *An Archaeology of Natural Places*. Routledge, London.
Chikhi, L., R. Nichols, G. Barbujani, and M. A. Beaumont
2002   Y Genetic Data Support the Neolithic Diffusion Model. *Proceedings of the National Academy of Sciences* 99:11008–11013.
Childe, V. G.
1940   *Prehistoric Communities of the British Isles*. W. and R. Chambers, London.
Colson, E.
1997   Places of Power and Shrines of the Land. *Paideuma* 43:47–57.
Cummings, V.
2002   All Cultural Things: Actual and Conceptual Monuments in the Neolithic of Western Britain. In *Monuments and Landscape in Atlantic Europe. Perception and Society During the Neolithic and Early Bronze Age*, edited by C. Scarre, pp. 107–121. Routledge, London.
Dronfield, J.
1996   Entering Alternative Realities: Cognition, Art and Architecture in Irish Passage-Tombs. *Cambridge Archaeological Journal* 6:37–72.
Drucker, P.
1951   *The Northern and Central Nootkan Tribes. Smithsonian Institution Bureau of American Ethnology Bulletin 144*. U.S. Government Printing Office, Washington, DC.

Green, C. P.
1997   The Provenance of Rocks Used in the Construction of Stonehenge. In *Science and Stonehenge*, edited by B. Cunliffe and C. Renfrew, pp. 257–270. Oxford University Press for the British Academy, Oxford.

Guenther, M.
1999   From Totemism to Shamanism: Hunter-Gatherer Contributions to World Mythology and Spirituality. In *The Cambridge Encyclopedia of Hunters and Gatherers*, edited by R. B. Lee and R. Daly, pp. 426–433. Cambridge University Press, Cambridge.

Guthrie, S. E.
1993   *Faces in the Clouds. A New Theory of Religion*. Oxford University Press, New York.

Helskog, K.
1999   The Shore Connection. Cognitive Landscape and Communication with Rock Carvings in Northernmost Europe. *Norwegian Archaeological Review* 32:73–94.

Hultkrantz, Åke
1996   Ecological and Phenomenological Aspects of Shamanism. In *Shamanism in Siberia*, edited by V. Diósvegi and M. Hoppál, pp. 27–58. Akadémiai Kiadó. Budapest.

Hunt, R.
1856   *Popular Romances in the West of England*. J. C. Hotten, London.

Insoll, T.
2004   *Archaeology, Ritual, Religion*. Routledge, London.

Jordan, P.
2001   The Materiality of Shamanism As a "World-View": Praxis, Artefacts and Landscape. In *The Archaeology of Shamanism*, edited by N. Price, pp. 87–104. Routledge, London.

Kus, S., and V. Raharijaona
1998   Between Earth and Sky There Are Only a Few Large Boulders: Sovereignty and Monumentality in Central Madagascar. *Journal of Anthropological Archaeology* 17:53–79.

Lewis-Williams, J. D., and T. A. Dowson
1993   On Vision and Power in the Neolithic: Evidence from the Decorated Monuments. *Current Anthropology* 34:55–65.

L'Helgouach, J.
1993   Du schématisme au réalisme dans la figuration anthropomorphe du mégalithisme armoricain. In *Les représentations humaines du néolithique á l' Age du Fer. Actes du 115e Congrès National des Sociétés Savantes (Avignon 1990)*, edited by J. Briard and A. Duval, pp. 9–19. Editions du Comité des Travaux historiques et scientifiques, Paris.

Mather, C.
2003   Shrines and the Domestication of Landscape. *Journal of Anthropological Research* 59:23–45.

Meaden, T.
1999   *The Secrets of the Avebury Stones*. Souvenir Press, London.

Meillassoux, C.
1972   From Reproduction to Production. *Economy and Society* 1:93–105.

Mérimée, P.
1836   *Notes de voyage dans l'ouest de la France*. Librairie du Fournier, Paris.

Morphy, H
1991   *Ancestral Connections: Art and Aboriginal Systems of Knowledge*. University of Chicago Press, Chicago.

Parker Pearson, M., and Ramilisonina
1998   Stonehenge for the Ancestors: The Stones Pass on the Message. *Antiquity* 72:308–326.

Peake, H., and H. J. Fleure
1929   *The Way of the Sea*. Clarendon Press, Oxford.
Peet, T. E.
1912   *Rough Stone Monuments and their Builders*. Harper and Brothers, London.
Renfrew, C.
1976   Megaliths, Territories and Populations. In *Acculturation and Continuity in Atlantic Europe*, edited by S. J. de Laet, pp. 198–220. De Tempel, Brugge.
Scarre, C.
2001   Modelling Prehistoric Populations: The Case of Neolithic Brittany. *Journal of Anthropological Archaeology* 20:283–313.
2002   A Place of Special Meaning: Interpreting Prehistoric Monuments in the Landscape. In *Inscribed Landscapes: marking and making place*, edited by B. David and M. Wilson, pp. 154–175. University of Hawai'i Press, Honolulu.
2004   Choosing Stones, Remembering Places: Geology and Intention in the Megalithic Monuments of Western Europe. In *Soils, Stones and Symbols*, edited by N. Boivin and M. A. Owoc, pp. 187–202. UCL Press, London.
Shanks, M. and C. Tilley
1982   Ideology, Symbolic Power and Ritual Communication: A Reinterpretation of Neolithic Mortuary Practices. In *Symbolic and Structural Archaeology*, edited by I. Hodder, pp. 129–154. Cambridge University Press, Cambridge.
Smith, G.
1752   Long Meg and her Daughters. *Gentleman's Magazine* 22:372.
Thomas, J.
1999   *Understanding the Neolithic*. Routledge, London.
Thorpe, R. S., and O. Williams-Thorpe
1991   The Myth of Long-Distance Megalithic Transport. *Antiquity* 65:64–73.
Tilley, C.
1994   *A Phenomenology of Landscape: Places, Paths and Monuments*. Berg, Oxford.
1996   The Power of Rocks: Topography and Monument Construction on Bodmin Moor. *World Archaeology* 28:161–176.
Tylor, E. B.
1871   *Primitive Culture: Researches into the Development of Mythology, Philosophy, Religion, Art, and Custom*. John Murray, London.
Vitebsky, P.
1995   *The Shaman*. Little, Brown, London.
Whitley, J.
2002   Too Many Ancestors. *Antiquity* 76:119–126.

NORTHERN LANDSCAPES, NORTHERN MIND: ON THE TRAIL OF AN *"ARCHAEOLOGY OF HUNTER-GATHERER BELIEF"*

Peter Jordan

"In fragile, birch-bark canoes, the Evenks moved with great mastery along the swift mountain rivers of the taiga ... the slightest negligence and the boat might be lost in the waves ... when he comes to a dangerous spot the Evenk, without fail, would throw something overboard as a sacrifice to the spirit, even if only a pinch of tobacco, because for him the concept of happiness and success consisted of a multitude of spirits, who were empowered to let him pass through 'their place' or to let him perish in the raging elements"

(Anisimov 1963:220–221)

Ethnographic descriptions of life in the north emphasize the centrality of human relations with the spirit world. Rivers, lakes and forests are inhabited by deities, and the fish, birds and game animals are owned and animated by powerful beings. In treading their way through life human persons cannot escape entanglement with these powerful presences, for northern spirituality isn't a formal religion that individuals may choose to worship or believe in. At the heart of this worldview is the constant, fearful and inescapable obligation to acknowledge and interact with the forces that make all life possible.

Anisimov's evocative account hints at the fragility of human existence in the Siberian taiga, but also captures the crucial requirement to tend *relationships* with the spirit world through repeated gestures of acknowledgment and respect. There are strikingly similar descriptions from across Fennoscandia, Siberia and North America, prompting speculation that many features of this distinctly northern worldview might stretch back into the deeper recesses of human prehistory. But what kinds of material traces might this fluid and socially-situated knowledge leave behind? Can archaeologists excavate the material expressions of pre-historic belief or amass only the more mundane evidence for diet and technology?

Across the discipline increasing numbers of archaeologists are now seeking to "humanise" their accounts of prehistory by grappling with the vexed question of prehistoric belief. In drawing on ethnographic insights, social theory and a wider range of interpretive methods their common desire is to move beyond empathy and imagination in order to find ways of comprehending more fully the material evidence for prehistoric cosmologies. While many of these efforts are laudable, it is also strik-ing that most contributors to the emerging "Archaeology of Religion" have tended to explore the roles of objects, built structures and landscape locations whose intrinsic cosmological significance is already well beyond doubt. As a consequence, current debate is less concerned with establish-ing that tombs, megaliths and temples might be the material expressions of some form of religion, and so greater energies are directed towards the more ambitious project of understanding the *specific* roles, meanings and embodied or "sensual" experiences of these places in past ritual practice. In this sense, the "Archaeology of Religion" is a project grounded on a general academic consensus that worldviews *can* be studied archaeo-logically. Disagreements only emerge when discussing *how* that research might proceed, or the level of detail that can be attained.

However, if we cast our gaze further it becomes clear that certain areas of the discipline continue to shy away from a more enthusiastic engage-ment with the study of past worldviews. In particular, hunter-gatherer archaeology remains one of the most curious anomalies to the wider "humanisation" of the past. The main aims of this chapter are to examine why research into prehistoric hunter-gatherer worldviews is still regarded as a rather questionable enterprise, and to signal how a more productive engagement with the topic might begin.

Several broad assumptions underpin the current approaches to hunter-gatherer archaeology: first, there is a lingering perception that prehistoric foragers—in contrast to farming populations—tended to be more mobile, maintained fewer fixed locations in the landscape, and left only limited material traces of their subsistence activities; second, because foragers were more directly dependant on the resources of the natural ecology their history is best envisaged as an adaptive response to changing envir-onmental settings. Finally, even if past hunter-gatherer societies practiced rituals, maintained beliefs and inhabited meaningful social worlds, these activities and perceptions would leave few, if any, material traces that might be identifiable archaeologically. For these reasons, excavations of hunter-gatherer deposits have tended to remain studies in the "archaeology of adaptation".

Interest in adaptation has also come to serve as a uniting feature of hunter-gatherers studies, and gives the field its coherence and distinct sense of identity (Ames 2004). However, the continuing dominance of this paradigm has also meant that other more social and symbolic aspects of forager behavior have seen much less attention (Kent 1996). Given these enduring research traditions what are the prospects for the development of an *"Archaeology of Hunter-gatherer Religion"*?

This chapter explores how the growing archaeological interest in religion might engage more fully with the hunter-gatherer archaeological record. One of the fundamental problems restraining further understanding of forager cosmologies is the poor ethnographic understanding of how the kinds of belief and ritual commonly practiced in hunter-gatherer settings might leave specific physical signatures. Archaeologists are simply not attuned to potential material articulations of forager belief, mainly through use of analytical models and explanatory vocabulary conditioned by primary emphasis on economy and adaptation (Jordan 2006).

The chapter opens with a brief review of hunter-gatherer studies, and examines why studies of adaptation have long overshadowed interest in more social and symbolic aspects of forager behavior. A case-study examines the characteristic worldview of hunting and gathering cultures in northern Eurasia, and explores how individuals articulate belief through narrative, seasonal movements, gifting ceremonies and ritual negotiation. The insights from these anecdotal accounts are 'scaled-up' to examine how activities in hunter-gatherer landscapes are structured by the scheduling of subsistence activities and also by cultural perceptions and ritual practices that generate distinctive material signatures. The chapter concludes with a summary of how further ethnographic work can contribute to the development of further research into the archaeology of northern spirituality.

The Archaeology of Hunter-Gatherers

General use of the term 'hunter-gatherer' is based on the assumption that populations subsisting on non-domesticated plant and animal resources will share characteristic features of economy, social organization and ideology. A broad distinction can be made between extensive ethnographic research into societies that hunt and gather, and the emergence of hunter-gatherer studies as a distinct sub-discipline of enquiry (Jordan 2008a).

The roots of the specialist field of hunter-gatherer research can be traced back to pioneering work of Julian Steward (1955) on 'cultural ecology' and to a series of conferences in the late 1960s "which had a tremendous impact on the anthropological view of hunter-gatherers ... and defined what was germane to know about them" (Binford 2001:21).

Steward's "cultural ecology" approach had a major influence on American scholarship in the 1950s and 1960s (Kelly 1995:43) and was attractive in proposing a natural science perspective on human behavior. This drew on 'materialist' explanations of human social life, which regarded extraction and control of material resources as the key determinant of broader patterns of behavior, especially amongst hunting and gathering societies, who were assumed to live in closest contact with natural ecosystems.

Early attempts to identify the universal features of hunter-gather adaptations led to major advances in the general understanding of foraging societies, their subsistence activities and social life (Lee and DeVore 1968), and also stimulated a new era of field research to collect the kinds of higher resolution data that was required to test new hypotheses. Eventually, the initial formulations of an archetypal foraging society were challenged by growing evidence for manifold variation in almost all domains of hunter-gatherer behavior. The core problem was that the basic economic definition of hunter-gatherers—populations reliant solely on non-domesticated plants and animals for subsistence—could also encompass immense variations in affluence and social complexity, as well as in territorial behavior, gender roles, health and diet (Bird David 1996).

Gradually, research interests shifted away from discussion of the typical behavior of archetypal foragers towards attempts to re-classify observed variations encompassed by the broader hunter-gatherer adaptation. A new series of "gross" categories was proposed, but importantly, analytical interest also shifted towards identification of the main factors generating these patterns of diversity (Kent 1996:1). While earlier work had employed the culture ecology framework to measure broader adaptive relationships between populations and environments (e.g., Lee 1969) later work shifted towards a behavioral ecology framework (Bettinger 1991; Kelly 1995; Winterhalder 2001; Winterhalder and Smith 1981). This deploys the assumption that humans will draw on an evolved rationality that promotes behaviors maximizing extraction of resources like calories at the lowest cost of time or energy expenditure (Bettinger 1991; Kelly 1995; Winterhalder 2001; Winterhalder and Smith 1981; Winterhalder and Smith 2000). Whether individuals actually conceive of the world in these terms is not of specific importance: the approach enables a rigorous and empirical assessment of the relative efficiency of different patterns of behavior, backed up with the general assumption that those selecting optimal patterns of behavior will tend to enjoy greater health and have more offspring. In contrast, less efficient strategies, and those individuals practicing them, will tend to decline and die off, especially in challenging northern environments with seasonal shortfalls of key resources.

Archaeologists also became increasingly interested in how materialist theories of behavior might improve understandings of long-term culture change (Trigger 1989). However, unlike anthropologists who could directly observe and measure different forms of human activity, archaeologists were left only with the static material remains. To resolve this problem archaeologists began to undertake their own ethnographic fieldwork in order to identify specific links between patterns of behavior and the likely material correlates (Binford 1977), a methodology broadly defined as 'middle range theory' (Binford 1981, David and Kramer 2001). Equipped with a diverse suite of insights archaeologists argued that they would eventually be able to reconstruct the behaviors that had generated the archaeological record, enabling the reconstruction of long term processes of culture change. Much early 'ethnoarchaeological' work focused heavily on the remaining hunter-gatherer societies in Africa and North America, concentrating, in particular, on key aspects of behavior, including site formation processes, settlement patterns and subsistence strategies. (see Binford 1978a, 1978b, 1980, 1982, 1987; David and Kramer 2001; Gamble and Boismier 1991; Gould and Yellen 1987; Kroll and Price 1991).

Classic ethnoarchaeological studies include Yellen's work amongst the !Kung San (Yellen 1977) in which he documented depositional behavior at campsites, and Binford's (1978b) study of "characteristic behaviors observed on [Nunamiut] hunting stands and the structured consequences of these behaviors in the archaeological record" (ibid 1978b:330). The legacy of this work is immense, and interests in ecology and evolution continue to dominate research into hunter-gatherer societies (Barnard 2004:6; David and Kramer 2001).

In hunter-gatherer studies the adaptive approach gradually began to endure critique from two main sources. First, the implicit assumption of many early culture ecology studies was that the remaining hunter-gatherer societies were optimal adaptations to local ecological settings. In this sense they were assumed to have survived as timeless and self-sufficient units from earlier periods of human history (Kelly 1995:47). Conclusions drawn from observations of their current patterns of behavior could easily be extrapolated back into the past in order to understand more general processes of human evolution. The main problem was that all recently documented hunting and gathering groups—and especially those of the Kalahari who were the focus of much early work—had endured extended histories of interaction with adjacent farming and pastoral societies. Some had even made repeated switches between foraging and other forms of subsistence, drawing in question whether these societies really did represent exemplars of an original form of human social life, or were perhaps better understood as recent products of colonial history and forager-farmer contact dynamics. Following the 'revisionist' critique hunter-gatherers now tend to be studied in wider regional and historical socio-political contexts (see Jordan 2008a, with references). Even though some continue to emphasize the integrity and cultural continuity of many hunter-gatherer groups (Barnard 2004:7), it is no longer standard practice to use modern foragers as direct analogies for the behavior of ancient humans and early hominids (Ames 2004:366).

The second source of criticism was that enduring "materialist" emphasis on adaptation was overshadowing a fuller "humanistic" understanding of other aspects of hunter-gatherer cultures (Kent 1996:17). In a series of papers Bird David (1990, 1992) explored underlying forager relationships with the environment, arguing persuasively that one of their core concerns is to maintain good and caring relationships with others and with the "giving environment" in which they live. Bird David (1996:302) later argued that "more attention should be given to symbolic worlds and worldviews" of hunter-gatherers, and notes that research into these themes lags far behind due to the comparative nature of the original hunter-gatherer project, which emphasized the importance of subsistence categories over expression of localized worldviews.

Despite critique from these two directions, archaeological research into hunter-gatherers remains heavily influenced by adaptive 'materialist' approaches to human behavior. While many would acknowledge symbolic dimensions to prehistoric forager behavior, the key question is whether these beliefs and subjective worldviews would actually generate material traces. We have an immense literature on the adaptive aspects of hunter-gatherer behavior (David and Kramer 2001), but without an accompanying suite of ethnoarchaeological studies demonstrating the material correlates to different forms of ritual activity we remain trapped into assuming that the archaeological record of hunter-gatherers reflects no more than community subsistence, with worldview a cognitive overlay on the world that is doomed to remain archaeologically invisible (Jordan 2006). As a result, hunter-gatherer archaeology has tended to remain the study of the spatial organization of economic activities.

In the rest of this chapter, I would like outline how ethnographic studies can open out new ways of approaching hunter-gatherer archaeology. Case studies from northern Eurasia explore the distinctive worldview of northern hunters and focus on some of the main material outcomes of common aspects of belief. The overall aim is to identify new ways in which hunter-gatherer archaeology might rethink many familiar categories of data in order to grapple more effectively with evidence for expression of prehistoric cosmology and belief.

The Worldview of Northern Hunter-Gatherers

Northern Eurasia is one of the few regions of the world in which hunter-gatherers survived until quite recently, and is an area in which many traditional communities remain. Their subsistence economies were based mainly on hunting and fishing, with dogs and reindeer employed for transport and hunting purposes (Forsyth 1992). Whilst in the seventeenth and eighteenth century many native groups of the Arctic zone shifted their subsistence to reindeer pastoralism, hunting and fishing groups persisted in the broad belt of boreal forest, or *taiga*, further to the south. In the difficult conditions of the forest, reindeer exploitation was limited, and most groups relied on local fishing and hunting for subsistence, using reindeer primarily for transport (Federova 2000; Golovnev 1993).

Like Canada, Siberia also has a long colonial history linked initially to the global fur trade, which led to various transformations in local indigenous hunting and fishing cultures, but did not necessarily lead to a shift to farming and cultural, linguistic or spiritual assimilation, (Forsyth 1992; Glavatskaia 2002; Jordan 2003). In western Siberia, many hunting, fishing and gathering communities were able to resist centuries or religious and ideological persecution and maintain their indigenous identities and worldviews (Glavatskaia 2002, 2004; Jordan 2003).

At a more general level, the worldview of these northern peoples is expressed through daily interactions with their natural environment, and central to this is the deep-seated belief that not only human beings, or even animals, but all animate and inanimate things possess souls. Acceptance of the existence of spiritual beings cannot be confined to the realm of religion, nor even the shamanistic tradition, as both are built on a deeper conception of the nature of reality that underlines the whole worldview. These notions of universe, soul, other spiritual beings, and related symbolic actions and activities converge in a total view of the world.

Cross cultural surveys of the circumpolar zone identify further recurrent themes in the northern worldview, including the notions of '*masterhood*' in which the souls of game are owned by higher beings who release individual animals to the hunter; the successful hunt constituting an act of world renewal in which essential forces are released to generate new life elsewhere; a vertical structuring of the conceptual universe into three domains of sky, earth and a watery underworld which creates potential for shamanic souls' flight between these worlds (Ingold 1986; Jordan 2003; Zvelebil and Jordan 1999).

Khanty

The Eastern Khanty reside along the Middle Ob' River in western Siberia (Figure 13.1: Base Map) and traditionally practiced hunting, fishing and small-scale reindeer herding. Each of the tributary rivers is inhabited by individual Khanty communities who distinguish themselves from one another through dress, dialect, material culture and minor variations in subsistence practice. The broader history of these communities has been described elsewhere (Federova 2000; Jordan 2003; Martynova 1995, 1998; Wiget 2002) and my concern here is to explore in more detail the

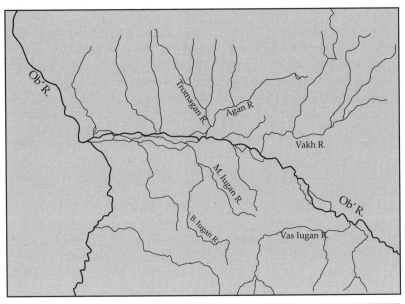

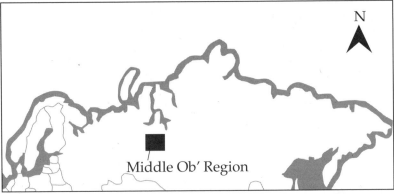

Figure 13.1 Rivers occupied by Khanty communities in western Siberia.

practical activities and personal understandings associated with northern spirituality.

The main tributary rivers run through a low-lying wetland landscape of taiga forest, lakes and bog (Figure 13.2). These rivers serve as a vital summer transport artery, and link a chain of remote base camps, or 'yurts', which are strung out along the bank and often several hours boat travel apart. The yurts consist of two to five households who occupy a row of single room log cabins during the Spring and Fall. In Winter individual households move off into their own hunting territories in the deeper forest and in Summer the entire river basin community travelled downriver to fishing spots on the lower tributary or main Ob' River. The strong seasonality and uneven distribution of resources at different times of the year meant constant journeying and generated complex routines of community aggregation and dispersal (Federova 2000; Golovnev 1993; Jordan 2003; Wiget 2002).

The extensive tracts of landscape also contain a rich sacred geography, comprised of ritual sites and other locations or natural features with divine or symbolic associations (Jordan 2003:135–153; Wiget 2002). In keeping with the more general themes of northern cosmology the Khanty

Figure 13.2   Boat travel along the Malyi Iugan (September 2005).

also understand that the universe exists on three distinct levels: an upper world of the sky, the middle world of the earth, and an underworld of the dead below the surface of the earth. Animal spirit masters reside in the upper world and "give" game to the hunters in return for appropriate offerings (*pory*) of gifts and food and fare, which include moose heads, cloth and vodka. Domestic animals—previously domestic reindeer but now also imported sheep and goats—are occasionally sacrificed and their souls offered up to the main deities. The master of the fish resides downstream on the main Ob' and drives fish up the tributaries where they can be caught. Each spring, as the ice breaks up, prayers are said at the water's edge, with gifts occasionally cast into the waters.

One of the main features of many local sacred sites is a stilted store house (Khanty: '*labas*') which houses carved wooden idols of the yurt's protector spirits (Figure 13.3). Communities visit and venerate these idols at the start and end of the hunting seasons, often when the yurt community regroups or as households are about to disperse for the winter. Cemeteries are also carefully placed in the landscape, and are never located upstream for fear that diseases of the dead will float downstream and into the households of the living community. The influence of spirits, dead relatives, and a range of other deities is experienced in every domain of human life, and this means that every part of the landscape, every human action, journey or movement involves some form of encounter or connection with another presence. This web of relationships cuts across social and species lines and grounds each human person into a wider set of obligations to acknowledge and come to terms with the divine forces that exist as an integral and immutable element of human nature and society (Kulemzin 1984; Jordan 2001, 2003).

From the numerous conversations and observations[1] generated by repeated fieldwork a picture gradually emerges of individual health, welfare and hunting luck being dependant on *two* sets of interlocking factors. The first finds expression through deep respect for the experience, judgment and practical abilities of individuals able to conduct their lives with calmness, autonomy and skill; the second is acknowledgment that human persons must also attend to the myriad of divine forces affecting daily travel, subsistence activity and their ultimate fate.

Hunting Luck and Reciprocity

Notions of reciprocity and exchange inform the general conduct of subsistence activity. On the Agan River, informants described how one hunter would take a length of white cloth—a common gift for the spirit masters—whenever he went hunting. Carrying this gift *in expectation*, he never came back without game, and took care to hang the cloth as *pory*.

Figure 13.3 Preparing *pory* at a sacred site on the Malyi Iugan River (Summer 1998).

Other accounts from the upper Malyi Iugan tell of one hunter suffering a particularly bad season. Finally, he dreamt that he should do *pory* at the *kot mykh* (sacred hill) located within his hunting territory, and upon awaking, went out and conducted this ritual. The next morning he skied out and found a valuable sable in every trap. A similar attitude to luck in procurement activities was expressed on the upper Bolshoi Iugan River where there is a large lake rich in fish, and where landing large catches is never normally a problem. Gradually, the fish catches deteriorated until eventually the community decided to cross the lake and "place a bottle" (another term for *pory*, as the ceremonies usually involve ritual consumption of alcohol) at the shrine located on the opposite lake shore. Record fish catches followed. But the leaving of gifts does not determine the outcome of hunting activities. In describing why his late brother had never killed a single elk one Malyi Iugan informant explained how the man had possessed "slow and nervous reactions" ensuring that even frequent sighting of game were rarely followed by an accurate rifle shot.

Sacred places are understood to be inhabited by a range of different deities who own, or remain active in procuring, the game and resources in and around sacred sites. Similar notions inform attitudes to the area in and around the cemetery where the dead are assumed to move at night and go about their business in reverse. As a consequence, these areas remain closed to procurement activity, with infringements causing deep offence and risking later retribution, even death (Glavatskaia 2002:87; Jordan 2003). Nevertheless, the explicit demarcation of boundaries around these locations is far from clear and exists more as a sense of having approached too far. One upper Bolshoi Iugan informant explained how it was "better not to" hunt game on sacred land. He'd once tracked a sable through the winter forest until the tracks ran up the side of a *kot mykh* (sacred hill). As he followed the tracks they suddenly disappeared: there was fresh snow all around; the animal had gone.

More formalized collective *pory* rituals are conducted at the local holy sites, which generally have deities housed in a stilted storehouse or labas (Figure 13.3) (Jordan 2003). At these times gifts of money and cloth are placed in the shrines. After the visits it is important to leave behind the bottles and other remains from the ritual meals, including fragments of moose skull, and the bones of sacrificed domesticates (Jordan 2008b).

Treatment of Animals

A sense of reciprocity also informs the more specific treatment of animal remains. The moose head is regarded as the tastiest part of the animal, and is often reserved for ritual meals, both at home and at sacred places. Prior to consumption of the head the spirit masters and other main deities are invited to attend the meal by reciting opening prayers, and this is regarded as an important gesture of thanks on the part of the hunter and wider household. There are older accounts from the Vas Yugan River of a major 'elk festival' which was held in the Spring. Separate parts of moose killed over the winter would be stored up and eventually cooked together at a sacred promontory as an act of world renewal (Kulemzin and Lukina 1977; Jordan 2003).

Symbolic treatment of moose bones in more routine spheres involves caching them in the "clean" areas of forest behind the base camp, or at some distance away from the winter hunting camp. As one Malyi Iugan River informant explained, the bones belong to the spirit master of animals, *Vojwort Iki*, and they need to be returned to quiet areas where dogs won't chew on them or disturb them, which might offend the spirit master and affect further hunting luck. Another informant described how clean areas are places of pure nature, where nobody had walked.

A more elaborate and ritualized treatment surrounds the treatment of bear bones and the entire process of hunting and consuming the animal often extends to a lengthy "bear festival" involving days of celebration by several households (Jordan 2003:115–123, with references). Trees are carved to communicate to the upper world deities that a bear has been taken, and this marks the symbolic passage of the newly killed bear from the world of the forest and into the human encampment, where the animal will be treated as an honored emissary from the spirit world. After the end of the festival the skulls are retained and placed on store house roofs, while the other bones are carefully disarticulated and cast into deep pools of stationary water where "not even a bird will disturb them." Here it is thought that the bones will eventually re-clothe themselves in flesh and blood.

Informants describe the complex relationships surrounding the successful discovery of an occupied bear den. At this moment it was thought that the bear's master had "seen" the hunter. The greater the number of bear kills the more fortunate the hunter and the more promising his relations with the deities. The notion of "being seen" extends to other domains of procurement activities and one of the main motivations for conducting *pory* at the start of a season, or when entering a new area of land, or fresh phase in the seasonal subsistence round was the desire to remain being "seen" during ensuing activities. Maintaining success in bear hunting is amongst the most challenging endeavors, for the animal can hear inside people's homes and listen to what they say. Notions of danger and revenge also come across in attitudes to the bear, with one Iugan hunter describing how the feeding of a bear skull to the dogs would result in the hunter encountering a bear later in the forest and being savaged as a reprisal.

Movement in the Landscape

With cemeteries and sacred sites inhabited by ancestors and deities the Khanty also believe it inappropriate to move in a full circle around these places. This results in a powerful sensitivity about the relative locations of these focal places. Even when they are not being visited, individuals will go to great lengths to retrace their route even whilst conducting subsistence activities. Ignoring these codes of conduct might affect luck in different ways, and may not bring immediate retribution, but direct the offender towards a different fate: a hand might be lost through a mysterious accident; a drowning may take place some time later. The most immediate results are often reflected in declining hunting luck. One Malyi Iugan informant recounted how, as a young man, he'd been out all day hunting and had ended up making a big loop around the local sacred site. With darkness falling he decided to return home without re-tracing his route. That night he recounted to his father what he'd done. His father became angry and warned him of the potential consequences, but he ignored the advice and went to sleep. From the next day onwards the man was unable to shoot a single animal, despite many sightings and frequent clear shots. He changed his weapon, and experimented with several others, but as the days passed, he was still unable to hit any game. Eventually, he gathered materials for making *pory* and visited the local sacred site where he left the offerings. The next day he shot a sable, followed by another each day, for several days. His luck was back.

Landscape Enculturation

If we "scale up" these insights we see that the entire seasonal round of the Khanty's semi-nomadic existence focuses on tending relationships with the ever-present spirit world. At the core of these concerns is fulfillment of the underlying obligation to acknowledge, communicate and reciprocate, often with material gifts, but also through appropriate patterns of bone and refuse discard, and the correct ways of journeying through the different features of the landscape. The more explicit ritualized activities include the maintenance of sacred sites which "mark" the land, and result in the enhancement of special topographic features, waterfronts and other landscape contexts through special deposits, construction of small structures, the carving of trees and making of offerings (Jordan 2003, 2008b).

This is not merely about cultural ways of *perceiving* otherwise natural landscapes, but deliberate modification and long-term active intervention in the landscape to maintain enduring focal places. From an ethnoarchaeological perspective, this symbolic ordering of the topography generates distinctive material signatures at a range of spatial scales, primarily in the form of deposited artifacts and distinctive bone scatters at the main ritual sites (see Jordan 2008b for a full analysis of sacred site activity areas and associated material residues).

From Ethnographic Insights to an Archaeology of Belief

These emerging insights also point to a more general need to review current subsistence-orientated understandings of hunter-gatherer landscapes: "hunter-gatherers … enculturate their landscapes using a number of practical and symbolic strategies, the signatures of which have often passed unnoticed" (Zvelebil 2003:65). However, a more fundamental "reappraisal of the symbolic perception and social use of landscape by hunter-gatherers … is only beginning" (Zvelebil 2003:65). More work might explore underlying variations in northern sacred landscape geography, including how it is dynamically interactive with different ecological settings and subsistence practices (Jordan forthcoming).

In particular, further research is needed to explore the potential for new forms of enduring "place", which fall outside the more usual "economic" notions of forager base camps and procurement sites. These new categor-ies might include focal places that are visited infrequently, but repeatedly, by a wider collective over many generations, serving as the location for collective consumption, and deliberate acts of artifact creation and material deposition. At the other end of the continuum, there may be smaller and more personal sites for other symbolic acts, including ritualized caching of selective animal parts in gestures repeated over a number of generations. The persistence of both kinds of location may also serve to express a wider "consciousness of place", which may structure more general forms of landscape movement and activity.

In the prehistoric past, such categories of place may have been marked out through distinctive deposits or the ritual embellishment of landscape features through caching, deposits or the creation of rock art, all serving as media to express and reproduce the imagined relationships linking the human collective with a wider sentient ecology. In seeking to understand the specificity of these meanings, we don't need to find general *answers* like "shamanism" or "animism" to fill the empty symbolic spaces; we require ways of understanding the relationships between the constitution of lives as lived, and the expression of a shared cosmological knowledge through repeated ritualized actions on an enculturated landscape.

While the broader patterns of ecological adaptation may define many of the outer limits of forager behavior, increased use of integrated ethnographic insights will expand the "analogical consciousness" (Cunningham 2003:393) and signal new ways to explore familiar datasets—places, subsistence residues, artifacts and rock art—generating a richer understanding of long-term trajectories of forager belief. These insights need not stand in contradiction to more typical materialist accounts of hunter-gatherers, but may signal ways to move beyond exclusively functional and ecological accounts through integration of more resolutely social and symbolic perspectives on hunter-gatherer lifeways (Jordan 2006).

These new approaches to the data may also prompt archaeological surveys of northern regions to reach beyond the investigation of mobility patterns and resource exploitation, and to start to seek out material reflections of hunting ethics, expressions of spirituality and consider evidence for sacred landscape geography. Iconographic evidence like rock art—often studied in isolation as a more overt material definition of hunter-gatherer 'religion'—may also benefit from a more contextualized treatment, which would ground the sites and panels within wider social, symbolic and subsistence landscapes (Jordan 2004).

Conclusions

This chapter began with a question: can archaeologists research the beliefs of prehistoric hunter-gatherers? Anecdotal ethnographic evidence for the spirituality inherent in northern hunter-gatherer lifeways is detailed and extensive, but has yet to see sustained theoretical attention from archaeologists. One major reason for this is the enduring "adaptive" paradigm, which continues to dominate hunter-gatherer research and provide the field with a distinct disciplinary identity. Documentation of the key economic and demographic factors underlying hunter-gatherer variability has been one of the great achievements of this approach (Kelly 1995), but more work is required to understand how hunter-gatherers actually *perceive* and express their understanding of the world through practices generating enduring material remains.

Looking to the future, these considerations highlight the crucial role of ethnographic analogies in opening out a new era of work on the "archaeology of hunter-gatherer belief":

- Systemic analysis of northern ethnographies is required to identify variability in the pervasive features of northern spirituality. Attention should be directed towards understanding how patterns of behavior are dynamically interactive with local cultural tradition, the broader ecology and wider trajectories of historical development, including the rise of the 'northern world' as a resource periphery to emerging urban markets and political states further to the south.
- Further ethnographic work is needed to understand the distinctive features of high latitude hunter-gatherer landscapes, in particular, the diversity and distinctive characteristics of *focal* places that may receive infrequent but repeated visits over many generations. Hunter-gatherers are not just reactants to the ecological forces of the natural landscape; nor do they merely overlay narrative and belief on natural features: they actively modify and "enculturate"

environments through social, economic and ritual activity, which reproduce a long-term structuring of the landscape.

- Within these landscapes, ethnographic studies also demonstrate that the procurement of animals includes the narrow provisioning of society with essential energy and raw materials, but also extends to encompass parting gestures of respect and symbolic return which also generate distinctive archaeological signatures (e.g., Binford 1978a:413).
- Research into the archaeology of the northern mind needs to move beyond the narrow quest to identify evidence for shamanism or animism, and should aim to develop greater understanding of how a worldview predicated on the ability to make direct "ecstatic" contact with the spirit world is made possible through broader routines of inter-generational practice (Jordan 2001).
- We should also seek new frameworks for advancing northern rock art studies, one avenue of hunter-gatherer research that has gone furthest in attempting to understand the expression of cosmology and prehistoric religion. Ethnographic insights demonstrate that we may need to rethink the role of this iconography as serving only as a static *reflection* of an underlying shamanic and animistic religion, and start to explore the "active" role of the images as direct material culture *derivatives* of repeated sets of ritual practices (Goldhahn 2002; McCall 2007:228). Forager rock art may better be understood as a palimpsest of repeated tradition extending over many generations (Jordan 2004), attracting the enactment of symbolic dialogues through the particular sensory experiences of place (Goldhahn 2002). Finally, ethnographies of landscape can indicate how rock art landscapes may *actively* structure, and be structured by, the wider features of forager behavior including long-term subsistence and mobility practices (McCall 2007:231; Zvelebil and Jordan 1999).

These conclusions indicate that hunter-gatherer archaeology has every potential to build on its long-standing focus on the spatial organization of economic activities and their direct material correlates, but that the field also needs to diversify towards a greater exploration of how ideology, worldview and belief are also incorporated into hunter-gatherer experience of the world through repeated use and embellishment of enduring focal places through deposition of material culture.

Acknowledgments

1. The author would like to express his heartfelt thanks to the numerous individuals and families who provided warm hospitality and much practical assistance during fieldwork. Research funding provided by the *University of Sheffield, Royal Anthropological Institute, Finno-Yugrian Society, British Academy and Leverhulme Trust* is gratefully acknowledged.

2. This chapter was originally presented as a paper in the session '*Faith in the past: theorizing ancient religions*' organized by Dave Whitley at the 2004 meeting of the *Society of American Archaeology* in Montreal, Quebec, Canada. I am very grateful to Dave for the invitation to

participate and for his gallant editorial efforts over subsequent months. Thanks also to the other session participants for lively comments and discussions.

Note

1. Primary data for this chapter were collected between 1997 and 2005 during seven field-work expeditions to various Eastern Khanty communities.

References Cited

Ames, Kenneth M.
2004   Supposing Hunter-Gatherer Variability. *American Antiquity* 69(2):364–374.
Anisimov, A. F.
1963   The Shaman's Tent of the Evenks and the Origins of the Shamanistic Rite. In *Studies in Siberian Shamanism*, edited by Henry M. Michael, Arctic Institute of North America. Translations from Russian Sources No. 4, University of Toronto Press, Toronto.
Barnard, Alan
2004   Preface. In *Hunter-Gatherers in History, Archaeology and Anthropology*, edited by A. Barnard, pp. ix–x, Oxford, Berg.
Bettinger, R. L.
1991   *Hunter-Gatherers: Archaeological and Evolutionary Theory*. Plenum Press, New York.
Binford, L. R.
1962   Archaeology as Anthropology. *American Antiquity* 28(2):217–225.
Binford, Lewis R.
1977   For Theory Building in Archaeology. Academic Press, New York.
1978a   *Nunamiut Ethnoarchaeology*. Academic Press, London.
1978b   Dimensional Analysis of Behavior and Site Structure: Learning from an Eskimo Hunting Stand. *American Antiquity* 43(3): 330–361.
1980   Willow Smoke and Dogs' Tails: Hunter-Gatherer Settlement Systems and Archaeological Site Formation. *American Antiquity* 45:4–20.
1981   *Bones: Ancient Men and Modern Myths*. Academic Press, New York.
1982   The Archaeology of Place. *Journal of Anthropological Archaeology* 1:5–31.
1983   *In Pursuit of the Past*. Thames and Hudson, London.
1987   Researching Ambiguity: Frames of Reference and Site Structure. In *Method and Theory for Activity Area Research*, edited by S. Kent, Columbia University Press, New York.
2001   *Constructing Frames of Reference. An Analytical Method for Archaeological Theory Building Using Hunter Gatherer and Environmental Data Sets*. University of California Press, Berkeley.
Bird David, Nurit
1990   The Giving Environment: Another Perspective on the Economic System of Hunter-Gatherers. *Current Anthropology* 31(2):183–196.
1992   Beyond "the Original Affluent Society." *Current Anthropology* 33(1):25–47
1996   Hunter Gatherer Research and Cultural Diversity. In *Cultural Diversity among Twentieth-Century Foragers: An African Perspective*, edited by S. Kent, pp. 297–304, Cambridge University Press, Cambridge.
Cunningham
2003   Transcending the "Obnoxious Spectator": A Case for Processual Pluralism in Ethnoarchaeology. *Journal of Anthropological Archaeology* 22:389–410.

David, N., and C. Kramer
2001   *Ethnoarchaeology in Action*. Cambridge University Press, Cambridge.
Federova, E. G.
2000   *Ryblovy i Okhotniki Basseina Obi: Problemy Formirovaniia Kultury Khantov i Mansi*. Evropeiskii Dom, Saint Petersburg.
Forsyth, J.
1992   *A History of the Peoples of Siberia: Russia's North Asian Colony 1581–1990*. Cambridge University Press, Cambridge.
Gamble, C., and W. Boismier (editors)
1991   *Ethnoarchaeological Approaches to Mobile Campsites: Hunter-Gatherer and Pastoralist Case Studies*. Ethnoarchaeology Series 1, International Monographs in Prehistory, Ann Arbor.
Glavatskaia, E.
2002   Khanty v Sostave Russkogo Gosudarstva v XVII–XX vv. In *Ocherki Istorii Traditsionnogo Zemlepol'sovania (Materially k Atlasu)*, edited by A. Wiget, pp. 75–123.
2004   Religious and Ethnic Revitalization among the Siberian Indigenous People: The Khanty Case. In *Circumpolar Ethnicity and Identity*, edited by T. Irimoto and T. Yamada, pp. 231–246. Senri Ethnological Studies No. 66. National Museum of Japan, Osaka.
Goldhahn, J.
2002   Roaring Rocks: An Audio-Visual Perspective on Hunter-Gatherer Engravings in Northern Sweden and Scandinavia. *Norwegian Archaeological Review* 35(1): 29–61.
Golovnev, A. V.
1993   *Istoricheskaia Tipologiia Khoziaistva Narodov Severo-Zapadnoi Sibiri*. Novosibirsk University Press, Novosibirsk.
Gould, R., and J., Yellen
1987   Man the Hunted: Determinants of Household Spacing in Desert and Tropical Foraging Societies. *Journal of Anthropological Archaeology* 6:77–103.
Ingold, T.
1986   *The Appropriation of Nature: Essays on Human Ecology and Social Relations*. Manchester University Press, Manchester.
Jordan, P.
2001   The Materiality of Shamanism as a "World-View": Praxis Artefacts and Landscape. In *The Archaeology of Shamanism*, edited by N. Price, pp. 87–104. Routledge, London.
2003   *Material Culture and Sacred Landscape: The Anthropology of the Siberian Khanty*. Rowman and Littlefield, London.
2004   Examining the Role of Agency in Hunter Gatherer Cultural Transmission. In *Agency Uncovered: Archaeological Perspectives on Social Agency, Power and Being Human*, edited by A. Gardner, pp. 87–104, University College London Press, London.
2006   Analogy. In *Mesolithic Britain and Ireland: New Approaches*, edited by C. Conneller and G. Warren, pp. 83–100. Tempus, Stroud.
2008a   In Press. Hunter-Gatherers. In *Handbook of Archaeological Theory*, edited by R. A. Bentley, Herbert D. G. Maschner, and Christopher Chippindale, AltaMira Press, Walnut Creek.
2008b   In Press. "Material Culture" Perspectives on the Worldview of Northern Hunter-Gatherers. In *Structured Worlds: The Archaeology of Hunter-Gatherer Thought and Action*, edited by Aubrey Cannon, Equinox, London.
Forthcoming (editor) *Landscape and Culture in the Siberian North*, University College London Press, London.
Kelly, R. L.
1995   *The Foraging Spectrum: Diversity in Hunter-Gatherer Lifeways*. Washington: Smithsonian Institution Press, Washington.

Kent, Susan (editor)
1996   *Cultural Diversity among Twentieth Century Foragers: An African Perspective.* Cambridge University Press, Cambridge.
Kroll, E., and T. D. Price
1991   *The Interpretation of Archaeological Spatial Patterning.* Plenum, New York.
Kulemzin, V. M.
1984   *Chelovek i Proroda v Veroianiiakh Khantov.* Tomsk University Press, Tomsk.
Kulemzin, V. M., and N. V. Lukina
1977   *Vasiugansko-Vakhovskie Khanty v Kontse XIX – Nachale XX vv.* Tomsk University Press, Tomsk.
Lee, R. B.
1969   !Kung Bushmen Subsistence: An Input/Output Analysis. In *Contributions to Anthropology: Ecological Essays,* edited by D. Damas, pp. 73–94. National Museum of Canada Bulletin 230. National Museum of Canada, Ottawa.
Lee, R. B., and I. DeVore (editors)
1968   *Man the Hunter.* Aldine Publishing Company, Chicago.
Martynova, E. P.
1995   "Obshchectvennoe Ustroistvo v XVII–XIX vv." In *Istoriia i kul'tura Khantov,* edited by N. V. Lukina pp. 77–121, Tomsk University Press, Tomsk.
1998   *Ocherki Istorii i Kul'tury Khantov.* Russian Academy of Sciences, Moscow.
McCall, G. S.
2007   Add Shamans and Stir? A Critical Review of the Shamanism Model of Forager Rock Art Production. *Journal of Anthropological Archaeology* 26:224–233.
Steward, J. H.
1955   The Concept and Method of Cultural Ecology. In *Theory of Cultural Change: The Methodology of Multilinear Evolution,* edited by J. H. Steward, pp. 30–42. University of Illinois Press, Urbana.
Trigger, B. G.
1989   *A History of Archaeological Thought.* Cambridge University Press, Cambridge
Wiget, A. (editor)
2002   Ocherki Istorii Traditsionnogo Zemlepol'sovania Khantov. Tezis, Ekaterinburg.
Winterhalder, B.
2001   The Behavioural Ecology of Hunter-Gatherers. In *Hunter-Gatherers: An Interdisciplinary Perspective,* edited by Catherine Panter-Brick, Robert H. Layton, and Peter Rowley-Conwy, pp. 12–38, Cambridge University Press, Cambridge.
Winterhalder, B., and E. A. Smith
1981   Preface. In *Hunter-Gatherer Foraging Strategies: Ethnographic and Archaeological Analyses,* edited by B. Winterhalder and E. A. Smith, pp. ix–x, University of Chicago Press, Chicago.
2000   Analyzing Adaptive Strategies: Human Behavioral Ecology at Twenty-five. *Evolutionary Anthropology* 9:51–110.
Yellen, J.
1977   *Archaeological Approaches to the Present.* Academic Press, New York.
Zvelebil, M.
2003   Enculturation of Mesolithic Landscapes. In *Mesolithic on the Move,* edited by L. Larson, H. Kindgren, K. Knutsson, D. Loeffler, and A. Akerlund, pp. 65–73. Oxbow Press, Oxford.
Zvelebil, M., and P. Jordan
1999   Hunter Fisher Gatherer Ritual Landscapes: Questions of Time, Space and Representation. In *Rock Art as Social Representation,* edited by J. Goldhahn, pp. 101–127. BAR International Series 794. Oxford University Press, Oxford.

ARCHAEOLOGY AND WOMEN'S RITUAL BUSINESS

Kelley Hays-Gilpin

*"We tend to see power in what men control, in the events and activities associ-
ated with men, and our questions about women and power are couched in
terms of the extent to which women control similar things or engage in similar
activities."*

—Jill Dubisch (1986a:24)

One would do well to keep gender in mind when pursuing the archaeology
of religion in any time period or location. Women as well as men had roles
in ritual practice. In many cultures, activities such as preparing and serving
food, lamenting the dead, and crafting ritually necessary textiles, ceramics, and other items may be women's work with vital religious dimensions;
such activities may support or subvert dominant religious hegemonies.
Gender as a structuring principle differs among cultures, and can change.
Ritual practice and iconography often involve actively manipulating gendered concepts. Material culture may reflect gender norms in relatively
straightforward ways, but gender indicators often may be combined or
inverted in ritual contexts and in the gender identities of ritual practitioners. Religion, ritual, and belief do not transcend sex and gender. Rather,
gender and religion are often inseparable.

Social scientists have long discussed definitions for the terms religion,
ritual, men, women, gender, and sex, but use of these terms often proves
problematic. A few simple comments about vocabulary will suffice here.
First, the words anthropologists use to generalize about gender categories tend to obscure the local meanings that really interest us. In many
societies, females, males, inter-sexed individuals, and people whose gender

identity and gender roles do not coincide with their biological sex often had socially approved ritual roles. Exceptions to social rules occurred as well. Second, by now all anthropologists realize that simplistic dichotomies such as sacred/secular and sacred/profane do not pertain in many non-Western societies, much less correlate with masculine/feminine domains of values or practice. But despite our superior and more nuanced understandings of such matters today, our vocabularies and our unconscious cultural biases still shape the way we think about the pasts of other people. Overcoming our own biases requires conscious effort. Concrete examples of other ways of thinking help that effort. My goal here is to provide three examples of how thinking outside dominant gender categories leads to a more interesting archaeology of religion. I focus here on the gender of ritual practitioners in a few recent studies of rock art and religion in Australia, the Pueblos of the southwestern United States, and the northern Plains.

Australian Women's Ritual Business

Spencer and Gillen's (1899) late-nineteenth-century ethnographic research on Australian Aborigines influenced early anthropological views of religion in the writings of the discipline's founding fathers, including Durkheim, Tylor, and Weber; psychologists such as Roheim also looked to Australia for evidence of "primitive" religious thought. Archaeologists who suggested hunting magic, totemic, and fertility interpretations for European Paleolithic rock art, such as Abbè Henri Breuil (1952), also looked to Spencer and Gillen and other accounts of Australian ritual. Australian data were first brought to bear on rock art by Reinach in 1903, so the link goes back to very early times in the development of archaeology. Australian ethnography therefore is central to the early foundation of the archaeology of religion. Spencer and Gillen portrayed Aboriginal women as submissive, subordinate to men, and lacking in ritual or artistic responsibilities. These male researchers saw many men's ritual activities and little or nothing of women's, though they noted in passing that women had ceremonies of their own. They saw a few Aboriginal men making paintings (1899:179–180) and assumed that only men painted. When early ethnographers discussed Aboriginal art and religion, they were referring to men's art and religion.

If Aboriginal women had rituals and made paintings, would male ethnographers have seen them? Probably not, because many Australian hunter-gatherer tribes divide ritual practice along gender lines, with enforced secrecy. In central Australia, for example, men and women avoid each other's "business." Diane Bell writes of central Australia that

> men avoid all paths which lead by or to the camps of women and not infrequently travel circuitous routes to avoid passing near or stumbling

upon women at business. The women, like the men, may keep men tactfully informed, for example, by wearing their ritual designs after the ceremony, the exact nature of which must remain unknown to the men. (1993:37)

Bell and other women ethnographers (see also Berndt 1981; Kaberry 1939) found that women have sacred sites, care for shrines and resource areas, and even play important roles in male initiation ceremonies. Claire Smith (personal communication 2004) reports the same for southern and central Arnhem land. Women paint their bodies, sacred boards, and other items with designs based on their hereditary rights to "Dreamings," their spiritual and religious connections to specific landscapes.

Did women paint on rocks in sacred places? Josephine Flood asked Wardaman consultants, "Who can paint?" They answered, "Anyone."

Q: Can men paint?
A: Yes, anyone.
Q: Can women paint?
A: Yes, anyone. (Flood, quoted in Smith 1991:46)

If women can paint and are known to retouch certain existing paintings (Kaberry 1939:206; Layton 1992:21, 47; Smith 1991:46) in some parts of Australia, why do many researchers attribute all rock art to men only? Probably because many male ethnographers accepted a basic dichotomy that categorized women and their activities as "profane," opposed to the masculine realm of the sacred (for example, Maddock 1974). As with most cultures, such oppositions are far too simplistic to be true.

Recently, several archaeologists have investigated Aboriginal Australian women's roles in making and using rock art and related paintings. Claire Smith (1993) studied contemporary Aboriginal acrylic paintings from the western desert region that draw on rock art and body art imagery to see if women and men use different motifs. She found that men's and women's design repertoires overlap a great deal, though some motifs are used more by painters of one gender than the other, and the most visually complicated motifs tend to appear in men's paintings. She concluded that both men and women have rights to paint designs based on their ancestral Dreamings.

Julie Drew (1995) surveyed published Australian rock art images for evidence of painters using gender-specific styles, and for the lack of such evidence. She found that most researchers had identified human figures with no distinguishing sex characteristics as male. Reanalyzing these figures in detail, she found that most did not have clearly differentiated male attributes such as penises; researchers had merely assumed a figure was male unless it had obvious feminine features, such as breasts and vulvas. Drew then produced a new typology for human figures, based on explicit and replicable attributes (1995:105). She compared anthropomorphic figures in five regions of Australia. Proportions of male and female figures vary a great deal, and so do their distinguishing features. Regional differences are strong and contexts vary. For example, in some areas women are distinguished from men by breasts, but in the Wardaman region, the females are instead identified by vulvas. Female figures in rock art panels are often central and are highly decorated in some areas, but not in others. Females are often paired with a male in other locations, and sometimes men and women are depicted together as "social actors" in groups. Across northern Australia, approximately equal numbers of males and females are depicted. In contrast, non-gendered human figures predominate in southern Australia, suggesting that the art is inclusive of both genders (see also Green 1997 for interpretation of "neutral figures" in European rock art).

In summary, ethnographic evidence suggests that both men and women had rights to paint. Archaeological evidence shows that the style and iconography of sex and gender in Australian rock art varies across time and space, but provides few (if any) clues about who made and used the images. Therefore, archaeologists cannot assume that only men made rock art. Nonetheless, Christine Stephenson (2000) reports that Aboriginal site guides interpreting Aboriginal rock sites in southern Australia tell visitors that men made all of the rock art, even at sites otherwise interpreted as women's camps. This may reflect a Native gender stereotype, or a European one, or both, or there may in fact be regional differences. Perhaps women in southern Australia did not make rock art. What we need is a critical examination of evidence for and against all these possibilities.

Pueblo Women's Ritual Sodalities

In contrast to the Australian case, nineteenth-century ethnographers working with the Hopi in the American Southwest recorded women's ritual activities and accorded Hopi women at least a small measure of respect. Early ethnographic accounts of ritual activities in the Hopi villages of northern Arizona show that both men and women took part (e.g., Stephen 1936; Voth 1903, 1912). Female members of the three Hopi women's ritual sodalities smoked tobacco and used prayer sticks and body paint, and they consecrated water, corn meal, and feathers, just like the men's groups. Hopi women had (and continue to have[1]) important roles in rituals undertaken by the men's sodalities. These often involve food preparation, such as grinding sacred meal and feeding participants. Sometimes women appear publicly in ritual roles that represent their status as clan mothers. Women's societies also include male priests who direct certain activities inside the kivas.

In spite of ethnographic accounts of women's activities, archaeologists working on ancestral Hopi sites have assumed that ritual activities and structures were a masculine domain. Most archaeologists oversimplify ethnographic, linguistic, and archaeological evidence when they refer to the subterranean rooms called kivas as men's spaces. Kivas are feminine-gendered structures, because they can be said to represent a womb and birth canal. They are mostly used by men, but women have activities in them as well, in rituals directed by both men's and women's societies. Women bring special ritual foods to the kivas during ceremonies directed by men, and are often present as observers. Initiations into women's own ritual societies, as well as other activities, take place in kivas. Ancestral Puebloan kiva structures, dating from the tenth to the thirteenth centuries, often include grinding stones and other tools usually associated with women's food preparation tasks (Perry and Potter 2006), and many sites include paired subterranean kivas and grinding rooms, suggesting shared and paired structures, respectively, for ritual activities and food preparation.

Today, several Hopi villages have three women's ritual societies, which have been documented since the nineteenth century. Each has distinctive performances and associated material culture. The *Lalkont* and *Owaqölt* perform "basket dances" holding flat round plaque baskets. In the Maraw Society's dance, members carry flat painted slats of wood adorned with feathers and the seed-heads of wild grasses. Sometimes items like these are consecrated and then placed in corn bins or fields. Similar dance wands are used by female dancers in Antelope and Buffalo dances. To look for evidence of the antiquity and cultural continuity of Hopi women's society practices, archaeologists can look for these distinctive objects or depictions of them. Unfortunately, the basket plaques used by the first two women's societies are not distinguishable from plaques made and used for non-ritual purposes, and they are mostly perishable items.

Dance wands, too, are made of perishable materials, but they may be depicted in petroglyphs. Some years ago, rock art researcher Patricia McCreery noticed that certain petroglyphs in the middle Little Colorado River area, southeast of the Hopi Mesas, look like Maraw *pahos* (prayer sticks) or dance wands (Figure 14.1). Some of these apparent dance wands are depicted in the hands of young women. We can tell that these are young women by their butterfly hair whorls, which are worn by females who have passed their puberty initiation ordeal but are not yet married (Hays-Gilpin 2002, 2003). The petroglyphs are located well away from known habitation sites, but are consistent with a style that dates to the AD 1200s, a period identified by both Hopi traditional histories and archaeological evidence as a century of extensive migration and aggregation.

Figure 14.1 Petroglyphs in the middle Little Colorado River area, Arizona. Drawings by Patricia McCreery.

"Other-Gendered" Ritual Practitioners

Shamans in many parts of the world do not conform to the same gender norms as non-shamans (Hollimon 2001; Mandt 2001; Price In press; Saladine d'Anglure 1992). Some probably become shamans because they are born with ambiguous sex or gender identities. Some cross-dress or blend indicators of more than one gender to disguise themselves in the spirit world or to merge their personal identities with spirit helpers of other genders and of other species. Anthropologists often suggest that because such ritual specialists mediate between life and death, this world and the spirit world, they also mediate between male and female realms by partaking of aspects of both or by standing outside normal gender conventions. Ritual specialists with non-conforming gender identities are not solely shamans (celibate Catholic priests come to mind; for Pueblo examples, see Parsons 1916; Perry and Potter 2006, and Roscoe 1991), nor are they all males. Rather than occupying one side of a set of oppositions such as nature/culture, pollution/purity, and profane/sacred, women in many cultures "are concerned with maintaining boundaries, mediating between realms, and transforming substances suitable for one realm into those proper for another" (Dubisch 1986b:208)—for example, by preparing and serving food in contexts that maintain the boundaries of social life. In rural Greece, women "tend the boundaries of life itself, for they both give birth and care for the dead" (Dubisch 1986a:37). Women's ritual laments in Greece have been described as implicit and explicit protests against official religion, and a "muted model" of the world, expressed by a subordinate sector of society (Caraveli 1986; Dubisch 1986a:31–32). Among the California Chumash, those who care for the dead are males who dress as women (Hollimon 1997). These examples of subaltern ritual expression and gender ambiguity would be difficult to detect archaeologically, even with ethnographic prompts, but approaching archaeological evidence with both ethnography and the guiding principle of gender as multi-dimensional, performative, and flexible is a necessary first step.

One interesting example of female ritual practitioners with non-conforming gender roles and identities is linked with a particular rock art complex in South Dakota. In nineteenth-century Lakota society, both men and women received visions or dreams related to healing, ceremonies, and warfare, but women most often received dreams conferring skills and designs for craft work, healing, or aid in securing a husband. Linea Sundstrom's (2002a, 2002b) analysis of northern Plains rock art and ethnography suggests that some rock art was produced by women who dreamed of "Double Woman," a spirit being who bestowed skills in making leather items with elaborate porcupine quill decorations. Village elders interpreted dreams for young people and guided them to choices appropriate for their gender and personalities. Women who dreamed of Double Woman could choose to become full-time craft specialists who did not marry or bear children. Because quill work patterns had spiritual power and were said to be derived from dreams, craft activities had important ritual aspects. Whether or not female Double Woman dreamers engaged in sexual relations with other women has apparently not been recorded, but it seems likely that at least some did. Likewise, men who dreamed of Double Woman could choose a non-conforming gender role if they were not inclined to become warriors and fathers. Some of these men did enter into domestic and presumably sexual partnerships with otherwise normative males.

Traditional stories associate Double Woman with petroglyphs, particularly complexes of awl-sharpening grooves. Double Woman dreamers may have made and maintained the bone awls used for hide and quill work, and obtained power from Double Woman, who is said to have lived in the rocks. Few ethnographic accounts actually attribute the petroglyphs to women. Following a pattern that was widespread in North America, the accounts claim instead that Double Woman herself made them, or that the petroglyphs simply appeared in the morning after villagers saw moving lights in the area at night and heard the raucous laughter of spirit beings. One needs to understand that the Lakotas telling the stories conflated Double Woman dreamers with their tutelary spirit herself to link these women with the rock art when telling these stories (Sundstrom 2002a, 2002b). That is, the ritual practitioner and the tutelary spirit become one and the same.

Implications for Archaeologists

These three examples show that few generalizations can be made about women and ritual practice, even in relatively egalitarian societies[2]. Men's and women's ritual activities may involve similar or different behaviors and material traces. These may be spatially segregated as in the Australian case; they may be temporally segregated in the same spaces, as in Pueblo kivas; or a subset of women may have their own ritual spaces and activities, as do Double Woman dreamers.

Australian Aboriginal cultures rigidly separated men's and women's ritual activities, but archaeologists are having a difficult time differentiating their respective material traces. Nonetheless, these archaeologists are correcting pervasive errors in earlier interpretations that left women's ritual activities out of the picture entirely. In contrast, Puebloan ritual practice intertwines the activities of men and women, but thanks to rich ethnography, certain historic continuities, good preservation of perishable artifacts such as basketry and wood, and fairly naturalistic representations of ritual activity in rock art, we can link rock art to other kinds of artifacts and trace some specific women's ritual practices through time, such as dance wands and the butterfly hair whorls specific to female puberty.

In Sundstrom's Lakota case, we do not see a contrast in masculine/feminine ritual practices, but can identify evidence for the activities of a subset of women who did not conform to the dominant feminine gender norm. Again, only a critical reading of the ethnography makes the interpretation of this archaeological evidence possible. One must recognize the probable biases of women consultants who did not take part in this ritual complex, as well as the biases of ethnographers.

Perhaps most important, most cultures recognize more than two gender categories and subdivide gender categories such that age or class may be more important than sex. For example, post-menopausal women may have ritual roles not filled by women of child-bearing age. This holds for hunter-gatherers in the western United States, where post-menopausal women can be shamans, and Crown and Fish's (1996) analysis of Classic Hohokam mortuary evidence in southern Arizona suggests that some high-status, post-menopausal women in this emerging complex society held priestly roles. In Siberia and Alaska, male shamans and other ritual specialists may "pose" as women or as gender-ambivalent (Saladine d'Anglure 1992), and one could argue that this is true in the Southwest Pueblos as well, where male personators fill the roles of female katsinas, deities, and other spirit beings. Or elite women may have specialist roles that non-elites cannot attain, as in the Inca Empire (Silverblatt 1987).

The lesson here for the archaeology of religion, I think, is that if relevant ethnography exists, one must read it critically, and use it carefully, but use it. In the absence of relevant ethnography, take care not to apply assumptions and generalizations about sex and gender drawn from Western stereotypes, as these are likely to be wrong. Stereotypes about active male ritual practitioners in the public domain and passive females confining their minimal ritual activities to the occasional fertility rite, childbirth charm, or hearth blessing will creep into anyone's interpretations if prior assumptions are not actively purged. At the very least, those bereft of ethnohistoric data should think critically about the complicated intersections of sex, gender, age, class, and productive specialization, with ritual roles and activities.

Acknowledgments

Many thanks to Pat McCreery, Claire Smith, Linea Sundstrom, and David Whitley for editorial, informational, and illustrative support.

Notes

1. These societies are alive and well today in several Hopi villages, but anthropological investigation has largely been prohibited. Pueblo ritual societies share information only with initiates; to share information more widely would undermine not only gender complementarity, but complementarity of ritual roles among kin groups, societies, and villages.
2. For studies of the roles of women ritual practitioners in complex societies such as states, see, for example, Nelson (1993) and Silverblatt (1987).

References Cited

Bell, Diane
1993   *Daughters of the Dreaming.* 2nd ed. University of Minnesota Press, Minneapolis.
Berndt, Catherine H.
1981   Interpretations and "Facts" in Aboriginal Australia. In *Woman the Gatherer*, edited by Frances Dahlberg, pp. 153–203. Yale University Press, New Haven, Connecticut.
Breuil, Henri
1952   Four Hundred Centuries of Cave Art. Centre d'Etudes et de Documentation Prehistoriques, Paris.
Caraveli, Anna
1986   The Bitter Wounding: The Lament As Social Protest in Rural Greece. *Gender and Power in Rural Greece*, edited by J. Dubisch, pp. 169–194. Princeton University Press, Princeton, New Jersey.
Crown, Patricia, and Suzanne K. Fish
1996   Gender and Status in the Hohokam Pre-Classic to Classic Transition. *American Anthropologist* 98:803–817.
Drew, Julie
1995   Depictions of Women and Gender Relations in Aboriginal Rock Art. In *Gendered Archaeology: The Second Australian Women in Archaeology Conference*, edited by Jane Balme and Wendy Beck, pp. 105–113. Australian National University, Canberra.
Dubisch, Jill
1986a   Introduction. *Gender and Power in Rural Greece*, edited by J. Dubisch, pp. 1–41. Princeton University Press, Princeton, New Jersey.
1986b   Culture Enters Through the Kitchen: Women, Food, and Social Boundaries in Rural Greece. *Gender and Power in Rural Greece*, edited by J. Dubisch, pp. 195–214. Princeton University Press, Princeton, New Jersey.
Green, Miranda
1997   Images in Opposition: Polarity, Ambivalence and Liminality in Cult Representations. *Antiquity* 71:898–911.
Hays-Gilpin, Kelley Ann
2002   Wearing a Butterfly, Coming of Age: A 1500 Year Old Pueblo Tradition. In *Children in the Prehistoric Puebloan Southwest*, edited by Kathryn A. Kamp, pp. 196–210. University of Utah Press, Salt Lake City.
2003   *Ambiguous Images: Gender and Rock Art.* AltaMira Press, Walnut Grove, California.
Hollimon, Sandra
1997   The Third Gender in Native California: Two-Spirit Undertakers among the Chumash and Their Neighbors. In *Women in Prehistory: North America and Mesoamerica*, edited by Rosemary A. Joyce and Cheryl Claassen, 173–188. University of Pennsylvania Press, Philadelphia.

2001   The Gendered Peopling of the North America: Addressing the Antiquity of Systems of Multiple Genders. In *The Archaeology of Shamanism*, edited by Neil Price, pp. 123–134. Routledge, London.

Kaberry, Phyllis M.
1939   *Aboriginal Women: Sacred and Profane*. George Routledge and Sons, London.

Layton, Robert
1992   *Australian Rock Art: A New Synthesis*. Cambridge University Press, Cambridge.

Maddock, Kenneth
1974   *The Australian Aborigines: A Portrait of their Society*. Penguin Books, Victoria, Australia.

Mandt, Gro
2001   Women in Disguise or Male Manipulation? Aspects of Gender Symbolism in Rock Art. In *Theoretical Perspectives in Rock Art Research*, edited by Knut Helskog, pp. 290–311. Novus, Oslo.

Nelson, Sarah M.
1993   Gender Hierarchy and the Queens of Silla. In *Sex Roles and Gender Hierarchies*, edited by B. Miller, pp. 297–315. Cambridge University Press, Cambridge.

Parsons, Elsie Clews
1916   The Zuni La'mana. *American Anthropologist* 18(4):521–528.

Perry, Elizabeth, and James Potter
2006   Materiality and Social Change in the Practice of Feminist Anthropology. In *Feminist Anthropology: Past, Present, and Future*, edited by P. L. Geller and M. K. Stockett, pp. 115–125. University of Pennsylvania Press, Philadelphia.

Price, Neil
In press The Archaeology of Shamanism: Beyond Rock Art. In *Seeing and Knowing: Ethnography and Beyond in Understanding Rock Art*, edited by B. Smith and G. Blundell. Witwatersrand University Press, Johannesburg.

Reinach, Salomon
1903   L'art et la magie. A propos des peintures et des gravures de l'image de renne. *L'Anthropologie* 14:257–266.

Roscoe, Hill
1991   *The Zuni Man-Woman*. University of New Mexico Press, Albuquerque.

Saladine d'Anglure, Bernard
1992   Rethinking Inuit Shamanism through the Concept of "Third Gender." In *Northern Religions and Shamanism*, edited by Mihály Hoppál and Juha Pentika inen, pp. 146–150. Etnological Uralica, Akadémiai Kiadó. Finnish Literature Society, Budapest and Helsinki.

Silverblatt, Irene
1987   *Moon, Sun, and Witches: Gender Ideologies and Class in Inca and Colonial Peru*. Princeton University Press, Princeton.

Smith, Claire E.
1991   Female Artists: The Unrecognized Factor in Sacred Rock Art Production. In *Rock Art and Prehistory*, edited by Paul Bahn and A. Rosenfeld, pp. 45–52. Oxford Monographs 10. Oxbow Press, Oxford.
1993   The Negotiation of Gender through Western Desert Art. In *Women in Archaeology: A Feminist Critique*, edited by Hilary du Cros and Laurajane Smith, pp. 161–170. Department of Prehistory, RSPS, Australian National University, Canberra.

Spencer, W. B., and F. J. Gillen
1899   *The Native Tribes of Central Australia*. Macmillan, London. Reprinted 1938.

Stephen, Alexander
1936   *The Hopi Journals of Alexander Stephen*, edited by Elsie Clews Parsons. Columbia University Press, New York.

Stephenson, Christine
2000   Women, Gender Relations, and Rock Art in Aboriginal Australia. Master's thesis, Department of Anthropology, Northern Arizona University, Flagstaff, Arizona.

Sundstrom, Linea
2002a Steel Awls for Stone Age Plainswomen: Rock Art, Women's Religion, and the Hide Trade on the Northern Plains. *Plains Anthropologist* 47:99–119.
2002b Prayers in Stone: Hoofprint-Vulva-Groove Rock Art in the Context of Northern Plains Religion. In *Rock Art and Culture Processes*, edited by Solveig Turpin, pp. 1–26. Special Publication 3. Rock Art Foundation, San Antonio, Texas.
Voth, H. R.
1903 The Oraibi Oaqöl Ceremony. Field Columbian Museum Publication 84, *Anthropological Series* 6(1), Chicago.
1912 The Oraibi Marau Ceremony. Field Columbian Museum Publication 156, *Anthropological Series* 11(1), Chicago.

TRADITIONAL KNOWLEDGE, RITUAL BEHAVIOR, AND CONTEMPORARY INTERPRETATIONS OF THE ARCHAEOLOGICAL RECORD—AN OJIBWA PERSPECTIVE

María Nieves Zedeño

"In the wonderment of [a] taxonomy, the thing we apprehend in one great leap, the thing that, by means of a fable, is demonstrated as the exotic charm of another system of thought, is the limitation of our own, the stark impossibility of thinking That."

—Michel Foucault

Prologue to *The Order of Things*

The implementation of federal laws aimed at preserving Native American religious practices and associated resources has opened an opportunity to revisit the vast body of accumulated knowledge about ancient religious beliefs and corresponding behavioral systems. Whether recorded in writing or held in the memory of contemporary people, this body of knowledge contains important clues for investigating the cultural logic of native worldviews that informed religious activity. Federally mandated research conducted in collaboration with Native Americans complements ethnography and archaeology by furnishing an explicit and systematic assessment and interpretation of material culture, archaeological deposits, and associated physiography by the descendants of prehistoric religious practitioners (Zedeño 2000). Unfortunately, as Shaafsma (2004) notes in a recent article about Navajo interpretations of archaeological remains, the politics of repatriation of human remains and sacred objects as well as the recalcitrance of archaeological epistemologies have overshadowed any potential benefits and contributions of sustained interaction with Native Americans.

This is a brief survey of the structure and state of traditional knowledge as it is manifested in contemporary Native American views of the past; the goal is to candidly evaluate the potential of this information for refining our understanding of the relationship between religion and the archaeological record. This survey entails an examination of the structure and state of traditional religious knowledge, and a discussion of the conceptual pathways followed by Native Americans to interpret the material remains of ancient ritual. Ethnographic literature and collaborative research involving the Algonquian-speaking Ojibwa of the western Great Lakes and Northern Ojibwa of the interior lakes illustrate key points.

Contexts for Interaction and Learning

In more than a decade of facilitating government-to-government consultation between federal agencies and Native American tribes and organizations as well as conducting archaeological and ethnographic resource surveys in public lands, it has become clear to participating scholars that traditional knowledge is a dynamic, continuously evolving body of principles and practices. This dynamism readily becomes apparent when native peoples encounter resources and places that historically and traditionally were a part of their lifeways and their homeland (Dongoske et al. 1997; Echo-Hawk 2000; Spector 1993; Stoffle et al. 2001). When confronted with an archaeological site, a resource of religious significance, or a museum collection, Native American consultants must appeal to different sources of knowledge to help them situate what they see within their present cultural frame of reference. Throughout this process, individuals follow various conceptual pathways that generally lead to the construction of inferences and analogical arguments that explain the manufacture, use, and discard of ritual artifacts and the activities leading to the formation of archaeological deposits in specific places.

Evidently, conventional analysts follow a similar interpretive process but from a vastly different cultural perspective (Mason 2000; Shaafsma 2004; Stein 2002). Thus the information obtained through consultation may diverge or even openly contradict archaeologists' reconstructions of the past. When conflict of opinion ensues during consultation, researchers may reject, politely dismiss, or uncritically accept native interpretation none of these responses constitute a fruitful venue for interaction or learning. Furthermore, many attempts at integrating oral traditions and archaeology in interpretations ranging from subsistence to migration and from craft production to religious practices without appropriate frameworks may become counterproductive (Anyon et al. 1997).

A better response is to scrutinize the components and structure of native interpretations as a means to apprehend the cultural logic behind specific past and present behaviors, and to isolate aspects of the native perspective that can be explicitly incorporated into archaeological analysis. A critical step toward this goal is to identify areas of stability or change in traditional knowledge systems and their relative contributions to the development of contemporary conceptual pathways and interpretive frameworks.

Clearly, there are areas of native culture and society that died out so early after European contact that they are no longer familiar to contemporary native groups. Thereafter, endemic warfare, epidemics, massacre, assimilation, removal, forceful suppression, Christian indoctrination, and apostasy acted in concert to change or destroy untold religious and other cultural knowledge. It is left to the archaeologist, then, to determine what types of information—ethnohistory, early ethnography, or contemporary ethnography—may be a good fit for interpreting the archaeological remains at hand. For example, the Algonquian Feast of the Dead, a ceremony attended by different ethnic groups, entailed mingling the bones of the ancestors and reburying them in ossuaries (Hickerson 1960; Schenck 1997). This politically integrative ceremony was recounted by Jesuit missionaries in the mid-sixteenth century and was last witnessed by French fur trader Pierre Esprit Radisson during his 1661 journey into the headwaters of the Mississippi River (Adams 1961). Historical memory of this practice does not extend to this day and thus early historical documents may be the most useful tools for documenting the existence of mass interments.

In contrast, the adoption of religious practices that grew out of European contact, such as the nineteenth-century Ghost Dance (Mooney 1896), not only represented new forms of ritual expression but also the reformulation of ancient ritual beliefs and practices in the face of tremendous cultural change. Although it is rarely practiced, the memory of this ceremony is fresh enough to use it as a reference point in the identification of places and features associated with the dance (Carroll et al. 2004; Stoffle et al. 2000; Vander 1997). There is yet another set of religious practices which, because of their centrality in group survival, have overcome the greatest odds, evolving and adapting to new conditions and constituencies. Such is the case, for example, of the Ojibwa "tent shaking" ritual (Hallowell 1940), which currently fulfills a central role in curing illnesses through magical performances that harness the powers of animals and other spirits. The same concepts and attitudes toward the animal and spirit worlds are still informing a multitude of practices in contemporary Ojibwa society.

In view of the great variation in the persistence of traditional religious practices, it is legitimate to ask, what is left of the aboriginal system and its cultural logic that can inform archaeology? Many archaeologists who engage the expert opinions of Native American elders and religious leaders hope for specific information on the nature and uses of ancient features and objects. When such information is not forthcoming, they conclude that the elders do not know, after all, the function and uses of archaeological remains nor the reasons for their depositional contexts. Such hopes for specificity and detail are ill-fated and naive, as they deny the possibility of evolution in belief and behavior. Ideally, from sustained, field-oriented interaction with Native Americans one should be able to identify relatively invariable concepts or practices that aid in the analysis of the archaeological record without requiring a level of empirical specificity that may no longer exist. Certain components of knowledge systems are nevertheless so resilient that they can continue to consistently inform contemporary religious practice and native interpretations of the past.

Knowledge Domains

When asked to review and provide opinions as to the nature of archaeological materials, Native American consultants make use of at least three sources of traditional knowledge: formative, historical, and experiential. Formative knowledge, which encompasses epistemology, ontology, and liturgy, situates people in the cosmos and furnishes tools for interacting with the forces and elements of the universe. Historical knowledge, ranging from origin stories and epics to single occurrences and to widespread events, situates people in time and place and furnishes arguments of causality. Experiential knowledge situates people in the actual context of ritual performance and lends authority to personal opinion. Experiential knowledge may be passive, or held by individuals who are not practitioners but who have directly observed religious performances at some point in their lives; or it may be active, or held by current practitioners of native religion.

This basic structure of knowledge domains has likely characterized traditional knowledge systems since prehistoric times. Today, native religious knowledge may also contain external elements acquired from Western culture and Western churches, and from sustained contact with members of the Native American Church. Not a negligible source, scholarly publications also inform native people's views of their own history and culture.

Knowledge and Power

The notion that Native American beliefs, knowledge of the world, and behaviors are unified was established early in American ethnology, in the works of Owen Dorsey (1894), Irving Hallowell (1976a, 1976b), James Mooney (1896), Washington Matthews (1897), Paul Radin (1957), and Henry Voth (1905), to name a few. This notion is central to understanding the role of formative knowledge—which allows people to comprehend how the universe works; where humans are placed in relation to the other things, beings, and forces that make the universe; and what the proper actions are that humans must take in order to establish harmonious relationships with the universal elements—in archaeological interpretation. The core component of formative knowledge pertains to epistemological principles, or what Roy Rappaport (1999:263–271, 446) calls "ultimate sacred postulates," which not only explain the workings of the universe but lend logic to the relationship between humans and the cosmos. Such is the case of the postulate generally referred to as *power*, which constitutes the single most important element in the structure of traditional knowledge systems across Native North America (Fogelson and Adams 1977).

The Numic *Puha*, the Algonquian *Manito*, or the Siouan *Wakan* are all terms that signify power. Among the Numa, for example, power is the cosmic force that, along with the living force, forms the fabric of the universe. *Puha* is causal and dynamic, as it flows through a web-like structure that connects all things and beings, human or otherwise (Miller 1983:78–80). The Siouan concept of power refers to a *mysterium tremendum*, or that infinite, ineffable, wholly "other" quality and quantity that resides in and takes the form of those things and beings that contain it— hence determining their properties and usefulness to humans (DeMallie and Lavenda 1977:164). Algonquians, specifically the Ojibwa, think of power as a simultaneously mortally dangerous and life-giving force that individuals must control and negotiate throughout their lives by observing rules of behavior (Black 1977a:142). These definitions illustrate the relationships among belief, knowledge, and behavior: whereas the Numic concept explains the essential role of Power in the makeup of the universe, the Siouan concept alerts one to the significance of understanding its concrete manifestations, and the Algonquian concept attests to the ubiquity of power in the structuring of human action, from everyday tasks to elaborate rituals.

Ontological Taxonomy

Native American taxonomies generally share one crucial trait: since power is neither fixed nor evenly distributed in the universe, categories of things and beings are distinguished from one another by the kind and amount of power they possess, and the manner in which they may acquire power from, or lend power to, the various universe components. Taxonomies are gateways to cultural logic, because they encode ordering principles that humans use to explain variation and to distinguish between the foreign and the familiar (Basso 1969:29). There are crucial links between experience and epistemology that become manifest through the application of classificatory systems that inform everyday actions and events and that, ultimately, bring the cosmos into human perspective. Taxonomies, in other words, mediate all relationships between humans and the universe.

Germane to any discussion of Native American taxonomy is, again, the notion of a unified system of belief, knowledge, and behavior. As Paul Radin ably put it, "the Indian does not make a separation into personal as contrasted with impersonal, corporeal with impersonal, in our sense at all. What he seems to be interested in is the question of existence, of reality; and everything that is perceived by the sense, thought of, felt and dreamt of, exists" (as cited in Hallowell 1976a:357). This unity is given by the existence of power. In Ojibwa taxonomy, for example, the Manito, that omnipresent, unpredictable, and often dangerous force, is inherent in the relationship between humans and the world and, in the words of William Jones (1905:183), "embodied in all forms of religious belief and practice, and intimately associated with customs and usages that bear upon life and its welfare." Jones's observations, I have found, remain current.

The Ojibwa taxonomy studied by Irving Hallowell in the 1940s (Hallowell 1976a), by Mary Black in the 1960s (Black 1977b), and again during an ethnographic resource survey in 1998 (Zedeño et al. 2001) and in my ongoing research among the Wisconsin Ojibwa, exemplifies the resiliency and consistency of traditional knowledge systems. Table 15.1, which integrates data from the four studies, attempts to capture (hopefully not too simplistically) the basic structure of Ojibwa ontology and the place occupied by humans in relationship to all other components of the universe.

Table 15.1   Ojibwa taxonomy.

Humans	Persons	Nonpersons
People	Certain spirits	Other spirits
Ghosts	Certain trees	Other trees
	Certain rocks	Other rocks
	Certain minerals	Other minerals
	Certain animals	Other animals
	Rifles	Other objects
	Kettles	Other landforms
	Pipes	
	Cannibals	
	Mermaids	
	Certain landforms	

Figure 15.1 Moose smoking a pipe, Basswood River, Boundary Waters Canoe Area, Minnesota (from Conway 1993:126).

Ojibwa taxonomy has three basic classes: humans, persons, and nonpersons. Humans encompass the living and the ghosts of the dead. Persons are those "born" with life-giving or life-taking power, including mythical figures, spirit helpers, "certain" animals such as bear, moose, and thunderbirds; flint, megis shells, native copper, true vermillion, pipes, kettles, grandfather rocks, grandfather trees, sun, moon, thunder, cannibals, and mermaids. Hallowell (1976a:364) refers to these as "other-than-human persons." The Ojibwa explain the logic behind the person/nonperson distinctions by appealing to human likeness: persons are self-propelling, sentient, and able to engage in social relations with humans and with one another. Figure 15.1, a pictograph on a sheer cliff overlooking a lake, shows how a moose, in addition to possessing the other-than-human power to walk on water (Conway 1993), can engage in activities normally associated with humans, such as pipe smoking.

The bestowal of personhood upon other-than-human things and beings is guided by epistemological principles as much as by historical events and human experience; it derives from the concatenation of human interactions with potential persons from time immemorial to this day, and it is lavishly illustrated by concrete examples of historical knowledge. This taxonomy is so ingrained in Ojibwa culture that, as linguist Kenneth Hill told me in 2004 (personal communication), it is reflected in a language structure that exhibits specific word endings to identify an object/person from a group of similar objects.

Power, Persons, and Ritual

In his ethnography of the Berens River Ojibwa, Hallowell (1992) noted that the currency of Ojibwa ontology, ambiguities and modern rationalizations notwithstanding, can be explained by the fact that individuals are continuously putting it to the test in the course of their daily struggle for survival. Recently I collected a contemporary story of curing illness associated with the magical powers of the shaman known as *Wabeno* who, through drumming and singing, can travel far in time and place to accomplish wondrous tasks, often impersonating an animal or an object. In this story, the Wabeno was able to visit a distant hospital where the victim of a car accident lay in a deep coma. Similar stories involving magicians are commonplace in everyday parlance; two additional stories were given to me by unrelated individuals over a period of seven years. The first story, dating back to the Sioux wars of the 1800s, tells how a magician from northern Wisconsin could send his war club to kill the enemy in battle while he sat at home singing and drumming. The second story, dating to the early twentieth century, explains that every time a particularly feared Wabeno from Lac La Croix, Ontario, sang and drummed, a bear would be seen leaving his lodge; the next morning, strings of human ears hung outside this Wabeno's lodge. This suite of Wabeno stories demonstrates not only that the concepts of person/object and other-than-human person occupy a prominent place in the fluid structure of Ojibwa ontology, but also that the quest for power control continues to permeate interactions between humans and the environment.

In traditional Ojibwa communities, individual experiences tend to prevail over socially sanctioned attitudes and practices, mainly because individual survival depends, first and foremost, on personally knowing how to control the unpredictable and dangerous nature of power, how to read the intention of potential "persons" who may have power here and now, and how to mask one's intent in order to avert contrary forces (Black 1977a). Causation, says Hallowell (1976b:403), is ultimately explained individually and behaviorally, and always in reference to the action of a "person." It is commonly said that a powerful human is one who lives to be old; thus for the average individual, power control is not an experience easily transferred in the form of a social sanction.

As with many other traditional knowledge systems (e.g., Southern Paiute; see Stoffle and Zedeño 2001), the northern Ojibwa have the concept of a knowledge "heaven" or repository, where deserving individuals may acquire songs, plant knowledge, animal languages, and any other type of knowledge necessary to harness the power to interact with the forces of the universe on an equal and competitive plane (Brown and Brighton 1988; Hultkrantz 1966). This knowledge may be tapped through individual revelation, formal training, or both. There are individuals who achieve extraordinary powers through training, dreams, visions, and encounters with powerful persons; who preside over group ceremonies; and who occupy special places in Ojibwa society. These are doctors, sorcerers, and priests of the Grand Medicine Society known as the Midewiwin. But even when these special individuals are sought for help or advice, the ultimate source of power control lies in the self; average individuals are routinely engaged in some form of ritual activity to maintain power control.

Pathways to Interpretation

Conceptual pathways used by Native Americans to interpret the archaeological record employ any and all of the domains of traditional knowledge. Of course, contemporary consultants also use modern technology (e.g., cartography, photography) to aid in interpretation; but ultimately, what guides their assessments and determinations of cultural significance are the principles governing traditional knowledge systems.

Repeated surveys of archaeological sites and examinations of artifact collections in the company of elders from different ethnic backgrounds have demonstrated that, despite the cultural diversity represented in the tribal groups doing surveys and providing interpretations (e.g., Stoffle et al. 2001), there exists a basic and largely replicable interpretive framework among contemporary native people, and that this framework, which I refer to as "conceptual pathways," constitutes a manifestation of culturally and historically informed worldviews. The four redundant pathways are these: (1) the intrinsic characteristics of an object, including the formal properties of raw material, shape, and color, as well as the properties that make the artifact a repository of power, such as human or animal likeness; (2) spatial associations between objects of any kind and objects of intrinsic power; (3) spatial associations between objects of any kind or power and powerful landscape features; and (4) any object, place, or feature used by humans in the performance of a ritual.

From this framework one may readily appreciate the roles played by formative, historical, and experiential knowledge in archaeological interpretation, particularly when it is accommodated to the more specific worldviews of different ethnic and linguistic groups. Objects of intrinsic power, for example, may vary from group to group, but there is nonetheless a core of items that crosscut many cultural and ethnic boundaries, for example, red paint, crystals, fossils, shells, copper, obsidian, and flint. The presence of these objects will most likely determine identification of ritual deposits and past ritual activities. Associations between common objects and features and powerful medicinal plants or animals (e.g., a bear tooth) can potentially influence interpretation. It is also important to note that, at least among Algonquian-speaking groups, human agency is at par with powerful forces in the transformative processes that make simple objects into "ritual objects" or "object/persons." Together, these pathways contain a rationale for interpretation that can help bridge the distance between native and archaeological-scientific understandings of artifact life histories and site formation processes (Walker 1999, 2002). Finally, it is important to note the significant role played by landscape and place associations in archaeological interpretations of ritual, as ceremonial loci were frequently selected on account of specific physiographic characteristics such as elevation, seclusion, view, lines-of-sight with prominent landmarks, and the presence of water sources and rock outcrops (Carroll et al. 2004; Zedeño 2000). It is perhaps from this conceptual pathway that the most fruitful lessons may yet be learned.

Conceptual Pathways in Contemporary Ojibwa Interpretation

The basic framework described above may be combined with Ojibwa taxonomy to explain how the Ojibwa worldview permeates contemporary interpretations of the archaeological record. To do so one must appeal to the concept of other-than-human persons or person/objects. When the taxonomy is applied to actual cases in which interpretation is elicited, the ontological principle that the Ojibwa appeal to most often is that of causation. For example, how is one to distinguish between a rock and a grandfather or a spirit rock? Well, the answer at hand may be that the grandfather rock with a human likeness opens its mouth to let medicine out. Yet, some grandfather rocks may not be distinguishable by appearances but by actions, including self-propelling travel, like the case of certain spirit rock that was repatriated from a mainland museum and later appeared, of its own volition, at the altar of a Midewiwin Lodge in Madeleine Island, Wisconsin. Grandfather rocks are also identified on account of personal experience: some rocks have brought luck or harm to people who came into close contact with them. So, *how does one know a grandfather rock?* I recently asked a Holy Man that question and he responded that some rocks are grandfather rocks by birth whereas others are apparently common rocks that lie waiting to be awakened by a particularly powerful human, spirit, or event. But overall one knows them by the fact that they like to live alone and in unexpected places (Zedeño et al. 2006).

Like many native cultures, Ojibwa conceptual pathways incorporate an element of percept ambiguity (Black 1977b), which carries as much weight in interpretation as readily observed intrinsic or acquired artifact characteristics, spatial associations, or participation in rituals. Historical knowledge, as well as experience, also provides Ojibwa consultants with sufficient and necessary elements to support and justify a wide range of interpretations.

Consider, for example, the ubiquitous lithic scatter, which elicits so few substantive interpretations from archaeologists. While working on ethnographic resource assessments in Sleeping Bear Dunes National Lakeshore,

Figure 15.2 North Manitou Island, Sleeping Bear National Lakeshore, Michigan.

Michigan, a group of Ojibwa elders came across a surface scatter near a lake on North Manitou Island (Figure 15.2). Upon close examination of the vicinity of the lithic scatter the elders determined that we were standing on sacred ground. How so? The elders had arrived at this conclusion by considering several pieces of evidence: First, the site was a flint scatter. Second, a stand of old birch trees grew only a few feet away from the site. Third, flint and trees were in close proximity to the island's lake; and fourth, while inspecting the lakeshore one elder acquired a new song, which he interpreted as an indicator of the sacred character of the place.

To build this inference, the Ojibwa elders followed three conceptual pathways directly associated with the traditional classificatory system: (1) formal characteristics of the artifacts—flint is a person; (2) spatial association between the flint and the Grandfather trees—also persons; and (3) location of both persons near a "lake within a lake"— a powerful landscape feature.

The elders, too, noticed that the area seemed to have been intentionally cleared of vegetation for use as a dance or ceremonial area. A deeper study of the ethnographic literature would reveal the prominent place of flint in creation stories. In explaining the animate nature of objects, for instance, the Berens River Ojibwa told Hallowell (1976a:367) that Flint and the Four Winds came from the same mother; when Flint was born he tore his mother to pieces, but in punishment he was, in turn, torn to pieces by the Great Hare. Similarly, old forests were the places where the primordial human and trickster *Nanabozho* met thunder, lightning, and wind; and where the ancestral keeper of the forests showed to him the power of the flintstone quarries (Benton-Banai 1988:47–48). The origin stories that lend power to resources are constantly reified in the landscape. As explained by the Lac Courte Oreilles Ojibwa storyteller J. Smith, flint found in association with material evidence of its power, such as a tree that has been struck by lightning, can give the person who finds it the power to make things happen (Zedeño et al. 2006). Those who learn the origin story of flint (or any other origin story, for that matter) are thus able to make the connection on sight and can tap into this power.

In addition, the understandably widespread use of flint artifacts as propitiatory offerings likely informed the site interpretation. Conway and Conway (1990:49), for example, observe that the Garden River Ojibwa shot flint tools tipped with tobacco as offerings at the Agawa rock art site in Ontario. For these elders, therefore, it would be impossible to consider the use or discard of flint artifacts, or even debitage, in anything but a ceremonial manner. By extension, any other artifact or feature found in proximity to the flint scatter and/or the grandfather trees would also be part of the ritual site, or in the elders' own words, "a sacred ground."

The inference made in regard to the properties of the lake water shows yet another angle of the complexity of Ojibwa ontology as it is applied to physiographic features, and also involves historical and personal knowledge. Lakes, particularly small lakes, are thought to be inhabited by mermaids. Other water spirits follow ravines in their travel to and from lakes. Furthermore, lake water has specific characteristics and may be prescribed as medicine. One elder explained that

> a particular medicine man may have a particular source of water that he would use in his medicine. He has a dream, which tells him what water is to be used for. Some cases require Lake Michigan water, other medicine needs spring or river water. I use medicine and water from a place—a very specific place told to me by a medicine man. Medicine men are very specific about the source of water.

Given that Ojibwa material culture was notoriously portable, perishable, and recycled, and then buried or traded, artifact assemblages alone are not always informative as to site or feature function. Physiographic features are, in most cases, determinant factors in ascribing religious significance to objects found in direct association with them. The Ojibwa have a highly developed geographical knowledge born out of a lifetime of travel along the lakeshores and rivers of the interior country, which provides the compass for any and all historical and experiential knowledge that is applied to archaeological interpretation (Zedeño 1999; Zedeño and Stoffle 2003).

In addition to appealing to historical knowledge in the construction of an interpretation, the Ojibwa acknowledge that when people engage in interactions with powerful persons, the objects they use and the places where interactions occur acquire ritual significance. Individual activities associated with everyday religious worship also result in the creation of sacred objects and ritual depositional contexts. An elder explains this concept in the following way:

> I could have one eagle feather and you could have another one, but it is how you use them that make them sacred. And that goes the same for the land: it is how you use it that makes the connection.

The cultural certainty that this transformation actually happens is at the core of Ojibwa belief, knowledge, and behavior, and in all likelihood it constitutes a critical factor in the long-term reproduction of the traditional knowledge system.

Conclusions

In conclusion, through this brief discussion of the Ojibwa worldview and its application to archaeological interpretation, I have attempted to show how belief, knowledge, and behavior become integrated in the construction of inferences. Regardless of time elapsed and cultural change, there remain a number of ancient components of traditional knowledge that continue to be called upon and tested for efficacy by contemporary religious practitioners and members of the culture. Whether hands-on experience or historical knowledge comes into play, the context for interpretation and the pathways followed to arrive there are founded upon the ontological principles that inform their taxonomy and by the epistemological principles that explain the functioning of the world. These knowledge domains are not only persistent, but continue to be enriched with new experiences and stories. The currency of such a knowledge system supports the authority of the information native consultants provide during assessments of sites and artifact collections, and encourages archaeologists to search for ways to fully and explicitly incorporate native conceptual pathways in archaeological interpretation.

However different, challenging, or downright amusing Native American interpretations of the archaeological record may seem to non-Native archaeologists, they nonetheless presuppose a rationalization of individual and group experience. Consultants must remove themselves from their everyday reality and use all knowledge available to them in order to construct an inference. The outcome of this process is a product of our recent times and thus seldom found described or discussed in the existing anthropological literature. In addition to teaching archaeologists how to read and evaluate the classic ethnographies, native perspectives can help refine analytical tools for the identification of ritual artifacts and resources and the formation of ritual sites. Finally, native perspectives of archaeology can substantively expand our current ability to associate the site or the artifact with the broader landscape, which is in turn essential to the documentation and explanation of ritual behavior, past and present.

References Cited

Adams, A.
1961   *The Explorations of Pierre Esprit Radisson.* Ross & Haines, Minneapolis.
Anyon, R., T. J. Ferguson, L. Jackson, L. Lane, and P. Vicenti
1997   Native American Oral Tradition and Archaeology: Issues of Structure, Relevance, and Respect. In *Native Americans and Archaeologists: Stepping Stones to a Common Ground*, pp. 77–87. AltaMira Press, Walnut Creek.
Basso, K.
1969   Western Apache Witchcraft. *Anthropological Papers of the University of Arizona No. 15.* University of Arizona Press, Tucson.
Benton-Banai, E.
1988   *The Mishnomis Book: The Voice of the Ojibway.* Red School House, St. Paul.
Black, M. B.
1977a   Ojibwa Power Belief System. In *Anthropology of Power*, edited by R. Fogelson and R. N. Adams, pp. 141–151. Academic Press, New York.
1977b   Ojibwa Taxonomy and Percept Ambiguity. *Ethos* 5:90–117.
Brown, J. S., and R. A. Brighton
1988   *"The Orders of the Dreamed:" George Nelson on Cree and Northern Ojibwa Religion and Myth, 1823.* Minnesota Historical Society Press, St. Paul.
Carroll, A. K., M. N. Zedeño, and R. W. Stoffle
2004   Landscapes of the Ghost Dance: A Cartography of Numic Ritual. *Journal of Archaeological Method and Theory* 11:127–155.
Conway, T.
1993   *Painted Dreams.* NorthWord Press, Minocqua, Wisconsin.
Conway, T., and J. Conway
1990   *Spirits on Stone: The Agawa Pictographs.* Heritage Discoveries Books, Echo Bay, Ontario.
DeMallie, R. J., and R. H. Lavenda
1977   Wakan: Plains Siouan Concepts of Power. In *The Anthropology of Power*, edited by R. Fogelson and R. N. Adams, pp. 153–165. Academic Press, New York.
Dorsey, O.
1894   *A Study of Siouan Cults.* Annual Report of the Bureau of American Ethnology No. 11. U.S. Government Printing Office, Washington, DC.
Dongoske, K., M. Yates, R. Anyon, and T. J. Ferguson
1997   Archaeological Cultures and Cultural Affiliation: Hopi and Zuni Perspectives in the American Southwest. *American Antiquity* 62:600–608.

Echo-Hawk, R. C.
2000   Ancient History in the New World: Integrating Oral Traditions and the Archaeological Record in Deep Time. *American Antiquity* 65:267–290.
Fogelson, R., and R. N. Adams (editors)
1977   *The Anthropology of Power*. Academic Press, New York.
Hallowell, A. I.
1940   *Magic: The Role of Conjuring in Saulteaux Society*. Connecticut Institute of Human Relations, papers presented at the Monday Night Group, pp. 94–115. Yale University, New Haven.
1976a   *Ojibwa Ontology, Behavior, and Worldview*. A. Irving Hallowell Contributions to Anthropology, pp. 357–390. University of Chicago Press, Chicago. Originally published in 1960.
1976b   *Ojibwa Worldview of Disease*. A. Irving Hallowell Contributions to Anthropology, pp. 391–448. University of Chicago Press, Chicago. Originally published in 1963.
1992   *The Ojibwa of Berens River, Manitoba: Ethnography into History*. Harcourt Brace Jovanovich College Publishers, Forth Worth.
Hickerson, H.
1960   The Feast of the Dead among the Seventeenth Century Algonkians of the Upper Great Lakes. *American Anthropologist* 62:81–107.
Hultkrantz, Å.
1966   An Ecological Approach to Religion. *Ethnos* 31:131–150.
Jones, W.
1905   The Algonkin Manitou. *Journal of American Folk-lore* 18:183–190.
Mason, R. J.
2000   Archaeology and Native North American Oral Traditions. *American Antiquity* 65:239–266.
Matthews, W.
1897   *Navajo Legends*. Memoirs of the American Folk-lore Society No. 5. Houghton Mifflin, Boston.
Miller, J.
1983   Basin Religion and Theology: A Comparative Study of Power (Puha). *Journal of California and Great Basin Anthropology* 5:66–86.
Mooney, J.
1896   *The Ghost-Dance Religion and the Sioux Outbreak of 1890*. Annual Report of the Bureau of Ethnology, vol. 14, Part 2, 1892–1893. GPO, Washington, DC.
Radin, P.
1914   Religion of the North American Indian. *Journal of American Folk-lore* 27:335–373.
1957   *Primitive Religion: Its Nature and Origin*. Dover Publications, New York.
Rappaport, R. A.
1999   *Ritual and Religion in the Making of Humanity*. Cambridge University Press, New York.
Schenck, T.
1997   *The Voice of the Crane Echoes Afar: The Sociopolitical Organization of the Lake Superior Ojibwa, 1640–1855*. Garland, New York.
Shaafsma, C.
2004   Truth Dwells in the Deeps: Southwestern Oral Traditions and Archaeological Interpretations. *Journal of the Southwest* 46:621–642.
Spector, J.
1993   *What this Awl Means: Feminist Archaeology at a Wahpeton Dakota Village*. Minnesota Historical Society Press, St. Paul.
Stein, J.
2002   *Vashon Island Archaeology: A View from Burton Acres Shell Midden*. Burke Museum of Natural History and Culture Research Report No. 8, University of Washington Press, Seattle.

Stoffle, R. W., and M. N. Zedeño
2001   Historical Memory and Ethnographic Perspectives on the Southern Paiute Homeland. *Journal of California and Great Basin Anthropology* 23:229–248.
Stoffle, R. W., L. Loendorf, D. Austin, D. Halmo, and A. Bulletts
2000   Ghost Dancing the Grand Canyon: Southern Paiute Rock Art, Ceremony, and Cultural Landscapes. *Current Anthropology* 41:11–38.
Stoffle, R. W., M. N. Zedeño, and D. Halmo (editors)
2001   *American Indians and the Nevada Test Site: A Model of Research and Consultation.* U.S. Government Printing Office, Washington, DC.
Vander, J.
1997   *Shoshone Ghost Dance Religion.* University of Illinois Press, Urbana.
Voth, H.
1905   *The Traditions of the Hopi.* Fieldiana Anthropology No. 8. Field Museum of Natural History, Chicago.
Walker, W.
1999   Ritual, Life Histories, and the Afterlives of People and Things. *Journal of the Southwest* 41:383–405.
2002   Stratigraphy and Practical Reason. *American Anthropologist* 104:159–177.
Zedeño, M. N.
1999   Ojibway Land Use in the Western Great Lakes. Paper presented at the Society for Applied Anthropology Annual Meetings, Tucson.
2000   On What People Make of Places: A Behavioral Cartography. In *Social Theory in Archaeology*, edited by M. B. Schiffer, pp. 97–111. University of Utah Press, Salt Lake City.
Zedeño, M. N., R. Stoffle, F. Pittaluga, G. Dewey-Hefley, M. Porter, and C. Basaldœ
2001   *Ojibway Traditional Resource Use in the Western Great Lakes.* Bureau of Applied Research in Anthropology, University of Arizona, Tucson.
Zedeño, M. N., and R. Stoffle
2003   Tracking the Role of Pathways in the Evolution of a Human Landscape: The St. Croix Riverway in Ethnohistorical Perspective. In *Colonization of Unfamiliar Landscapes: The Archaeology of Human Adaptation*, edited by M. Rockman and J. Steele, pp. 59–80. Routledge, London.
Zedeño, M. N., J. Smith, and V. Fletcher
2006   A Companion to the NPS Ethnographic Resource Inventory, St Croix River National Scenic Riverway. Bureau of Applied Research in Anthropology, University of Arizona, Tucson.

INDEX

ABOUT THE CONTRIBUTORS

ELISABETH CULLEY is a Ph.D. student in the School of Human Evolution and Social Change at Arizona State University, Tempe, where she is studying the origin of art and human modernity. She was recently co-editor (with J. Huang) of *Making Marks: Graduate Studies in Rock Art Research at the New Millennium* (ARARA Occasional Paper No. 5, 2005).

ROBERT DECAROLI is an Assistant Professor of Art History at George Mason University, Fairfax, Virginia. His research focuses on the early Buddhist art of southern and southeast Asia. His recent publications include *Haunting the Buddha: Indian Popular Religions and the Formation of Buddhism* (Oxford, 2004).

THOMAS E. EMERSON is an Adjunct Professor of Anthropology and the Director of the Illinois Transportation Archaeological Research Program at the University of Illinois at Urbana-Champaign. His research focuses on the prehistory of the North American Midwest, especially Cahokia. His books include *Cahokia and the Hinterlands: Middle Mississippian Cultures of the Midwest* (edited with R.B. Lewis, University of Illinois, 1991) and *Cahokia and the Archaeology of Power* (University of Alabama, 1997).

LARS FOGELIN is an Assistant Professor of Anthropology at Albion College, Michigan, whose archaeological research emphasizes religion, especially Buddhism on the south coast of India. He recently published *The Archaeology of Early Buddhism* (AltaMira, 2005).

KELLEY HAYS-GILPIN is Professor of Anthropology at Northern Arizona University and the Danson Chair of Anthropology at the Museum of

Northern Arizona. Her research interests include rock art, gender, and ceramics. Her book, *Ambiguous Images: Gender and Rock Art* (AltaMira, 2004), received the Society for American Archaeology Award for best professional publication of the year.

PETER JORDAN is a Senior Lecturer in the Department of Archaeology at the University of Aberdeen, Scotland. His primary research focus involves ethnoarchaeological studies in Siberia, where his interests emphasize landscape and belief. His recent publications include *Material Culture and Sacred Landscape: The Anthropology of the Siberian Khanty* (AltaMira, 2003).

J. DAVID LEWIS-WILLIAMS is Professor Emeritus and University Mentor for the Rock Art Research Institute and Archaeology Department at the University of the Witwatersrand, South Africa. His research focuses on southern African and European Paleolithic rock art, and he was awarded the Society for American Archaeology's Award for Excellence in Archaeological Analysis in 2004. He is the author of numerous books, including *The Mind in the Cave: Consciousness and the Origins of Art* (Thames and Hudson, 2002), which received the American Historical Association's James Henry Breasted Award in 2003.

JOHANNES LOUBSER is a consulting archaeologist, rock art conserva-tor and artist working for Stratum Unlimited, LLC., in Alpharetta, Georgia. His research interests include the southern African Iron Age and the prehistory and ethnography of the Native American southeast. His books include *Archaeology: The Comic* (AltaMira, 2003) and *The Ethnoarchaeology of Venda Speakers in Southern Africa* (Bloemfontein National Museum, 1991).

MARIA NIEVES ZEDEÑO is an Associate Professor at the Bureau of Applied Research in Anthropology, University of Arizona, Tucson. Her research involves the prehistory, ethnography, and ethnology of Native America. Her books include *Sourcing Prehistoric Ceramics* at Chodistaas Pueblo, Arizona (University of Arizona, 1994), and *American Indians and the Nevada Test Site: A Model of Research and Cooperation* (with R.W. Stoffle and D.B. Halmo, U.S. Government Printing Office, 2001).

TIMOTHY K. PAUKETAT is Professor of Anthropology at the University of Illinois at Urbana-Champaign where his research interests include the prehistory of the North American Midwest and archaeological method and theory. His recent books include *Chiefdoms and Other Archaeological*

Delusions (AltaMira, 2007) and *Cahokia's Big Bang and the Story of Ancient North America* (Viking-Penguin, 2008).

NEIL PRICE is Professor and Head of the Department of Archaeology at the University of Aberdeen, Scotland. His research focuses on the Viking archaeology and shamanism. Recent books include *The Archaeology of Shamanism* (edited, Routledge, 2001) and *The Vikings (Ancient Peoples)* (Routledge, 2008).

ANDRZEJ ROZWADOWSKI is an archaeologist at the Institute of Eastern Studies, Adam Mickiewicz University, Poznan, Poland. His research emphasizes the rock art of central Asia and Siberia. His recent books include *Spirits and Stones: Shamanism and Rock Art in Central Asia and Siberia* (edited with M.K. Kosko, Institute of Eastern Studies, Adam Mickiewicz University, 2002) and *Symbols through time: interpreting the rock art of Central Asia* (Institute of Eastern Studies, Adam Mickiewicz University, 2004).

CHRIS SCARRE is Professor of Prehistory in the Archaeology Department at the University of Durham, England, where his research emphasizes the prehistory of the Atlantic region of Western Europe. His recent books include *Monuments and Landscapes in Atlantic Europe* (edited, Routledge, 2002) and *The Human Past* (Thames and Hudson, 2005).

DAVID S. WHITLEY is a consulting archaeologist with W&S Consultants in Fillmore, California, and an Adjunct Professor in the School of Geographical Sciences at Arizona State University, Tempe. His research interests are Native American prehistory, ethnography and rock art, and the cognitive neurosciences of religion. Recent books include *Introduction to Rock Art Research* (Left Coast Press, 2005) and *Cave Art and the Human Spirit: The Origin of Art and Belief* (Prometheus Books, 2008).

MICHAEL WINKELMAN is an Associate Professor in the School of Human Evolution and Social Change at Arizona State University, Tempe. His research interests include shamanism, applied medical anthropology, and cross-cultural relations. His recent books include *Psychedelic Medicine: New Evidence for Hallucinogenic Substances as Treatments* (with T. Roberts, Greenwood/Praeger, 2007) and *American Ethnic History* (Kendall-Hunt, 2006).